1966

PANORAMA

OF

AMERICAN POPULAR MUSIC

Other Books by David Ewen

Panorama
of
American
Popular Music

by DAVID EWEN

The Story of Our National Ballads and Folk Songs—The Songs of Tin Pan Alley, Broadway and Hollywood—*New Orleans Jazz, Swing and Symphonic Jazz.*

PRENTICE-HALL, INC.
Englewood Cliffs, N. J.

TO IRA *and* LEE GERSHWIN

NOTE

Our popular music is a fertile field that yields many crops. This fact is often ignored by partisans of one kind of popular music to the exclusion of all others. The authority of folk music tends to ignore jazz; and the authority on jazz tends to look disparagingly on the songs of Tin Pan Alley. But a single branch does not make a tree; and it is the tree that is important, rather than some of its random fruits.

In this book, the writer has attempted—possibly for the first time—to tell the *complete* story of American popular music: not just the story of jazz, but also that of Tin Pan Alley; not just the story of our folk music, but also that of our national balladry; not just the story of Broadway and Hollywood music but also that of symphonic jazz heard in Carnegie Hall. Since the writer is not the follower of any single cult, but is interested in everything that pertains to our popular musical expression, he has tried to discuss every facet of our popular music with equal objectivity and completeness, as well as to relate one facet of popular music to every other.

TABLE OF

CONTENTS

PANORAMA

OF

AMERICAN POPULAR MUSIC

PRELUDE

OF ALL the contributions made by Americans to world culture
—automation and the assembly line, advertising, innumerable
devices and gadgets, skyscrapers, supersalesmen, baseball,
ketchup and hot dogs and hamburgers—one, undeniably native, has been taken to heart by the entire world. It is American popular music.

In some lands America is criticized for its politics, in others
envied for its wealth and power. Certain groups of intellectuals
in world capitals are hypercritical about Hollywood movies
and have not as yet been won over completely to our theater,
literature, and art. And many of the world's serious-music audiences have still to respond enthusiastically to our best concert
music. But popular music has proved to be an ambassador of
good will, welcomed into the homes and hearts of people of
every land.

Within living memory it has been fashionable to be snobbish
about jazz, both the hot and the symphonic variety. No more.
Such jazzmen as Louis Armstrong and Dizzy Gillespie were
given a regal welcome when they recently performed in foreign
lands. In every part of the civilized world an all-Gershwin

concert is invariably an assurance of a sold-out auditorium. In this country, leading symphony orchestras under the greatest conductors repeatedly perform works by Gershwin, Grofé, or Morton Gould. Conservatories and universities give courses on jazz; jazz has found a shrine in an annual festival in Newport, Rhode Island; and great jazz artists like Benny Goodman and Louis Armstrong have been invited to appear with major symphony orchestras.

In the past it has been acceptable to be condescending about the songs of Tin Pan Alley. But in recent times some of our foremost concert artists and stars of the Metropolitan Opera have sung publicly the songs of George Gershwin, Jerome Kern, Cole Porter, Irving Berlin, and Richard Rodgers, while these songs are also loved the world over. And it must also be recalled that an opera like Gershwin's *Porgy and Bess*—whose epoch-making tour in virtually every part of the world has won more enthusiasm than any opera of our generation—has its stylistic roots deep in Tin Pan Alley.

In former years our musical comedy was often subjected to harsh criticism. But particularly since World War II we have developed a musical theater that has acquired the status of a native art. More then one serious-music critic has been tempted to call the musical plays of Kurt Weill or Rodgers and Hammerstein "American operas." At the same time, musicals like *Kiss Me Kate, Oklahoma!,* and *South Pacific* have been given in foreign translations in many European capitals and have been wildly acclaimed.

Imitation, the sincerest form of flattery, is proof of the world-wide acceptance of this art form. Hot-jazz *boîtes* have mushroomed in virtually every capital of Europe; significantly, many of these jazz artists are Europeans. And most of Europe's current popular hits show an unmistakable family resemblance to our own.

Its present status is international, but the origin and growth of our popular music is truly American. Of course, the colonists

and immigrants brought with them musical ideas and traditions: ballads and melodies from England, Ireland, and Scotland; dances from central Europe; harmonies and rhythms
from Africa. But all these elements were fused by American
history, evolution, and experiences into something new, personal, and distinctive: into a native art that reflects our way of
life, thought, and backgrounds; that speaks to us and to the rest
of the world about us.

chapter one

MY COUNTRY 'TIS OF THEE—
Our National Ballads
and Patriotic Songs

RELIGION and politics were the dominant influences in the popular music of the English Colonies of North America. And, appropriately, our first popular composer, William Billings, was a psalm composer (the culmination of the era of psalmody in New England) who, during the Revolution, turned from religion to politics to write our first great war song.

Fate had not dealt kindly with him. Born in Boston in 1746, he came into the world with one blind eye, one withered arm, legs of uneven length, and an irritatingly rasping voice. As he grew into manhood he helped Nature along in making him a physical monstrosity by becoming increasingly slovenly, adopting an outlandish and frequently quixotic dress, and assuming the manners of a boor. Despite his native or assumed disfigurations he managed to convince two different women to marry him—the first in 1764, the other a decade later—and to have them bear him six children.

Music was his passion. By profession a tanner, he often neglected his work to spend hours scribbling tunes with chalk on

[6]

the hides or the walls of the tannery. At other times he absorbed voraciously every psalm book he could put his hands on, and tried acquiring some technical guidance by memorizing Tansur's *Musical Grammar*.

Eventually he gave up tannery for music, and in doing so became America's first native born professional musician. Outside his door he hung a sign of his new calling reading: "Billings—Music." Since he was convinced that everybody should sing—and since he was violently opposed to the haphazard singing practices then existing in the church—he formed in 1774 a singing class in Stoughton, the first of its kind in the colonies; after his death, this group became the nucleus of the Stoughton Musical Society, America's first major musical organization. The example he set in forming a singing class led to the formation of several singing schools where Americans could learn to read music. Billings, father of the singing school, was also a pioneer in other musical directions: as the founder of the American church choir, as the first musician to use a pitch-pipe, and as the first to introduce a violoncello into church services.

None of his activities were able to provide him with a livelihood. He died, as he had lived, in appalling poverty. Not even occasional benefit concerts and publications by kindly disposed neighbors and friends could relieve his misery. He died a pauper in 1800, and was buried in the Boston Common in a neglected and unidentified grave.

He was an opponent of the psalm music of his day. To point out a new direction for the psalm he published in 1770 a psalter of his own called *The New England Psalm Singer*. Each of the melodies was a "fuguing piece"—not a formal fugue in the textbook acceptance of that form, but vocal pieces utilizing the technique of imitation. His music had all the crudity of the man who wrote it. Billings defied convention, rule, cleanliness, the *status quo*—partly because he was an iconoclast and an innovator, partly because he did not know the rules and conventions. In the preface to his book he rationalized his limitations: "For my own part, I don't think myself confined to any Rules. . . . I think it is best for every composer to be his own learner. . . . Nature lays the foundation. Nature must give the thought."

What Billings actually accomplished was to "jazz up" the psalm music of his day. His pieces—both in his first volume, and in those that followed, notably *The Singing Master's Assistant* in 1778 and *The Psalm Singer's Amusement* in 1781— were, as he wrote, "more than twenty times as powerful as the old slow tunes, each part striving for mastery and victory." He employed a faster tempo, his rhythms were more rugged, and his bass moved with greater vigor than had been habitual with the older psalms. His harmonic and contrapuntal writing, filled with practices forbidden by authorized texts, was as virile as it was uncouth. As Louis Ritter wrote in 1890, Billings' music was filled with "illogical progressions of octaves," "hideous consecutive fifths," "chords and harmonies tumbling upon each other without order or euphony." This was no longer English psalmody, with its usually slow and stately and well-measured tread. This was a rough and homespun product made in the colonies.

The better informed, the better schooled musicians of Billings' day laughed at his crudities, awkwardness, sloppiness, and ignorance. As an expression of their derision, a few of his contemporaries one day hung two cats by their tails on Billings's signpost—the howling of the victims probably intended by the perpetrators of this prank as an audible example of the kind of music Billings was writing. The composer, who was not without a sense of humor, laughed right back at his critics by writing a piece called "Jargon" filled with all kinds of intentional discords and harmonic irregularities.

And it was Billings who had the last laugh. For even before his death there were few psalm collections in the colonies that did not contain at least one of his fuguing tunes; nor was there an important singing group that did not perform one of them. More than this: By 1790 Billings had written a war song which was sung so extensively, and proved so influential in arousing the martial spirit among the rebel colonists, that it has since been described as "the 'Marseillaise' of the American Revolution."

II

As the political cauldron began to bubble and boil in the Colonies, as rebellion against the English motherland passed from hot words to hotter deeds, the tensions of the times found an outlet in song. Thus the political song succeeded the psalm in public favor. The Sons of Liberty interrupted their practices of terrorism to write and spread numbers like "A New Song" which hotly denounced tyranny. Samuel Adams organized singing groups in Boston where political songs like "The Liberty Tree" with lyrics by Thomas Paine were taught. These and other lyrics, written either in the white heat of anger or else in cool deliberation for propaganda purposes, were printed on broadsides and distributed in the streets a penny apiece. Broadsides were highly effective for propaganda use, since they were cheap to print and sell, were quickly distributed, and could be hawked on the streets to publicize an important political event while the news was still hot. The colonists bought these broadsides avidly, and quickly learned the new lyrics. At a time when entertainment was none too plentiful or varied, singing at home or at public meetings provided not only a safety valve for pent-up, explosive emotions, but also a welcome form of recreation.

It is surely ironical that most of the political lyrics in which the colonists expressed their defiance of their mother country should have been set to English music, the prevailing practice being to borrow the melody of a familiar English song or ballad for new words. Thus, through the medium of English tunes, the colonists expressed their defiant denunciation of the Writs of

Assistance, the taxes on stamps and tea, and the other abuses which finally invoked the Revolution.

"The Liberty Song"—words by John Dickinson set to the popular English tune, "Hearts of Oak" by William Boyce—was one of the most popular of these inflammatory songs of defiance, sometimes described as "the first American patriotic song." Its inspiration was the Circular Letter which was distributed in 1768 to denounce unfair taxation. One of the fiery lines of the lyric reads: "Not as slaves but as freemen our money we'll give." So popular did "The Liberty Song" become that the Tories had to respond in kind—with numerous parodies. One of these cried out that "not as men but as monkeys the token you give." Another warned the "simple Bostonians" that "if ye chance to return to this town, your houses and stores will come tumbling down."

Once the shot was fired at Lexington, the Revolution was on. In a large sense it was a people's war, and as such it found expression in the songs of the people. The Revolution was fought almost as savagely with music as with ammunition. As had been the case before 1776, England was attacked with her own melodies. "God Save the King" became "God Save the Thirteen States." The old English tune, "Derry Down," reappeared in "What a Court Hath England" to reply to a satirical Tory description of the patriots. Joseph Warren's combustible admonition to the colonists to "oppose, oppose, oppose" was set to the melody of "The British Grenadiers" and was called "Free America." Our first sentimental song, John Tait's "Banks of the Dee" (in which a Scotchman bids farewell to his beloved as he leaves to join the British troops in America) came from "Langolee."

The colonists sang as they fought. Joel Barlow, writer of patriotic verses, wrote in 1775: "I have great faith in the influence of songs and shall continue, while fulfilling the duties of my appointment, to write one now and then to encourage the taste for them which I find in camp. One good song is worth a dozen addresses or proclamations."

Fife songs were sung and played on the field of battle; "My Dog and Gun" and "On the Road to Boston" were particular favorites. The words and music of the most celebrated fife song of all—"Yankee Doodle"—actually became popular some years before the Revolution. Like most of the colonists' war songs, the melody came from England. Its precise source is unknown; attempts to place its origin are numerous and contradictory. One of the best known uses of the melody was in an English nursery tune called "Lucy Locket." The melody first appeared in the colonies in 1755. At that time, General Braddock gathered colonial soldiers for war on the French and Indians at Niagara. In their ragged costumes, the colonists appeared a sorry lot. Dr. Richard Shuckburgh, a British Army soldier, mocked this decrepit army by telling it that "Yankee Doodle" was the latest British song hit. He taught the tune with his own improvised nonsense lyrics; but colonial troops took him seriously, learned the song, and frequently sang it in battle. For the next two decades, "Yankee Doodle" was used by British soldiers to taunt the colonials. British troopers would come to a New England church and disturb the services by singing the tune and its silly verses at the top of their raucous voices. As if in eloquent retribution, the colonists accepted the song as their battle cry of freedom once war with England erupted. They marched to its jaunty rhythm to Lexington in 1775. When the British troops were dispersed at Concord they heard "Yankee Doodle," and they heard it again when Cornwallis surrendered at Yorktown and when they later marched as prisoners through New England.

During the Revolution an amusing parody of "Yankee Doodle" was written by Francis Hopkinson—statesman, friend of George Washington, one of the signers of the Declaration of Independence, and one of our earliest serious native composers.

His verses were inspired by an amusing incident which he had witnessed. David Bushnell, the inventor of a man-propelled submarine boat that had proved ineffectual, devised an ingenious scheme for attacking British ships. He filled kegs with powder and floated them down the river toward the British vessels then anchored in Delaware River outside Philadelphia. When the British saw the kegs floating in their direction they began firing at them wildly. This sight proved so amusing to Hopkinson that he then and there wrote a set of satirical verses entitled "The Battle of the Kegs," for which he borrowed the familiar melody of "Yankee Doodle." There is good reason to believe that he sang it to George Washington and his staff at their army headquarters in Virginia.

But not all of the songs of the Revolution were based on English melodies. Our first native popular songs—the melody as well as the lyric—emerged from the heat of the battle. One of these was "The American Hero," whose lyrics, by Nathaniel Niles, were set to the melody of Andrew Law's "Bunker Hill." Both the words and the music date from 1775. Modeling his melody after the pattern of the English ballad, Law created in "Bunker Hill" a tune that was more melancholy than rousing. Nevertheless, when joined to the spirited words of "The American Hero," it became a rallying cry for people prepared to die for their freedom—reflecting the hopes and fears of the colonists when, immediately after Bunker Hill, they realized that they had come to grips with one of the great military powers of the world.

The most popular and important native war song of the Revolution, however, came from none other than the deformed and greatly mocked New England psalmodist, William Billings. As a friend of Samuel Adams and Paul Revere, Billings allied himself with the cause of the Revolution from its very inception, and in the only way he could. He enlisted his music in the struggle by writing new martial lyrics for his psalms, and distributing them in army camps. "Many of the New England soldiers who . . . were encamped in southern states had his popular tunes by heart and frequently amused themselves by singing in camp to the delight of all those who heard them." So recorded a writer for the *Musical Reporter*. The colonists "wept as they remembered Boston"—to the tune of Billings' psalm "By the Waters of Babylon." Another Billings' psalm, "Chester," was destined to become the most famous native song of the Revolution. The angular melody, with its even meters and formal cadences, betrayed its church origin, and made it hardly suitable for the set of belligerent lyrics which Billings wrote after the Revolution. But since the new words caught and fixed the spirit of the times, "Chester" spread like a contagion through all the army camps to become, as we have already noted, the *"Marseillaise"* of the American Revolution.

III

During the first half century of American independence many different kinds of songs became popular. There were, first of all, the often poignant tunes of the street vendors (ancestors of the present-day singing commercial). Since the early eighteenth century, vendors hawked their wares in the streets with their highly personalized street cries. Some of these tunes, like the commodities they advertised, passed on from seller to buyer. It was not unusual for tunes like "Come Buy My Woodenware" or "Oyster Sir" to become part and parcel of the song literature of that day. Even up to about 1840, street cries were so prevalent throughout the states that the New York *Mirror* complained editorially about "tradesmen who make music enough every day of the week to set every citizen's teeth on edge. . . . You cannot pass a pile of pine boxes without music, or dodge through a defile of empty brandy cakes without encountering a concert." A century later, George Gershwin successfully simulated the street cries of Charleston, South Carolina, in his Negro folk opera, *Porgy and Bess*.

Other popular songs of the period spoke of everyday experiences: fires and disasters, the gaiety and the pitfalls of the big city, the peace and rewards of farm life, contemporary fashions, the problems of the heart (usually expressed in metaphorical and highly euphuistic language), and love.

Sentimental ballads were especially favored. Indeed, one of the most substantial song hits before 1840 was "Woodman, Spare That Tree," whose lyrics by George P. Morris grew maudlin over the fate of a tree. Its composer, Henry Russell, was a baritone who came from his native England in 1833 to tour the United States in concerts devoted mainly to his own ballads. Russell was a highly theatrical performer, given to excessive dramatics; his rendition of his own sentimental ballads always excited his audiences. When he first sang "Woodman, Spare That Tree," in 1833, he touched the hearts of his listeners so deeply that one man in the audience suddenly arose to inquire whether the tree had *really* been spared. When Russell assured him that this was actually the case, the questioner muttered "Thank God" and the rest of the audience burst into applause. Still another Russell ballad caught on in 1840: "The Old Armchair," a tearful tribute to a chair once belonging to a mother was in all probability the "mammy song" making its initial appearance.

One of the sentimental ballads of this period has deservedly acquired permanence in our song repertory: "Home, Sweet Home," lyrics by John Howard Payne, who was born in New York City in 1791. Early in his manhood Payne went to London where for a while he acted and wrote plays. While there he collaborated with Sir Henry Bishop, an eminent English composer and conductor, in writing an opera, *Clari,* first produced in London on May 8, 1823. One of its principal arias, "Home, Sweet Home" was sung by the heroine as a nostalgic recollection of her home. Actually it was Payne himself who expressed his deepest feelings, for destiny had made him a lifelong wanderer in foreign lands.

Bishop's beloved melody had not been written directly for

Payne's libretto. The composer had created it a few years earlier as a Sicilian air for a collection of folk tunes which he edited. Its inclusion here led many to accuse Bishop of having stolen a Sicilian folk melody for his "Home, Sweet Home," and he had to go to court to prove his authorship, which he did to the full satisfaction of all concerned. After its appearance in *Clari,* the song acquired extraordinary popularity halfway around the world, not only among the masses, but even in the concert hall and opera house. In 1823, the year of its première in London, it was introduced in New York and published by George Bacon in Philadelphia. "How often," commented Payne sadly in his diary, "have I been in the heart of Paris, Berlin, London, or some other city, and have heard persons singing or hand organs playing 'Home, Sweet Home' without having a shilling to buy myself the next meal, or a place to lay my head."

Since the growing pains of a young democracy were a subject dominating the thinking and dreaming of most Americans after acquiring their independence, politics is a favorite theme for the popular songs of this era. As had been the case before and during the Revolution, many melodies were borrowed from Europe—mostly from English songs and ballads, sometimes from Irish and Scottish tunes. The lyrics, however, were of local origin, and many of these paid tribute to American heroes. Hymns were written to honor George Washington for his birthday, to describe his victories and achievements, to commemorate his inauguration as President, and in the end to mourn his death. There were lyrics signalizing or providing editorial comment on major political events; one of the best known was "Jefferson and Liberty," by an unidentified lyricist, set to an Irish reel, and expressing public resentment against the Alien and Sedition Laws. Songs commemorated the anniversary of independence. They were written for and used in Presidential campaigns—at a time when such campaigns provided a welcome form of public entertainment—often powerful factors in carrying a candidate into office: "Jefferson," in 1800, "The Aristocracy" for Henry Clay in 1824, and "Tippecanoe and Tyler, Too," for Benjamin Harrison in 1840, are three examples. A fourth Presidential campaign song, "Adams and Liberty," was written by Robert Treat Paine in 1798 to an old English melody, "Anacreon in Heaven"; before long, the same melody would be used again for our national anthem.

The importance of politics in our early popular music is pointed up by the preponderance of political songsters circulated during the first half century of American independence. Songsters were of pocket size, inexpensive in price, and contained only lyrics. They had a wide distribution, often selling out an entire edition as soon as they were hawked in the streets. With singing a principal form of entertainment at home, meeting places, political rallies, quilting bees, men's club dinners, and public ceremonies of all kinds, the songster assumed a prominent role in the social life of our country.

The first such volume, *The American Musical Miscellany*, came out just before the end of the eighteenth century. Here we find such political songs as "Rise Columbia," lyrics by Robert Paine to the melody of Arne's "Rule Britannia," and "Washington," music as well as words by Samuel Holyoke. After 1798 numerous songsters appeared devoted entirely either to political subjects (*Nightingale of Liberty, The American Naval and Patriotic Songster*) or to prominent political personalities (*The Clay Minstrel, The Harrison*, and *The Log Cabin Songster, or The Polk Songster*). *The Missouri Songster*, issued in Cincinnati in 1808, was one of those used most widely at camp meetings; young Abraham Lincoln, and his sweetheart Ann Rutledge, sang from it at the Rutledge tavern in New Salem.

IV

It was out of the political storms and stresses of our early history that our first national ballads emerged.

"Hail Columbia" appeared in 1798 when war with France seemed imminent following actual skirmishes between French and American ships on the high seas. Joseph Hopkinson (son of Francis) was asked by Gilbert Fox, a Philadelphia singer, to write some patriotic verses for him. It was Fox's idea that a patriotic song might become the *tour de force* of his concert, planned for the New Theatre in Philadelphia on April 25, 1798. Hopkinson accepted the assignment eagerly, for he sensed that stirring patriotic lyrics might "well get up the American spirit," as he put it, and make Americans "look and feel exclusively for our honor and rights." For his melody, Hopkinson chose a stirring tune by the name of "The President's March," which Philip Phile had probably written to honor George Washington and which had been published in Philadelphia in 1793. Since President Adams had also become convinced that the new song might help unite the American people by arousing their national consciousness, he joined his cabinet in attending the Gilbert Fox concert. To dramatize the performance, Fox performed "Hail Columbia" (accompanied by chorus and brass band) with a huge portrait of President Adams behind him. The hymn proved a sensation, and two days later it was published in Philadelphia by Benjamin Carr. For a quarter of a century after that, "Hail Columbia" was our national anthem, played on every American ship at the lowering of the colors at sunset. For still another half century it shared its status as our national anthem with "The Star Spangled Banner." During the Civil War, "Hail Columbia" was one of the most frequently played anthems of the North. We learn from Charles Coffin's *Four Years of Fighting* that in 1861 the hymn was "everywhere the music of the streets, vocal as well as instrumental."

An actual war, rather than the threat of one, gave birth to "The Star Spangled Banner." In the summer of 1814, during the War of 1812, the British fleet was anchored off the city of Baltimore, facing Fort McHenry. That September, a Maryland physician, Dr. William Beanes, was captured by the British and held prisoner on one of their vessels. Francis Scott Key, a young Baltimore lawyer, headed a truce commission to effect Dr. Beanes' release. The party was treated cordially, but since the British were just then planning a secret attack on Fort McHenry, they refused to allow the party to leave ship until the battle had ended. On the night of September 13-14, Francis Scott Key, from the vantage point of an enemy ship, watched a blistering attack on Fort McHenry. When, at dawn, he saw the American flag still flying atop the fort, his excitement found outlet in verses, which he then and there scribbled on an envelope. The melody he had in mind for his verses was "Anacreon in Heaven," a tune he himself had previously used for another of his lyrics, "The Warrior's Return." "Anacreon in Heaven" was an English song believed to have been written by John Stafford Smith in 1775 for a group of esthetes and art lovers known as the London Anacreontic Society. The melody became popular in America, having been used by several lyricists, including Robert Treat Paine for "Adams and Liberty."

The day after the termination of the battle of Fort McHenry, when the truce party had been released and returned to Baltimore, Key's verses were printed on a broadside under the title of "The Defense of Fort McHenry," and distributed in the streets. The same evening it was sung by Ferdinand Durang in a Baltimore tavern where it proved so successful that for the next few weeks it was heard there regularly. On September 20, Key's verses appeared in a Baltimore newspaper, *The Patriot*, which remarked editorially: "The following beautiful and animatory effusion, which is destined long to outlast the occasion and outlive the impulse which produced it, has already been extensively circulated." Still another Baltimore newspaper, *The American*, printed the poem a day later. The anthem became popular throughout the East after the Civil War, and throughout the rest of the country after the Spanish-American War. For many years both the Army and the Navy regarded it as our national anthem, before it was officially made so by an act of Congress on March 3, 1931.

No war, battle, or political conflict was the immediate inspiration for still another patriotic ballad of the period, "America." In 1831, Lowell Mason, the distinguished musical educator, brought several volumes of songs to Samuel Francis Smith, a clergyman. Mason suggested to the clergyman that he use one of the melodies for a new patriotic hymn. "Accordingly," recalled Smith, "one leisurely afternoon, I was looking over the books, and fell in with the tune of "God Save the King," and at once took up my pen and wrote the piece in question. It was struck out at a sitting, without the slightest idea that it would ever attain the popularity it has since enjoyed. . . . The first time it was sung publicly was at a children's celebration of American independence at the Park Street Church, Boston, on July 4, 1831. . . . If I had anticipated the future of it, doubtless I would have taken more pains with it."

V

Probably no American war yielded such a profusion of national ballads as did the Civil War. All the varied passions aroused by the conflict, every phase of the struggle, echoed and re-echoed in the popular music of the day. John Tasker Howard goes so far as to maintain that "the Civil War produced hundreds of songs that could be arranged in proper sequence to form an actual history of the conflicts; its events, its principal characters, and the ideals and principles of the opposing sides."

The first Civil War songs rallied the men around their flags. The South sang "Dixie"; the North, "The Battle Hymn of the Republic." Each song was perhaps more effective in maintaining morale and generating the martial spirit than hundreds of slogans, speeches, and editorials. Paradoxically, however, the Southern hymn, "Dixie," was written by a Northerner, while the battle song of the North, "The Battle Hymn of the Republic," was the work of a Southerner.

"Dixie"—or, as it was first called, "Dixie's Land"—was written by Daniel Decatur Emmett, a native of Ohio who was one of the creators of the minstrel show. "Dixie" was originally meant not as a war song but as the closing number (the "walk-around" in which the entire company paraded as a finale) for a minstrel show produced at Bryant's Theatre in New York in November, 1859. Emmett wrote his song one rainy Sunday afternoon in his boarding-house after Bryant had asked him to write a new "walk-around" for his show. Emmett later recalled: "A line, 'I wish I was in Dixie,' kept repeating itself in my mind, and I finally took it for my start. The rest wasn't long in coming." Emmett had heard the word "Dixie" during his travels south, where even before the Civil War it was a synonym for the Southland.

When first introduced, "Dixie's Land" created such a furore that other minstrel companies appropriated it, and performed it throughout the North. It first came south in a burlesque production, *Pocahontas*, performed in New Orleans where it was sung by Susan Denin while serving as a march for zouaves. Before the week was over, everybody in New Orleans was singing "Dixie." The words were printed in a broadside and proved a sell-out. A New Orleans publisher, Philip Werlein, issued it and was so successful that before long he had to meet the competition of over a dozen pirated editions; in 1860, the powerful New York firm of Firth, Pond & Co. released it. The tune was now heard in many public places, often with improvised lyrics of local interest. Since Emmett had sold his copyright for five hundred dollars he realized only a pittance from what virtually overnight became one of the great song successes of the pre-Civil War period.

In the bitter Presidential campaign of 1860, the South used the melody of "Dixie," with new appropriate words, as a campaign song against Lincoln. Then, when war erupted, "Dixie" —once again with new words—became the song which sent Southern soldiers bravely into battle. It was played by command of General George Pickett at the charge at Gettysburg. The fact that a Northerner had written the song was conveniently forgotten. Its authorship was ascribed to an unidentified Negro who spoke here of his attachment to the Southern homeland. Up North, however, Emmett was frequently subjected to bitter criticism and even verbal attacks for having written the battle song of the South. Unable to convince these critics that he was innocent of treason—that the South had merely confiscated his minstrel-show tune for its own nefarious uses—he prepared new lyrics for his melody exhorting the North to meet "those Southern traitors with iron will" and "to remember Bunker Hill." Notwithstanding his new version, "Dixie" remained the hymn of the Southland. Abraham Lincoln confirmed this southern identity when, after the surrender at Appomattox, he remarked that since the rebel army had been conquered so had "Dixie" been, and exhorted a band outside the White House to play it for him.

Only the lyric of "The Battle Hymn of the Republic" was a child of the Civil War. The music had first appeared in the middle 1850s as "Say, Brothers, Will You Meet Us?" by William Steffe, a camp-meeting song popular in many colored congregations. As was then so habitual with popular melodies, new parodies were set to the tune, some topical, some ribald. The most famous is still remembered: "John Brown's Body," a favorite of one of the battalions of the 21st Massachusetts Regiment stationed at Fort Warren. The "John Brown" in this version is not the celebrated fanatic who headed a band of anti-slavery zealots in an attack on Harper's Ferry. He was rather a member of the 21st Massachusetts Regiment whose naïveté made him a helpless butt for jests and taunts. This "John Brown" version was sung by Northern troops and used by them as a marching song as they moved southward at the beginning of the war.

One day, in December 1861, Julia Ward Howe—poetess, pioneer suffragette, and the wife of a noted physician—heard

"John Brown's Body" and was greatly impressed. When asked by a minister friend to write for the virile melody new and more suitable words she complied willingly. That very night, at the Willard Hotel, the opening line suddenly came to her in her sleep: "Mine eyes have seen the glory of the coming of the Lord." With that as a starting-point, she wrote the rest of the lyric by candlelight, completing it before dawn. Her poem was published in *The Atlantic Monthly* in February, 1862, for which she received a payment of ten dollars. Soon after this, her poem was republished in numerous magazines and Army hymn books, and issued as sheet music with the melody by at least three publishers. After the chaplain of the 122nd Ohio Regiment of Volunteers taught it to Union soldiers everywhere, "The Battle Hymn of the Republic" became a Union favorite. It is said that when Lincoln first heard it sung by the same chaplain he wept and begged for a repetition.

"The Battle Hymn of the Republic" was only one of many Northern war songs. "When Johnny Comes Marching Home" was written by the celebrated bandleader, Patrick S. Gilmore, while he was the official bandmaster of the Union Army. Apparently he thought so little of this effort that he published it in 1863 under the pseudonymn of "Louis Lambert." Union soldiers liked it and sang it frequently. The Confederacy took cognizance of its popularity by writing to its melody a comic verse entitled "For Bales!" After the Civil War, "When Johnny Comes Marching Home" was revived several times. It grew so popular during the Spanish-American War that it became one of the identifying songs of that conflict. It returned once again during World War I, this time in the modern dress of a fox trot. The melody has been given serious musical treatment by several modern American composers, including Roy Harris and Morton Gould.

Lincoln's call for 300,000 additional volunteers inspired "We Are Coming, Father Abraam," words by James Sloan Gibbons, and music by Luther Orlando Emerson. (Stephen Foster also wrote a song to the same lyric.) Emerson's melody had great sobriety, reflecting the increasing gravity with which the North was then regarding the war. Sobriety and gravity also prevail in "Tenting On the Old Camp Ground," one of the most poignant songs of the Civil War period. Walter Kittredge wrote it in 1862 as an emotional reflex action to being called for the draft. The thought of leaving his wife and child stirred somber thoughts and aroused painful feelings which became crystallized in his mind in a single recurring line: "Many are the hearts that are weary tonight, wishing for the war to cease." That night he wrote his song—first the lyric, then the music. The next morning he was turned down for the Army, since he had once suffered from rheumatic fever. Kittredge then tried marketing his song. One Boston publisher, to whom he offered it outright for fifteen dollars, turned it down as too lugubrious, too lacking in the martial spirit. However, a famous group of concert singers, the Hutchinson Family, included it in one of their concerts. Their influence was responsible for getting the song published by Oliver Ditson in 1864. Long after the war, the song continued to hold its appeal, often heard at picnics, camping expeditions, political meetings, and soldier rallies. In 1893, a chorus of five hundred rendered it with telling effect at the Chicago Columbian Exposition.

The singing Hutchinsons were responsible for the success of another Civil War classic, "The Battle Cry of Freedom," words and music by George F. Root. Before he had become a composer, Root had been a pioneer in the field of music education in the public schools and one of the founders of the New York Normal Institute which trained music teachers. Then, in 1851, in his thirty-first year, he started writing the words and melodies for popular songs, using for his first published pieces the pseudonymn of "Wurzel" (German for "root"). One of these was a sentimental ballad, "Rosalie," which came out in Boston in 1855 and became so popular that it brought him a royalty of about $3,000—not an inconsiderable figure at the time. Another of his successes was an evangelical hymn, "The Shining Shore," words by Rev. David Nelson. Root, then, was a song composer of some standing when the Civil War turned him to writing war songs.

The stimulus for "The Battle Cry of Freedom" was Lincoln's second call for volunteers in 1863. At that time, Root was his brother's partner in the Chicago music shop of Root and Cady. On the day he wrote his song, Frank and Jules Lombard, a singing duo, came to his shop seeking a good war song for a program scheduled that day for a rally in the Chicago Court House Square. Root showed them his fresh manuscript, which the Lombards liked so well that they took it for their performance. The audience was so stirred that, at one of the repetitions of the refrain, it spontaneously joined in the singing. After that, the Hutchinsons incorporated it into their own programs during their tours. The song then passed on from the public auditorium to the army camp. One unidentified Union soldier is quoted as having said: "It put as much spirit and cheer into the army as did a splendid victory. Day and night you could hear it by every campfire and in every tent."

"The Battle Cry of Freedom" was Root's most famous war song. He wrote several others, including the ballad "Just Before the Battle, Mother," in 1863, and one year later the marching song, "Tramp! Tramp! Tramp!"

George F. Root was one of two composers most prolific in writing Civil War songs. The other was Henry Clay Work, the author of "Marching Through Georgia." Before the outbreak of the war, Work was an active abolitionist in Illinois and Missouri, imprisoned for helping thousands of Southern Negro slaves escape. After his release in 1845, he became a printer of music. A decade later he settled in Chicago as a printer, where he started writing songs. "We Are Coming, Sister Mary" was published by Firth, Pond & Co., and was performed by the Christy Minstrels.

It was to be expected that Work would regard the Civil War

as a crusade for freedom, and that he should turn to writing war songs. "Kingdom Coming," published by Root and Cady in 1862, was so successful that it brought its composer a song-writing contract enabling him to give up printing for writing music. Other war songs soon enhanced his reputation, notably the humorous "Grafted into the Army" in 1862, "Babylon Is Fallen!" in 1863, and his masterpiece, "Marching Through Georgia," inspired by Sherman's historic march to the sea, published just before the war's end in 1865.

"The Battle Cry of Freedom" and "Marching Through Georgia" belonged to the North. The South had their equivalents in "The Bonnie Blue Flag" and "Maryland, My Maryland." The former was written in 1861 by Henry Macarthy, a Variety entertainer. He was appearing in New Orleans when as a finale for his act he wrote a march, "The Bonnie Blue Flag," in which he recounted the different steps of secession; for his melody he selected an old Irish tune, "The Jaunting Car." The audience thundered its enthusiasm; not many months passed before this enthusiasm was echoed by Confederate soldiers.

The lyric of "Maryland, My Maryland" was by James Ryder Randall, professor of English literature at Pydras College in Louisiana. While reading a newspaper account that Northern troops were fired upon as they passed through Baltimore, Randall instantly recognized that this incident might well provoke the recalcitrant Maryland to join the Southern cause. "That night I could not sleep, for my nerves were all unstrung," wrote Randall. "About midnight I rose, lit a candle, and went to my desk. Some powerful spirit seemed to possess me, and almost involuntarily I proceeded to write the song of 'My Maryland'." The poem was published in Baltimore in 1861 without giving credit to its author. Soon after this, Jennie Cary of Baltimore held a meeting at her home for advocates of the Southern cause. She sang Randall's poem to the melody of a German song, "O Tannenbaum," which had already become familiar in many American homes as a Christmas carol, and

in some American colleges as *"Lauriger Horatius."* Such enthusiasm met her rendition that people in the street flocked to her
window to see what was happening. Cary also sang the song
before the men of Beauregard's army at a concert at the Fair-
fax County House in Virginia. It was on this occasion that the
popularity of the song can be said to have begun, for it was
then that the soldiers of the Confederacy adopted it. The song
was published with due recognition to its author in New
Orleans in 1862, and soon after that appeared in various
pirated editions both in the North and South. James Russell
Lowell described it as the best poem produced by the war.

In the battle of songs, as ultimately on the field of conflict,
the North had the edge over the South. It has been written that
shortly after the surrender of General Lee, a few Northern
soldiers gave a potpourri of Northern war songs for several
Confederate men. A southern major remarked: "Gentlemen, if
we had had your songs, we'd have licked you out of your
boots."

VI

Though written for and during the Civil War, "When Johnny
Comes Marching Home" is most often identified with the Spanish-American War. This jaunty and cocky melody apparently
struck a responsive chord with an *opéra bouffe* war like that of
1898 in which the enemy was no match for American forces
and where the casualties were few and far between. Also in
the spirit of this war was Paul Dresser's jingoistic "Our Country, May She Always Be Right," and a vigorous minstrel-show
tune, "A Hot Time in the Old Town Tonight." The latter actually became the most famous song of the war, but like
"When Johnny Comes Marching Home" it antedated the conflict by several years, having been written in 1886 by Theodore
Metz, bandleader of the McIntyre and Heath Minstrels, and
published a decade later by Willis Woodward & Co. Metz
wrote his song after witnessing from a train a fire in Old Town,

Louisiana, being put out by some Negro children. When one of his minstrels remarked, "there'll be a hot time in Old Town tonight," he knew he had the idea for an effective minstrel-show number. For some years after its composition, the song was used as a march by the McIntyre and Heath Minstrels for its street parades, but it never quite caught on with the general public as an instrumental number. However, with lyrics by Joe Hayden carrying out the idea of a "hot time in the Old Town," it began to make an appeal, and was often heard as an opening chorus in minstrel shows. During the Spanish-American War, Theodore Roosevelt's Rough Riders adopted it as their personal anthem, and after that American soldiers in Cuba often sang it in an anticipation of a joyous return home.

Sentimentality was not absent from the songs of this war. The apostle of the sentimental ballad, Charles K. Harris—author of "After the Ball"—took the line "just break the news to mother" from William Gillette's play *Secret Service,* and, in 1897, published a tearful ballad called "Break the News to Mother" about the death of a fireman. When the Spanish-American War began, Harris revised his lyric to change the fireman into a soldier. "Break the News to Mother" suddenly acquired timeliness and became a hit.

After the Spanish-American War, the United States became a power earning the respect of the entire world. As if in anticipation of this development, there appeared three years before that war a patriotic song reflecting the citizen's pride in his land. In 1895, Katharine Lee Bates, an English professor at Wellesley College, paid a visit to Pike's Peak and was so moved by the grandeur of this sight that she wrote the verses of a hymn, "America the Beautiful," whose opening line read "O beautiful for spacious skies." The poem was first published in *The Congregationalist,* a Boston magazine, on July 4, 1895. Subsequently—though no one can say precisely when—these words were combined with the melody of "Materna," by Samuel A. Ward, written in 1882, and first performed in Boston six years later. Though never originally intended for each other, the words of Katharine Bates and the music of Samuel A. Ward proved perfect mates and combined into one of America's most effective anthems.

Another piece of music symbolic of the growth of American prestige and power also appeared before the Spanish-American War. In 1897, John Philip Sousa, former bandmaster of the United States Marine Corps, was returning from a trip to Europe which had been aborted by the sudden death of his manager. While on his way home aboard the *Teutonic,* he kept hearing in his mind's ear the strains of a military march which gave him no rest until he put it down on paper. His nostalgia for home and country undoubtedly was responsible for giving this melody its stirring virile character, and it became a reflection of his own love for, and pride in, his country. As it was finally crystallized, the melody became "The Stars and Stripes Forever," surely one of the most celebrated marches ever written. The self-assured, strong-muscled, proudly assertive music speaks not only for its composer, but also for a people grown conscious of the increasing importance of their country. From then on, Sousa's marches continued to speak for American patriotism.

America's march king was born in Washington, D.C. six years before the Civil War. As a boy he witnessed the frenetic activity and excitement attending the war—the marching troops, flying banners, martial songs, military bands. Their influence on a young and impressionable mind was inescapable. He was not yet fourteen when he enlisted in the Marine Corps, in whose band his father had played the trombone. Being highly musical, and having received a musical training in boyhood, young John Philip also joined the Marine Band. There followed various musical engagements outside the periphery of the armed services: as violinist in various orchestras and as conductor and musical director of several different theater companies. In 1880 he was appointed director of the United States

Marine Band, a post held with eminence for a dozen years. In this office he wrote his first famous marches, though he had been producing march music since boyhood. In 1888 came "Semper Fideles," written to provide his band with a stirring piece of music for parades and outdoor concerts. A year later he wrote "The Washington Post" and "The Thunderer."

In 1892, Sousa left the Marine Band to form his own concert organization, with which he made numerous tours both of this country and Europe. It is estimated that he gave over 10,000 concerts, for which he continued writing many stirring marches. Among them were "The Liberty Bell" in 1893, "King Cotton" in 1895, "El Capitan" (which originated as a male chorus in the second act of a comic opera of the same name) in 1896, "The Stars and Stripes Forever," in 1897, and "Hands Across the Sea," in 1899. By the time he died in Reading, Pennsylvania, in 1932, he had left behind him an impressive library of marches without equal in American music. He had also written ten operas and comic operas and made effective band arrangements of many of our national anthems and patriotic hymns.

VII

By World War I, Tin Pan Alley had become a well organized, efficient factory, capable of producing songs on every conceivable subject on an assembly belt. In 1917 it geared itself for war production. Singing war tunes was a practice that prevailed during the war years to strengthen morale at home and on the fighting front. Tin Pan Alley met the huge demand for war songs by producing them on every conceivable subject. There were some to fire the fighting spirit, to inflame patriotic ardor, and to incite hate for the enemy. There were songs of optimism, hope, sentiment, and nostalgia for home; songs glorifying every branch of the war effort; humorous songs to provide relief from war tensions. From the Tin Pan Alley production line came such songs to remember as "Till We Meet

Again" by Richard A. Whiting (Raymond B. Egan);* "Hello Central! Give Me No Man's Land," by Jean Schwartz (Sam M. Lewis and Joe Young); "K-K-K-Katy," words and music by Geoffrey O'Hara; "Rose of No Man's Land," by Joseph A. Brennan (Jack Caddingan); "Goodbye, Broadway, Hello France!" by Billy Baskette (Francis Reisner and Benny Davis); "How Ya Gonna Keep 'Em Down on the Farm?" by Walter Donaldson (Sam M. Lewis and Joe Young); and "Send Me Away With a Smile," words and music by Louis Weslyn and Al Piantadosi.

The classic of World War I, however, was none of these, but George M. Cohan's "Over There." When on the morning of April 7, 1917, Cohan read the news that America had just entered the war, something deep within him was stirred. As he himself later recalled: "I read those war headlines and I got to thinking and to humming to myself—and for a minute I thought I was going into my dance. I was all finished with both the chorus and the verse by the time I got to town, and I also had the title."

His song, "Over There," was introduced by Charles King at a Red Cross benefit at the Hippodrome Theatre in New York in the fall of 1917. It brought down the house. Nora Bayes later sang it up and down the stages of the country. Before the war ended, "Over There" had sold over two million copies of sheet music and over a million records; even the great Enrico Caruso recorded it. Cohan turned over all his royalties to war charities. President Wilson described it as "a genuine inspiration to all American manhood." By a special act of Congress, it brought Cohan a Congressional Medal from President Franklin D. Roosevelt.

During World War I, Irving Berlin (already a recognized king of ragtime) was called to uniform and stationed at Camp Upton. There the commanding officer, General Bell, asked him

---

*From this point on, and for the rest of the book, a name appearing in parentheses after a song title will be that of the lyricist.

to write and produce an all-soldiers show to raise $35,000 for a badly needed service center. Drawing from his own experiences as a sad rookie, Berlin not only wrote all the songs, sketches, and dialogue, but even planned all the dance routines for *Yip, Yip, Yaphank*, which opened at the Century Theatre in New York on July 26, 1918. The cast was headed by Berlin himself who appeared in one scene as a badly mauled K.P. whining, "I scrub the dishes against my wishes, to make this wide world safe for democracy"; and, in another, being dragged from his cot by the merciless call of reveille, lamenting "Oh, how I hate to get up in the morning!"

There was an ovation after the final curtain. *Variety* called *Yip, Yip, Yaphank* "one of the best and most novel entertainments Broadway has ever witnessed." It played to capacity houses for four weeks, earning $83,000 for Camp Upton's service center; the sum swelled beyond $150,000 after a brief tour of Boston, Philadelphia, and Washington, D. C. Eventually, the show earned many times that amount for the composer. While Berlin drew no salary or royalties during the War, he was, of course, free to capitalize on his songs once he discarded his uniform. Two of these songs passed a million-copy sale: "Oh, How I Hate to Get Up in the Morning," and "Mandy," the latter interpolated into the *Ziegfeld Follies of 1919* where it was sung by Marilyn Miller.

VIII

Irving Berlin, then, played a not inconsiderable part in the song history of World War I. But he was to fill an even more heroic role during World War II. Actually he was the song laureate of the second war—and even before the first Nazi bombs fell on Poland.

In 1938, Kate Smith asked him to write for her a new patriotic song. Berlin liked the idea. Having recently returned from a European trip and having seen the shadows of Fascism lengthen across Europe, he had gained a new awareness of the meaning of American liberty and a new feeling of pride in democracy. But he seemed incapable of putting on paper the kind of sentiment he felt would echo his true feelings. Then he remembered a melody he had written in 1918 as an optional finale for *Yip, Yip, Yaphank,* but which had not been used. He retrieved the manuscript from his trunk and wrote new lyrics.

As "God Bless America" it was introduced over the radio by Kate Smith on Armistice Day, 1938, and after that was popularized by her on records and through innumerable broadcasts. The song caught fire. It became our second national anthem. In 1939 both major political parties used it as the key song for their Presidential nomination conventions. A year later the National Committee for Music Appreciation gave it a special citation. Having done more to create a national consciousness in this country than any other piece of music, "God Bless America" was honored by President Dwight D. Eisenhower when, on July 16, 1954, he approved a bill authorizing Congress to strike a special gold medal for the composer.

Like Cohan before him, Berlin refused to capitalize on his patriotism. He created the "God Bless America Fund" in 1940, allocating all royalties (over $200,000) to the Boy Scouts, Girl Scouts, and Campfire Girls. Later on he dedicated himself more and more completely to writing songs for patriotic causes and war agencies—for the sale of war bonds, to spur arms production, for Navy Relief, for the March of Dimes, for the Red Cross—and he continued to contribute all royalties from these efforts to war charities.

But his greatest single effort for World War II was—just as it had been in the earlier war—in writing and producing an all-soldier show. The idea came to him soon after Pearl Harbor, when he recognized the acute need among American soldiers for stage entertainment. Army officials, faced with the grim business of quickly transforming civilians into seasoned troops, frowned on his suggestion for a soldiers' show. But he persevered in his aim, and finally won a grudging consent from the Pentagon.

He was assigned a small room in a barracks in Camp Upton (the same camp where he had been stationed during World War I, and had produced *Yip, Yip, Yaphank*) so that he might gain first-hand army experiences. He found a wealth of material for his acts, routines, sketches, songs, and production numbers—on the training-field, in the service club, the mess hall, the P-X. Since the army had insisted that this be no gold-brick assignment, rehearsals usually had to take place after the regular army details and duties had been completed. Often in fits and starts, and often late into the night, the show was slowly whipped into shape. Starring Sgt. Ezra Stone, Cpl. Philip Truex, Pvt. Julie Oshins, and Mr. Irving Berlin, and including a cast of about three hundred, many of them amateurs, *This Is the Army* opened on Broadway on July 4, 1942. This was a picture, in song, dance, and humor, of army life during World War II. But there was also a poignant reminder of the first World War. For the number that always stopped the show was the song, "Oh, How I Hate to Get Up in the Morning," retrieved from *Yip, Yip, Yaphank*, and once again sung by Irving Berlin, wearing his World War I uniform.

So great was the demand at the box office that a four-week engagement was extended to twelve weeks. A nation-wide tour followed, culminating in Hollywood where the production was made into a motion picture by Warner Brothers. The tour swung back east and across the ocean to England, Scotland, and Ireland. By special permission, it then visited the combat areas of Europe, the Near East, and the Pacific. Two years and three months after it had opened, *This Is the Army* gave its last performance—in Honolulu, on October 22, 1945. It had earned almost $10,000,000 for the Army Relief Fund and another $350,000 for British War Charities. It had also brought the joy of song, laughter, and dance to about 2,500,000 war-weary American soldiers. In gratitude for this monumental achievement, General George C. Marshall presented Irving Berlin with the Medal of Merit.

American soldiers fighting in the Pacific owed still another debt to Berlin. One of Berlin's songs, "White Christmas," brought them in swamps and jungles nostalgic recollections of home and Yuletide peace and good will. "White Christmas" was written for *Holiday Inn,* a screen musical starring Bing Crosby and Fred Astaire. As sung by Bing, "White Christmas" stepped out of the screen to become an American classic. It sold several million copies of sheet music and phonograph records in its first year. Since then the sales figures have soared to almost 20,000,000 records and 4,000,000 copies of sheet music, a total still without parallel in our song history. It has become a permanent holiday staple, bringing to each Christmas season an added radiance: the Gallup poll has placed it second only to "Silent Night" as a Yuletide song favorite.

Among the songs rising out of the emotions and experiences of World War II were "The White Cliffs of Dover" by Walter Kent (Nat Burton); "The Last Time I Saw Paris" by Jerome Kern (Oscar Hammerstein II); "Comin' In on a Wing and a Prayer" by Jimmy McHugh (Harold Adamson); and "I'll Walk Alone" by Jule Styne (Sammy Cahn). But the first major song inspired by American participation in the war came from a novice: Frank Loesser who, up to 1941, had only written lyrics, but who made his first solo flight as a composer immediately after Pearl Harbor. It was that tragedy that stimulated him to write an unusual lyric called "Praise the Lord and Pass the Ammunition"—the title phrase attributed to Father Maguire, fleet chaplain of the Pacific Fleet during the sneak attack on Pearl Harbor. Since Loesser had never before written a melody without assistance, he planned to turn his lyric over to a professional composer. But before doing so, he created a dummy tune to test the singableness of his words. It was a melody that happened to spring to mind as he wrote the words, and he put it down on paper without revision. When he tried out his lyric with its dummy tune for friends, they insisted that his melody be retained. In this haphazard and casual way, Loesser had created a song with an American hymnlike character, rich with folk flavors. It was not the kind of melody that a Tin Pan Alley troubadour would regard as commercial —this, perhaps, was its inherent strength. Loesser published his song, and it swept the country. But for the fact that some members of the clergy complained over the juxtaposition of the Lord with the passing of ammunition, and that Father Maguire himself expressed displeasure at being associated with the now-famous slogan—developments that did much to arrest the floodtide of popularity for the song—"Praise the Lord" might easily have become one of the half dozen or so most successful American war songs ever written. As it was, even with an arrested development, it sold over two million records and a million copies of sheet music.

"Praise the Lord" was Loesser's first contribution to the war. That contribution was soon to grow to formidable proportions. He was, like Irving Berlin, one of the war's songwriting heroes. As a Private First Class in Special Services, Loesser helped write soldier shows (to which he contributed all the songs, music as well as the words), packaged and distributed to army camps everywhere. He also created individual songs for different branches of the armed services. One of these, "What Do You Do In the Infantry?" is now one of the official songs of that branch of the service. Loesser also wrote songs for the WACS, the Service Forces, and even the Canadian Tank Force.

Before the war ended, Loesser produced one of its most poignant songs: "Rodger Young." He wrote it at the request of Infantry officials who wanted to advertise the heroism of some infantryman. Loesser wrote to Washington for a list of infantrymen posthumously awarded the Medal of Honor. Rodger Young's name was one of these. He was a twenty-five-year-old soldier who attacked a Japanese pillbox in the Solomons, sacrificing his own life to save his buddies. Like "Praise the Lord," his ballad has such a homespun American quality that it is likely to find a permanent place in our folk-song literature.

IX

Any survey of American national ballads and political songs should include at least a passing word on some of the better and more prominent ones dedicated to the various branches of the armed services. We have already commented upon Loesser's "What Do You Do In the Infantry?". The field artillery march, "The Caisson Song," or "The Caissons Go Rolling Along," was for a long time believed to have been written by John Philip Sousa, largely because he issued an excellent band arrangement in 1918 and introduced it successfully at a Liberty Loan drive at the Hippodrome Theatre. Strange to say, Sousa himself helped support the long-held belief that he was its author, and the first publication in 1918 gives credit to the march king. Later incontrovertible evidence, however, proved that Edmund L. Gruber wrote both the words and music in 1908, while serving as a lieutenant with the 5th Artillery in the Philippine Islands. A 1936 publication by Shapiro, Bernstein and Co. gives full and sole credit to Gruber.

The Army Air Corps Song appeared in 1939 as the winner in a song contest sponsored by the Army Air Corps. Its author was a civilian, Robert Crawford, who taught voice at Princeton University. The song was immediately adopted by the air forces and from that time on has helped to identify it. During World War II, the song was used with telling effect as the *Leitmotif* for the Air Corps production, *Winged Victory*, written by Moss Hart, successfully presented on both stage and screen.

The Navy song, "Anchors Aweigh," was published in 1906, words by A. H. Miles and R. Lovell, music by Charles A. Zimmerman. The Marines' Hymn, "From the Halls of Montezuma," first appeared in 1918 in an uncopyrighted version, "printed but not published by the United States Marine Corps Publicity Bureau." One year later, the song was copyrighted by the Marine Corps. The music was taken from an aria from an obscure *opéra bouffe* of Jacques Offenbach, *Geneviève de Brabant*. Considerable doubt exists concerning the author of the lyrics. One account (a sheet-music edition issued by the Marine Corps Publicity Bureau) has it that it was the work of an unidentified marine, who wrote it in 1847. In *The Book of Navy Songs*, published in 1926, Col. Henry C. Davis of the Marine Corps is credited; and the marine copyright of 1919 identifies the lyricist as L. Z. Phillips.

chapter two

THE PEOPLE SING—
Our Folk Music

FROM the dawn of our history, Americans have sung of their experiences, troubles, and aspirations. Thus, as our democracy grew to maturity, a folk music has been evolved which, in a large measure, expresses and interprets our national growth. Songs followed the frontier, and they accompanied industry in its expansion; they went into the mines and penetrated the hills; they were inspired by work in the fields, forests, and on ships.

At the beginning of the eighteenth century, lumbering was already a major industry in New England; and in the nineteenth century it went further west. The lumberjacks, or shantyboys, were a polyglot lot, embracing Scottish, Irish, German, and French Canadians. "Into the woods flocked the adventurers like beehives," wrote James Cloyd Bowman in the *Michigan History Magazine*. "Many . . . were drawn into the camps by their love of hardy, out-of-door, roving life with men. Many others were recent emigrants, and came eagerly to try the first chance that fortune offered in the new land of opportunity. Some were natural 'floaters,' dominated entirely by an insatiable wanderlust. Occasionally, one proved a fugitive from justice and took to the friendly forest. And almost every nationality was represented."

Work was hard, beginning at four in the morning and continuing right up to sunset. Danger was ever present, either from falling logs or from log jams on the river. Diversions were few and far between. A favorite form of entertainment for lumberjacks was to listen to minstrels sing songs and tell tall stories after the evening meal. The word shantyboy—derived from the French word *chanter,* meaning "to sing"—points up the significance of song in the life of these lumberjacks. So does the legend of George Burns. One evening, during the height of a blizzard, Burns staggered into a log camp, frozen and half-starved. When he recovered, he asked for food, offering to pay for it with songs. These made such an impression on the men that they insisted he stay with them all winter and entertain them every evening. Burns was not a good lumberjack. But his shortcomings with ax were more than compensated for by his gift at song invention. Burns was typical of the wandering minstrel who habitually went from one log camp to the next practicing his folk art.

The songs of the shantyboy were usually about experiences closest to him. "A Shantyman's Life" told of his rigid daily routine, "The Little Brown Bulls" of his work on the river, "The Logger's Boast" of his pride in his work. "The Jam on Gerry's Rocks" described a log jam, the dread of all lumberjacks. Sometimes the songs told the stories of legendary lumberjacks. There was the mythical Paul Bunyan, and his blue ox "Babe," who inspired a long skein of tall tales. Bunyan scooped out the Grand Canyon by dragging his pick, and he worked in such freezing weather that his profanity froze into ice and did not thaw out until the following July. Then there were Jimmie Whalen and Johnny Stiles, actual shantyboys, both of whom came to their tragic end in a log jam.

The songs, like the life of the men who sang them, were filled with loneliness, bleakness, nostalgia for home, dreams.

Dramatic impact came through free rhythms and the declama-
tory nature of the melody. Sometimes old English ballads,
sailor chanteys, Negro spirituals, or railroad songs were adapted
for shantyboy lyrics; but just as often the melody was original
with the singers and had the same improvisational character
as the lyric. Rough, brusque, and masculine in spirit, the songs
of the shantyboy project emotions self-consciously. Many have
the restrained sadness of sad men too stout of heart to give
voice to their inmost feelings. Poignancy comes from understatement. Occasionally, a rough-and-tumble humor is inter-
posed. But whether in joy or sorrow, these songs are the voice
of vigorous men who led robust lives, and they have the lusty
stride and the steel-like muscle of such men.

II

The songs of the shantyboy were generally concerned with
his work, sung in retrospect when the day's labors had ended.
On the other hand, chanteys—or sailor songs—were *work*
songs, sung during the performance of menial duties. Work on
American ships, as in the forests, was hard during a long day.
Singing helped sailors to ease their terrible strain. As Richard
Henry Dana noted in *Two Years Before the Mast:* "A song is
as necessary to sailors as the fife and drum to soldiers."

Chanteys fall into four categories. Songs for tasks requiring
short, heavy pulls were called "Short Drags." They had
abrupt rhythms, crisp accents, clipped phrases—as in "Haul
Away, Joe" or "Haul on the Bowline." Songs for more sustained and heavier tasks, such as hoisting sails or casting anchors, were called "Halliards." A halliard like the famous
"Blow, Boys, Blow" had a more even rhythm than the short
drag, a more monotonous meter, a more flowing melody, and
more sustained choruses. For still more monotonous jobs
there were "Capstans," long and sustained melodies with
slow march-like rhythms like "Santy Anno." Finally, there
were the "Foc'sle Songs." These were not work songs but

songs meant to entertain the crew when off duty; songs about ladies of easy virtue, epics of whaling and fishing, ballads about naval heroes.

Chanteys were originally accompanied by an accordion or a violin. But as the work on deck grew more complex and arduous, and as all hands were needed to complete the daily chores, instrumental accompaniment had to be dispensed with. In these unaccompanied chanteys, a leader would render the solo lines, with the rest of the crew joining in the refrain. The leader was permitted full latitude in improvising and embellishing upon his solo part, and it was he who most usually made up the original tunes. Since leaders were chosen for their pleasing voices, Negroes or Irishmen (generally the best singers of the crew) filled that role. It is for this reason that stylistic traits of Irish balladry and Negro spirituals are so predominant in the music of the chanteys. But other musical sources also provided a fund of melody: foreign ballads, national anthems, cowboy songs, and Vaudeville ditties.

III

The migration westward, and its accompanying song literature, began almost as soon as the War for Independence was over. By 1790, over 170,000 settlers had crossed the mountainous regions of the South to the western lands of Kentucky and Tennessee. Throughout the nineteenth century this flow continued uninterruptedly, penetrating ever further and deeper west.

Out of this migration came a new storehouse of folk songs. Bullwhackers, who drove the wagons, sang as they traveled. Stout-hearted pioneers who lived dangerously and worked hard, they sang of their new lives in the open country.

The entertainments of the city—the theater, social gatherings, card games—were virtually nonexistent in a place where one's nearest neighbor lived many miles away. Men and women of the West sang to while away their leisure hours, sometimes making up their own songs—virile, wind-swept, and energetic, of the open spaces, with vigorous rhythms and wild and stark melodies.

These pioneers were free men. They could build their lives in their own way. They developed their own government freed of any vestiges of imperial rule. A spirit of equality was born on the frontier, where each man's courage, energy, and complete lack of snobbery made him the equal of his neighbor.

The same spirit of equality, independence, and love of freedom entered their songs. These men looked contemptuously upon the popular tunes of the Eastern seaboard—"Federalist tunes," they called these aristocratic songs of a snobbish people. In the East, people sang of the fashions of the day or politics; many eastern popular songs were bathed in sentimentality describing a railroad wreck, or a ship on fire, or even the agony of a parent seeing her child snatched by a vulture. Musically, these eastern songs were stereotyped and formal, following the rigid pattern of the English ballad.

What the frontiersman wanted in his song were words and melody suitable for a plain, common, democratic people. He had no use for sentimentality or sensationalism, and only contempt for snobbish descriptions of fashions and talk of city vice. At the same time, he swept aside the formal academic style of eastern songs. To his popular music he brought a gust of fresh wind and a spirit that was proud and free. "To the West" or "Shoot the Buffalo" had a lusty energy and manly vigor that would have been out of place in the stuffy atmosphere of the eastern parlor. The pioneer was not afraid to be original in his musical thinking. A melody like "The Star of Columbia" was built on a scale with a pentatonic character, structurally far different from the invariable diatonic writing of the east. The rhythmic pattern had an unorthodox variety.

The fiddle was the favorite instrument of the frontiersman. Bob Taylor, one-time Governor of Tennessee, wrote: "The fiddle, the rifle, the ax, and the Bible . . . were the trusty friends and faithful allies of our pioneer ancestry in subduing the wilderness and erecting the great commonwealth of the Republic." For their social gatherings, the pioneers would either play old tunes or spontaneously improvise new ones on their fiddles. These social gatherings included square dances and play parties. The latter were instituted by the more religious pioneers for the young folk as a modified substitute for dancing; with involved gestures and steps, the young people would sing and move to the rhythm of songs like "Here Comes Three Dukes," "Weevily Wheat," and "Skip to My Lou."

Originally borrowed from many different sources (most usually Irish reels and minstrel-show tunes), the melodies of the frontiersman underwent a radical change of feeling, structure, and style at the hands of the fiddlers. These melodies would gain new figurations as the performer allowed his imagination to wander freely about a given tune. Abrupt intervals (usually that of the open fifth) would dramatize the lyric line. Rhythms would be dynamic and incisive. Men of strength and individuality had to express themselves in songs that were strong and free. Before long, borrowed melodies came to be considered original homespun pioneer products, and—truth to tell—they had become original with their performers.

There was primitivism in these social songs, and there was primitivism in the frontiersman's religious music ("white spirituals"). A religious song like "The Promised Land" was rugged, crude, and powerful. There were no formal religious services on the frontier. The circuit-riding preacher would come to a settlement to conduct a revival meeting and lead the pioneers in the singing of hymns. Sometimes secular tunes were adapted for religious functions. Where new religious tunes were created (and the preachers sometimes invented them while riding horseback from one settlement to the next) they had the passionate and savage feelings found in the pioneer secular song. During religious worship the melodies became almost barbaric as the pent-up emotions of the frontiersman were allowed an outlet in religious ritual.

IV

Others who pushed westward also sang as they traveled. There were the Forty-Niners who, lured by gold in Sutter's Creek, poured into California by covered wagon, horse, steamer, sailing boat, and some even on foot. "No earlier cause ever called together in the New World such a strange medley of men, so curious a mass as this Golden Army," wrote A. B. Hulbert in his diary. "There they lie, amid their fading fires of prairie grass, of tepee poles, of cottonwood stumps . . . rich men, poor men, beggar men, thieves; farmers, lawyers, doctors, merchants, preachers, workmen; Republicans, Whigs, Federalists, Abolitionists, Baptists, Methodists, Transcendentalists; Germans, Russians, Poles, Swiss, Spaniards; sailors, steamboat men, lumbermen, gamblers; the lame, squint-eyed, pockmarked, one-armed; squaws in royal blankets, prostitutes in silk, brave women in knickerbockers; fortune-tellers, phrenologists, mesmerists, harlots, card sharks, ventriloquists, and evangelists . . . dreaming of gold."

This adventure led to the making of songs like "Sweet Betsy from Pike," a classic of the Gold Rush days, in which the adventures of "Betsy" and "Ike" epitomized the experiences of all others who braved the unknown to cross the wide prairies into California. Other songs were parodies—of Stephen Foster's "Oh! Susanna" and "Camptown Races," for example, or of the chantey, "Rio Grande." To these three melodies, and to many others, new lyrics were invented to describe the hardship of travel, to retell of the excitement and exhilaration of the grand adventure, to depict the swelling hopes for riches, and finally to speak of the disenchantment that set in when these hopes did not materialize. "Sacramento" had two versions; One was filled with the bluster and enthusiasm of a people convinced that "there's plenty of gold on the banks of the Sacramento." The other version, sung on the homeward trek, was touched with bitterness and disillusion.

The opening of the West brought still other songs into existence. The cowboy created them to rally his herd or to lull it to sleep, "up the trail" from Texas to the shipping point in Dodge City, Kansas. A simple person, close to the fundamentals of living and working, the cowboy sang songs that were so simple in design as to be almost ingenuous—with little variety of rhythm, meter, or structure. He was a lonely man; his songs overflow with nostalgic sentiments for home, a girl, peace of heart, rest. His best friend was his horse, and his one dread, a lonely grave. He frequently sang about both. When he was happy, he spoke of breaking loose in Dodge City. When he was sad he lamented dying alone and being buried in a solitary grave on the wide prairie.

One of the songs most often heard among cowboys was "The Old Chisholm Trail," to which they always improvised fresh lyrics as they made their way to Kansas. "It was a dull day on the drive when one of the cowboys did not make a new verse to 'The Old Chisholm Trail'," wrote an unidentified cowboy. The brisk melody was a perfect companion to the lyrics describing the life and activity of cowboys as they herded their cows north: "Come along, boys, and listen to my tale, I'll tell you of my troubles on the old Chisholm Trail." Other cowboy songs were more poignant, reflecting the cowboy's terrible loneliness. The best were "Goodbye Old Paint," "The Cowboy's Dream," "Poor Lonesome Cowboy," "Bury Me Not on the Lone Prairie," and "The Dying Cowboy." Into most of these songs, the cowboy interpolated familiar cowboy calls, such as "whoopee-yi-yi," or "yipee," or "comma tiyi yoppy," or "hi-oo, hi-oo." In some of the songs we can detect the rhythm of the clattering hoofs of his horse.

The most familiar of all cowboy songs, "Home on the Range," was once described by John A. Lomax as "the cowboy's na-

tional anthem." Its authorship has long been hotly debated.
There are some supporters to the claim of Dr. Brewster Higley
and Dan Kelly that they wrote the words and music respectively
in or about 1873. At that time, the song was introduced by
Clarence Harlan (who later also made a recording of it), and
the verses were published in the *Smith County Pioneer*.
Others insist that the author of both the words and music was
C. O. Swartz. However, a court action in 1934 decreed that the
song was in the public domain. A copyrighted version appeared
in 1905, but not until Lomax heard it sung in Texas by a
Negro saloon-keeper, made a record of it then and there,
and then printed it in the 1910 edition of his *Cowboy Songs*
did it make a first bid for public attention. In 1925, a Texas
publisher issued it in a sheet-music edition, and five years
later a Texas musician, David Guion, made an arrangement
that soon became famous. "Home on the Range" first became
popular over the radio in the early 1930s. It was then said
that this was President Roosevelt's favorite song—an unfounded
rumor, but one that helped to spread its popularity.

The men who built the railroads drove their spikes on sun-
baked prairies to the tunes of swinging work songs. A leader,
frequently chosen either for his gift at improvisation or for
the pleasing quality of his voice, would chant the saga of some
legendary railroad hero like John Henry, or an actual one like
Casey Jones, or a ballad about a famous train wreck. The workers would then join in the chorus, accenting the beat with
the pounding of their hammers on the spikes.

It was the wreck of a mail train near Danville, Virginia, in
1903, that inspired the well-known "The Wreck of the Old
'97," set to the music of an old ballad by Henry C. Work,
"The Ship That Never Returned." An early Victor Company
recording was so popular that it sold over a million disks and
earned a profit of over $150,000. The author of the lyric is
unknown. When the song became a success many stepped forward to claim it—one or two in the law courts—but to no avail.

Still another wreck was responsible for what is surely the best known of all railroad songs—"Casey Jones." This wreck occurred just outside the town of Vaughn, Mississippi, in 1906, when a crack train of the Illinois Central crashed into a line of box-cars. The engineer, Casey Jones, shouted to his fireman, Sim Webb, to jump and save his life. Webb was saved, but Casey himself was a victim. When his body was found one of his hands was on the whistle and another on the airbrake lever. A few days later, Wallis Saunders, a Negro engine-wiper—who had wiped Casey's blood off the throttle handle—improvised lyrics about the death of his heroic friend, using for his model a Negro ballad called "Jimmie Jones." His song was taken over by railroad workers everywhere. Two actors heard it in New Orleans and introduced it on the vaudeville stage. With the interpolation of a ragtime lyric, the song acquired national fame in 1909, a fame that has not died down to the present day.

V

Still another repository of folk songs was preserved in the Appalachian and Cumberland mountains of Kentucky, Tennessee, North Georgia, the Carolinas, and Virginia. British settlers had penetrated these parts during the seventeenth and eighteenth centuries. Since access to these mountain places, either by road or rail, was difficult, the settlers led a cloistered and comparatively primitive existence, often untouched by changes and developments of the world outside the hills. The barter system, an archaic language, and an old-world folk-song literature imported from the mother country, were kept alive.

Shortly after World War I, several musicologists—among them Cecil Sharp of England, and Howard Brockway of Brooklyn, New York—explored these mountain communities and helped to bring this rich repertory of American folk songs to national acceptance. "We stepped out of New York into the life of the frontier settler of Daniel Boone's time," wrote

Howard Brockway in describing his expedition. "Here are people who know naught of the advance which has been made in the world outside of their mountains. It surpasses belief. . . . In the 17th century, their ancestors had brought the songs from England, Scotland, Ireland, and Wales, and they have been handed down orally from generation to generation. Songs that died out in the old country a century ago are still sung every day in the Appalachian region. The statement has been made that amongst these people one can find nearly all the folk songs ever sung in the British Isles, and perhaps the claim is not far wrong."

In his monumental edition of these mountain tunes, *English Folk Songs from the Southern Appalachians,* Cecil Sharp remarks that these songs are by no means faded and obsolete museum pieces, but living and vital music. Everybody sang in the mountains; there were few homes without some musical instrument, usually a fiddle, guitar, or banjo. Everybody seemed born with a gift for making ballads. Thus a rich storehouse of ballads was either preserved or created, including such gems as "Barbara Allen," "Pretty Polly," "Sourwood Mountain," and "The Two Sisters," each of which exists in numerous variants. Such songs were called "lonesome tunes" because they were sung solo, and without accompaniment. Their technical individuality lay in their free intonation and in their fluctuating rhythm. Some, like "Pretty Polly," are unmistakably British in character and style. Others, like "Sourwood Mountain" and "The Two Sisters," are more intrinsically American, having acquired subtle nuances of expression and little melodic idiosyncrasies that are foreign to the English ballad.

VI

American folk ballads, of actual or spurious, historical or mythical heroes, sprang up in every part of the country. We already had occasion to comment upon a few of these ballads inspired by Paul Bunyan, or Jimmie Whalen, or Casey Jones. There were many others.

One of them glorified John Henry, a Negro railroad worker reputed to be a steel-driving champion. In or about 1873, during the construction of a mountain tunnel on the C & O Railroad, he met his death—during a competition with a steam drill, say some; from a falling rock, according to others. Another ballad, "Johnny Appleseed," pays tribute to Jonathan Chapman of the Northwest, who traveled with bags of appleseed planting orchards up and down Ohio, Indiana, and Illinois. A third ballad, "Cumberland Gap," spoke of Daniel Boone, the brave Indian fighter.

Some ballads are about disreputable characters whose lives and deeds inflamed the imagination of writers. In the West there were numerous songs of bad men—"Jesse James," for example, in which the outlaw is portrayed as a western Robin Hood who "robbed from the rich and he gave to the poor." The East had its own Robin Hood in Jim Fisk. Fisk was an unsavory character who had amassed wealth in Wall Street, and had acquired power in politics, both through illegitimate methods; becoming involved with pretty Josie Mansfield, he was murdered by Josie's boy friend in 1872. In "Jim Fisk" he becomes a hero who might defraud the rich, but whose heart belonged to the poor.

Two other no less ignoble characters appear in the most celebrated of all such folk ballads. One was a prostitute, Frankie; the other a loose character named Johnny who "done her wrong." Many variants of "Frankie and Johnny" exist— several hundred no less—and in most of them Frankie finally shoots her man and is acquitted.

It is impossible to say when and where "Frankie and Johnny" first appeared. In *The Covered Wagon*, Emerson Hough places the song as far back as 1840. Thomas Beer wrote in *The Mauve Decade* that it was sung at the siege of Vicksburg. In *The American Songbag* Carl Sandburg fixes its year of birth sometime in the 1880s.

When "Frankie and Johnny" was made into a motion picture starring Helen Morgan, an interesting litigation ensued. A Portland, Oregon lawyer brought action against Republic Pictures, Helen Morgan, and several others, for defaming the character of his client, a certain Negro woman named Frankie Baker. He maintained that this woman had killed her boy friend in 1899 and was the inspiration for the famous ballad. The case was dismissed, and the plaintiff had to defray all court costs.

VII

For many years, our folk music was to most Americans *terra incognita,* the exclusive hunting grounds for scholars. But within the last few decades folk songs have begun to reach out to an ever-widening public, and have come to be accepted by it. Thanks to the patient labors of many musicologists; thanks to the increasing frequency with which folk singers have begun to appear in the theater, on the concert stage, on records, and over the radio; thanks, too, to the numerous recordings and popular-priced publications that have inundated the music and book markets during the past few years—Americans have come to know and love folk songs almost as they do current commercial hits.

One consequence of the growing popularity of folk music has been its effect on Tin Pan Alley. Many of the song hits of recent years have been patterned after the style, structure, idiom, and mood of western and mountain ballads, cowboy songs, railroad songs, work songs.

One of the most successful composers to carry folk-song styles and techniques into Tin Pan Alley was Billy Hill. Hill was born in Boston in the last year of the past century. After some musical training at the New England Conservatory he played the violin in the renowned Boston Symphony Orchestra. In his seventeenth year he answered the call of adventure and travel. For the next few years he wandered shiftlessly throughout the West, often riding from one destination to the next on the rods of freight trains, and just as often holding down menial jobs. When the mood was upon him he wrote songs; and on one occasion he organized and led what is believed to have been one of the first jazz bands in the West.

He returned to New York in the early 1930s determined to make a career of song writing. To earn his living, he worked as an apartment house doorman. His poverty was so intense that there were times when he was unable to pay his rent or gas bill, when the local food stores refused to trust him any longer, and when even the maternity ward of one of the city hospitals refused admission to his wife. Only a generous loan from Gene Buck, President of ASCAP tided him over one of these difficult periods.

In 1933, Hill wrote the words and music of "The Last Roundup," a frank imitation of a cowboy ballad. Only the loan he had just received from Buck kept him from selling his song outright for $25.00. Published in 1933, it was introduced the same year by Joe Morrison at the Paramount Theatre in New York, and one year after that interpolated into the *Ziegfeld Follies of 1934*. "The Last Roundup" was a succes of major proportions. Hill could now give up his job and live in comparative affluence at the Park Plaza Hotel near Central Park. Other songs in a folk style—many written some years earlier—were now published and performed, assuring him of a prosperity which happily continued up to the time of his death on Christmas Eve of 1940. Among them were "Wagon Wheels," "The Old Spinning Wheel," and "Empty Saddles."

The influence of the American folk song on Tin Pan Alley was felt by many other composers, too, and was responsible for numerous commercial hits. Here are a few since the middle 1930s: Johnny Mercer's "I'm an Old Cowhand"; Cole

Porter's "Don't Fence Me In"; "Buttons and Bows" by Jay Livingston and Ray Evans, a Motion Picture Academy Award winner in 1948; Dimitri Tiomkin's "Do Not Forsake Me, Oh My Darling" (Ned Washington), recipient of the Motion Picture Academy Award in 1952; "The Ballad of Davy Crockett" by George F. W. Bruhns (Tom Blackburn); "Sixteen Tons" by Merle Travis; "The Wayward Wind" by Stan Lebowsky and Herb Newman.

chapter three

GONNA SING ALL OVER GOD'S HEAVEN — The Songs of the Negro

THE FIRST Negro slaves landed in Virginia a year before the arrival of the *Mayflower*. By the early eighteenth century there were about 75,000 slaves in the Colonies; a century later that number swelled to about a million.

The slaves brought with them from Africa their musical instincts, a natural aptitude for expressing their feelings in rhythm and melody, a flair for dancing. Thomas Jefferson was probably the first white man to make note of the musical nature of his slaves. "In music they are more generally gifted than the whites," he wrote in the *Notes on Virginia,* "with accurate ears for tune and time, and they have been found capable of imagining a small catch." They also imported from Africa various kinds of African drums, and an African instrument that came to be known in the Colonies as a "banjo." Finally, they introduced into the music of the Colonies stylistic traits indigenous to African music: syncopated beats, shifting accents, variety of rhythm, and the "call and answer" format of voodoo chants.

Africans frequently sang and danced during working hours. On slave ships bound for the new world, and later on the plantations in the Colonies, Negroes were encouraged by their masters to sing, since it was felt that music was an opiate to dull the sharp edge of rebellion on the part of slaves. Transplanted into a new cruel world where he was despised and rejected, the Negro found solace in his songs.

In the new world, the Negro came into contact for the first time with European melody and harmony. He was too innately musical not to be affected by them. Before long, his music-making tried to combine European idioms with African rhythms and musical approaches. Still one other powerful new-world influence helped to give the Negro song its character and personality: Christianity. In Christianity, the Negro found an escape from his own miserable existence; in it he found the promise of a new life in the hereafter to compensate him for his terrible ordeals on earth. The Negro began to identify himself with Christ who had been crucified. Christianity taught the Negro patience and resignation.

To the Negro in the new world, religion and song often became one and the same thing. The religious songs of the Negro were sometimes "sorrow songs": elegiac lamentations expressing the woe of an oppressed people. Sometimes, too, the religious songs were "Shouts": orgiastic outbursts of religious ecstasy.

II

The Negro spiritual had techniques and processes that set it sharply apart from other American folk songs. Generally speaking, the spiritual was characterized by mobile changes from major to minor without the benefit of formal modulations; by the freedom of its rhythm and intonation; by its plangent moods; by the injection of notes, like the flatted third or seventh, foreign to the formal scale; by the variation of the rhythmic pattern.

Unlike so many other American folk songs, the spiritual was created not by an individual, but by groups; it was meant to be sung not as a solo, but chorally. Consequently, the interest in the spiritual lies not only in the melody but also in the harmony.

The spiritual—particularly the "Shout"—was often produced spontaneously, inspired by the excited emotions of the moment, and carried to ever greater intensity and depths of feeling by an uncontrolled momentum on the part of virtually hypnotized singers. As R. Emmett Kennedy wrote in *Mellows,* the "Shout" was evolved "partly under the influence of association with Whites, but in the main, original in the best sense of the word; the inspiration of a moment of ecstasy, the expression of religious elation curiously intermingled with emotions of intrinsically barbaric character; the changed prayer of a simple, child-like mind, the melodious cry of a soul on its knees."

There were three classes of spirituals. One employs the call-and-answer technique found in African tribal songs. Here one line is provocatively thrown out by a leader, and is answered by a repetitious word, phrase, or sentence, by a group of voices. The tempo is fast, the melodies are spirited, the mood intense and passionate. In this category belong "Shout for Joy," "Joshua Fit the Battle of Jericho," and "The Great Camp Meeting."

A second type has a slower tempo, a statelier movement, and greater majesty. A long sustained phrase is the core of the melody, as in "Deep River," "Nobody Knows De Trouble I've Seen," "Sometimes I Feel Like a Motherless Child," and "Swing Low, Sweet Chariot."

The third kind of spiritual is perhaps the most famous of all. It consists of a highly syncopated melody made up of snatches of rhythmic patterns. In this group we find "Little David, Play On Your Harp" and "All Gods Chillun Got Wings."

The Crucifixion was a subject close to the hearts of Negroes. When they sang of Christ on the Cross, they brought to their music the immense and shattering sorrow of people who feel themselves crucified. Perhaps nothing more moving or noble has been spoken in tones about the Crucifixion than spirituals like "Never Said a Mumbalin' Word" or "Were You There When They Crucified My Lord?" (The possessive pronoun in the singular in the second spiritual is significant. To the Negro, the Lord was someone personal to whom he could speak his heavy heart openly as if to a sympathetic friend.) In spirituals like these, the expression of sorrow is all the more poignant for its restraint and understatement; they achieve sublimity comparable in many ways to the unforgettable closing page of Bach's *The Passion According to St. Matthew.*

The Old Testament also struck a personal note with the Negro, for in the captivity of the Jews in Egypt he found a counterpart to his own slavery. "Let my people go," rings out firm and clear in "When Israel Was in Egypt Land" because the Negro was sounding a plea for his own emancipation. He could not speak openly of his dreams for freedom. But in the appropriate allegory of the Old Testament he could sound his inmost hopes without fear of reprisal. "Steal away to Jesus, steal away home, I ain't got long to stay here," or the fervent belief that "I am bound for the Promised Land" was as much a hope for escape to places of liberation as it was an affirmation of deep religious conviction in a future world. Frederick Douglass emphasized this point when he wrote: "A keen observer might have detected in our repeated singing of 'O Canaan, Sweet Canaan, I'm bound for the land of Canaan,' something more than a hope of reaching heaven. We meant to reach North, and the North was our Canaan. . . . On our lips, it simply meant a speedy pilgrimage to a free state, and deliverance from all evils of slavery."

While many spirituals possessed an awesome majesty, others

like "The Old Time Religion" and "I Know the Lord Has Laid His Hand on Me" are almost savage, carrying in their womb the seeds of later ragtime music. Still others—the "Shouts"—were even hysterical, and show the closest resemblance of all between the American spiritual and the African song. "Shouts" developed during religious services. What started out with dignity and devotion usually ended in hysteria. James Weldon Johnson has vividly described one of these "Shouts" in *The Book of American Negro Spirituals:* "A space is cleared by moving the benches, and men and women arrange themselves, generally alternately in a ring, their bodies quite close. The music starts, and the ring begins to move. Around it goes, at first slowly, then with quickening force. Around and around it moves on shuffling feet that do not leave the floor, one foot beating with the heel in a decided accent in strict two-four time. The music is supplemented by the clapping of hands. As the ring goes around it begins to take on signs of frenzy. The music, starting perhaps with a Spiritual, becomes a wild, monotonous chant. The same musical phrase is repeated over and over, one, two, three, four, five hours. The words become a repetition of an incoherent cry. The very monotony of sound and motion produces an ecstatic state. Women, screaming, fall to the ground, prone and quivering. Men, exhausted, drop out of the Shout. But the ring closes up and moves around and around."

Johnson explains further that the "Shout" often proved to be for the worshipers an illicit adventure. "It was distinctly frowned upon by a great many colored people. Indeed, I do not ever recall seeing a 'ring Shout' except *after* the regular service. Almost whispered invitations would go around: 'Stay after church! There's going to be a ring Shout.' The more educated ministers and members, as far as they were able to brave the primitive elements in the churches, placed a ban on the 'ring Shout.'"

These "ring Shouts" produced much spiritual music that is

wild and febrile. Some of these "Shouts" were adaptations of familiar and stately spirituals grown primitive and savage during the rite; others were new songs improvised in the delirium of worship.

III

The first spiritual to appear in printed sheet music was "Roll, Jordan Roll," published in Philadelphia in 1862. After that several other spirituals were published until, in 1867, there appeared in the Port Royal Islands the first collection of Negro spirituals: *Slave Songs of the United States*, edited by William Francis Allen, Charles Pickard Ware, and Lucy McKim Garrison.

Thus the spiritual came north by way of a few scattered publications. But before this happened it traveled northward by other paths. Passengers on Mississippi river boats brought back north the sounds of the strange new music the Negro was producing in the southland. Also, some Negro spirituals were introduced into the North by abolitionists who used them as propaganda for their rallies.

Not until 1871, and in the ensuing few years, did the spiritual come into general popularity throughout the country. In that year of 1871, a group of singers from Fisk University, in Nashville, Tennessee—"The Jubilee Singers"—toured parts of the country in concerts devoted exclusively to Negro songs.

Here is how "The Jubilee Singers" came to be organized. George L. White, the treasurer of Fisk University, had often heard some of his students sing in groups. He felt that the entire country, whites as well as dark-skinned, would be interested in the poignant music of his race. He had another idea in mind as well. From the time of its founding in 1866 to provide education for liberated Negroes, Fisk University had been harassed by financial problems. Public concerts by the students might provide a sadly needed source of revenue. The University authorities reluctantly gave White permission to form a choral group made up of twelve students, but only on the condition that White himself defray all expenses. For two years, White trained the ensemble until it acquired artistic finish. On October 6, 1871, the group left Nashville for its first tour. Initially, the concerts were met with cool reserve. But as the tour proceeded, and as the music grew more familiar, the enthusiasm of the audiences mounted. The road was finally paved with unexpected triumphs. At the Gilmore Music Festival in Boston in 1872, an audience of some 20,000 rose to its feet and shouted: "Jubilee Forever!" In 1878, when the Fisk Jubilee Singers returned to the University, they brought back with them over $150,000—testimony that the spiritual had won the heart of America.

The fame of the Negro spiritual—or "Jubilee Songs" as they were first known—now spread rapidly. The New York music critic, Henry E. Krehbiel, spoke for its musical importance and helped to win many converts. One of them was Anton Dvořák, the famous Bohemian composer, who had come to America in 1892 to become director of the National Conservatory of Music in New York. Dvořák became an avowed enthusiast of the spiritual. He wrote: "In the Negro melodies of America I discover all that is needed for a great and noble school of music. They are pathetic, tender, passionate, melancholy, solemn, religious, bold, merry, gay. . . . It is music that suits itself to any mood and purpose." Dvořák himself began to use authentic Negro material in his serious compositions, notably in his *Symphony from the New World*, written in this country. In the first movement there is a passing quotation from "Swing Low, Sweet Chariot"; and in the second, there appears a famous melody that has the unmistakable character of an authentic spiritual, even though it is original with Dvořák.

The Negro composer, Henry T. Burleigh, coming under Dvořák's influence, was encouraged by the master to make arrangements of many Negro folk songs. This was still another potent force in propagandizing the spiritual among music lovers. His "Deep River" arrangement, for example, was performed by the Flonzaley Quartet, Maud Powell, and Fritz Kreisler, and was sung by Frances Alda—a fact that gave further confirmation to the general belief that the spiritual had acquired artistic significance.

IV

Not all Negro songs were spirituals. Being a people who are musical to the tips of their fingers and toes, Negroes have always made music for any and every situation in which they found themselves. They not only sang in worship, or in lamentation over their destiny, but also in work and play.

Some Negro songs were born on the banks of the Mississippi. Laboring on the southern docks to load river boats with cargo, Negroes accompanied their tasks with songs called "roustabouts." These lyrics and melodies were usually improvised. The former told of the difficulty of the work at hand, but often digressed to comment on the elegance of the river boats, on the personal idiosyncrasies of different captains, on a love affair, a fight, or trouble with the police. At times the lyrics lapsed into sheer nonsense:

> *Ducks play cards and chickens drink wine*
> *And de monkey grown on de grape vine,*
> *Corn starch pudding and tapioca pie,*
> *Oh, de gray cat pick out de black cat's eye.*

Traits of the Negro spiritual are found in these songs, particularly in the languorous melody and the highly syncopated beat. But these songs also had a unique rhythmic motion not found in other Negro songs. As the Negroes sang, they went through the physical gesture of loading and unloading with a peculiar motion and gait: a slouching motion of the body and rhythmic movements of the hands synchronized with a slow dance-like gait.

Songs were also born in the mines and tunnels of Virginia, in the cotton fields of the South, and on the rock piles of prison camps in Georgia, Tennessee, and Texas. If this music is not so imaginative or musically as distinctive as the spiritual (after all, these work songs came from the humdrum monotony of a muscular job, and not from a stirring emotional experience), they nevertheless have interest. Sung out-of-doors, and never to the accompaniment of a musical instrument to set the pitch and guide the intonation, these songs developed their own curious intonation. The voice was permitted to slide to tones foreign to the scale, and to intervals smaller than the half tone. The melody was sprinkled with grunts and groans which became a part of the melodic texture; these grunts and groans were inspired by the physical strain of smashing a rock with a hammer or piercing through a hard substance with steel drill. Out of this intonation there developed a unique melody and harmony; many years later this intonation became a distinguishing feature of authentic jazz.

The peculiar melody and harmony set an atmosphere of bleakness, arising from the feeling of utter hopelessness with which Negro laborers did their jobs and sang their songs. These work songs are touched with pathos; even humorous verses are frequently couched in melodies filled with melancholia. The work was unspeakably arduous, and the conditions most trying. In prison camps, the Negro was the victim of barbarous overseers; in work camps, his pay was poor and uncertain and his treatment at the hands of foremen ruthless. Work songs frequently describe the appalling conditions under which these men labored.

> *Told my cap'n my hands was cold*
> *Said, 'Damn your hands, boy*
> > *Let de wheelin' roll.*
> *Raised my hand, wiped de sweat off my head,*
> *Cap'n got mad, Lord, shot my buddy dead.*

"I works from kin to can't"—from the time I can see until I can't see anymore—sighs the Negro in lamenting his long hours. "O Cap'n, has de money come? Tain't none o' yo' bizness, I don't owe you none," he sang sadly about the uncertainty of his wages. These songs may well be said to have been the progenitors of the blues.

Many songs were improvised during the progress of the work. The leader would raise his voice in the opening refrain of a song like "Boll Weevil," classic of the cotton pickers or "Nine Foot Shovel," which originated with the Georgia chain gangs. The leader was a specialist who knew not only the technique of the work, but also the songs best suited for that work; a good leader could inspire his men to harder effort. After the leader gave the cue, the work gangs would chime in with the chorus in convention-defying harmonies. For hours, verse after verse would be sung. Lines were freely interpolated. The melody was varied with each repetition, the rhythm always permitted flexible changes. At the end of the song, the melody might appear in a form completely different from what it had been at the start. Sometimes new melodies would be evolved to familiar words—as one voice after another would make its own individual contribution after the leader had thrown out a phrase—and sometimes new words were created for familiar tunes.

His work done, the Negro found relaxation in dancing, and dancing helped to produce the social song. The work song was strictly *a cappella* (unaccompanied); the social song was accompanied by instruments. The work song was choral; the social song, solo. In the social song, improvisation played an even more important role than it had done on the work fields. A singer (accompanied by banjo, guitar, or violin) gave his invention wings, as he discoursed musically on a great variety of subjects ranging from love to death, from heroes to notorious villains. The singer would add embellishments to the monotonous melody each time the principal theme was repeated; often, at the inspiration of a moment, he would spontaneously make up a new melody to a familiar text.

Because social songs were primarily intended to encourage dancing, they were strongly rhythmic, much more so than the spiritual or work song. And since instrumental accompaniment was used, social songs often revealed a harmonic resourcefulness not usually found in other types of Negro folk songs.

V

It would be difficult to exaggerate the influence of the Negro song on our popular music; that influence has been decisive and permanent. The physiognomy of American popular music has been shaped by spirituals, "Shouts," and Negro work and social songs. The techniques and idioms, moods and atmospheres, personality and idiosyncrasies of Negro songs have formed the bone and tissue of our popular musical expression. The song and dance of the minstrel show, the ragtime of New Orleans, the blues of St. Louis, the boogie-woogie of Chicago, the sophisticated jazz of New York, and the commercial melody of Tin Pan Alley—all these, as we shall see in later chapters, owe a profound debt to Negro musical sources.

chapter four

MR. TAMBO AND MR. BONES—
The Minstrel Show
and Its Songs

THERE has always been a musical theater in America. Even before the Revolution a musical performance took place in a courtroom in Charleston, South Carolina, on February 8, 1735: a ballad-opera, *Flora*. Fifteen years later the most celebrated of all the ballad-operas, John Gay's *The Beggar's Opera,* was seen in New York.

The ballad-opera, as popular in the Colonies as in England, interpolated songs and airs into a spoken play. The melodies were tunes then popular with the public but adapted to new lyrics. Simple in approach and materials, usually concerned with everyday subjects written in the people's English, and filled with popular songs mostly of English origin, the ballad-opera was the ancestor of the American musical comedy.

The ballad-opera was an importation from England. Just before the Civil War, an indigenous stage production came into vogue in America—the minstrel show.

The minstrel show grew out of a stage routine devised and

popularized by a popular entertainer of the early nineteenth century, Thomas "Daddy" Rice. In 1828, while appearing in Baltimore, Rice happened to see an old deformed Negro slave with a peculiar limp, who moved his body with strange contortions. Something else attracted Rice's attention: as the slave ambled along in his strange, shuffling motion, he muttered to himself a silly ditty that began, "Wheel about an' turn about and do jis so, an' ebry time I wheel about I jump Jim Crow."

This scene made such an impression on Rice that he decided to imitate the old slave and to introduce his gibberish chant into his own act. Negro songs and black-faced performers on the stage were nothing new in 1828. "The Bonja Song" (with which the banjo is reputed to have become popular) in 1820, and "Coal Black Rose" in or about 1827 were two songs about the Negro that achieved considerable popularity in our early musical theater. As for black-face performers—even as far back as 1769 Negroes were being caricatured on the stage in song and dance, while in 1799 a performer named Gottlieb Graupner was acclaimed for his rendition in black-face, and to his own banjo accompaniment, of "The Gay Negro Boy" at the Federal Theatre in Boston.

But Daddy Rice's routine, which he called "Jump Jim Crow," was the first major Negro act on our musical stage. Such was the measure of its success that the song, "Jump Jim Crow," became a rage not only in this country but also in England. Rice's Jim Crow act was imitated by black-faced performers everywhere; and the term "Jim Crow" entered the American vocabulary to designate segregation. Thus the Negro had secured a permanent place on the musical stage, and the embryo of the minstrel show was slowly taking shape.

"Zip Coon"—better known to us today as "Turkey in the Straw"—was another Negro-inspired song to become popular on the musical stage in the era before the minstrel show. Like "Jump Jim Crow," "Zip Coon" had more or less nonsensical verses. The song was published in Baltimore in 1834, and was introduced by Bob Farrell at the Bowery Theatre in New York on August 11 of the same year. It was also used and popularized by one of the most highly esteemed black-face entertainers of that period, George Washington Dixon. Farrell and Dixon each insisted that he wrote the song, but there is little validity to either claim. In all probability, the melody was usurped from an old English or Irish tune.

II

The first minstrel show was introduced in the early 1840s. With box-office receipts at all theaters emaciated by the national depression of 1842, many actors were thrown out of work. Solo acts had to merge into a group and seek a single booking. One of those compelled to join up with other performers in a new single act was Daniel Decatur Emmett, better known as Dan Emmett, born in Mt. Vernon, Ohio, in 1815. His career in the theater (which included the writing of a Civil War classic, "Dixie") began in his boyhood when he was employed as a drummer for the Spalding and Rogers Circus. He later joined a troupe headed by Daddy Rice, the first occasion upon which he came into contact with Negro song and dance. Rice's Jim Crow act made such an impression on young Emmett that he decided to write a similar routine of his own. In or about 1839 he began writing Negro songs, and then appeared in his own black-face act, singing Negro songs and accompanying himself on the banjo. His act was victimized by the 1842 economic holocaust.

One day in 1843, he and three friends tried out a few numbers at Emmett's room in a New York boardinghouse. The idea was suddenly raised, and enthusiastically received, for the four men—Emmett, Billy Whitlock, Frank Brower, and Dick Pelham—to join forces in a single act and possibly with a new kind of stage format. The four men gave themselves the collective name of "The Virginia Minstrels," and tried out a few of their numbers in a New York billiard parlor. The response to their performance encouraged them to make a more official debut at the Chatham Square Theatre on February 17, 1843.

Theirs was a new kind of stage entertainment. Besides appearing in black-face, they assumed the unorthodox dress of blue swallow-tail coats, striped calico shirts, and white pantaloons. They sang songs, played the banjo, exchanged light banter, did "The Essence of Old Virginia" and "The Lucy Walk Around." The audience was delighted at each of their efforts. Before long, imitators of their act mushroomed in different parts of the country.

Besides helping to create the prototype of the minstrel show, Dan Emmett was also one of its principal composers. In 1843, he wrote "Old Dan Tucker," introduced by his minstrels, and a gem of the old minstrel show days. The protagonist of this song was an evildoer who caused havoc wherever he went; in Emmett's song, Dan Tucker is admonished to "git out de way." So instantaneous was the acceptance of the song by the general public that in less than a year it was used (with new lyrics) as the battle cry of a group of New York farmers in their revolt against feudal conditions. A few years after that, it was adapted for abolitionist verses to propagandize the abolition of slavery. Today, "Old Dan Tucker" is still a favorite at square dances.

"Old Dan Tucker" was only one of several important songs which Emmett wrote for his minstrel shows. Others include "The Blue Tail Fly," more familiar to us under the name of "Jim Crack Corn," "The Boatman's Song," "Walk Along, John," "My Old Aunt Sally," and the song that made him immortal, "Dixie," discussed in an earlier chapter.

If Dan Emmett suggested a pattern for the minstrel show it was Ed Christy who definitely formalized the production and who once and for all established the form and refined the techniques it would henceforth utilize. Ed Christy organized his first minstrel show in 1840. Two years later he made his first New York appearances. For the next six years, Christy and his troupe gave over 2,500 performances in New York alone. He also toured England where he was a great favorite.

It was Ed Christy who made the minstrel show popular throughout the United States. The format he used was borrowed by such popular minstrel groups of his time as The Virginia Serenaders, The Ethiopian Minstrels, The New York Minstrels, The White Serenaders, and The Bryant Minstrels, among others. After that, Christy's pattern became the accepted one for all troupes everywhere.

Christy divided his production into three parts. The first consisted of variety entertainment—or, to use a term technical with minstrel shows, the "olio." In this part, the performers sat in a single row on the stage, with Mr. Tambo and Mr. Bones as end men and Mr. Interlocutor in the center. Mr. Interlocutor asked questions, to which Mr. Tambo and Mr. Bones responded with all kinds of gags. From time to time, individual members offered songs and dances, and the group as a whole performed popular choral numbers. The second part was a fantasia, or free for all, without any set form. Here, individual performers were given an opportunity to strut their stuff. The concluding part burlesqued what had previously transpired.

Some of the most popular songs of the era preceding the Civil War were incubated in the minstrel show, not only those by Dan Emmett, but also many others: "The Big Sunflower," by Bobby Newcomb, made famous by the minstrel Billy Emerson; "Lubly Fan," written by Cool White and introduced by him with the Virginia Serenaders, and now sometimes remembered as "Buffalo Gals"; and the delightful nonsense song, "Polly Wolly Doodle."

III

The minstrel show produced not only important popular songs but also important popular-song composers. Dan Emmett was one. Another, and even more significant, was his contemporary, Stephen Foster—America's first major composer, and one of the world's outstanding writers of songs. Foster's first song classics were written for and introduced in the minstrel shows of his day; like Emmett, he was essentially a product of the minstrel show.

Foster was not a trained musician. His knowledge of musical technique was perfunctory; his use of harmony, elementary, consisting only of a few stereotyped chords. He lacked self-criticism to a point where he not only could write a hackneyed potboiler and a song masterpiece with alternate strokes of the pen, but often was incapable of accurately evaluating the merits of either. But he was born with the gift of melody. He might have said, as Goethe's minstrel did, "I sing as the bird sings." For him, melody was such a natural and spontaneous expression that his biographer, John Tasker Howard, was tempted to remark that had Foster been a trained musician "his charm might have vanished." When inspired, Foster produced beautiful lyricism with facility and simplicity; it seemed to come from him as inevitably as his breath. That lyricism has never failed to touch hearts or to stir sentiments. Foster's best songs remain to this day one of the proudest legacies of our musical heritage.

He was a voice of his times. When he wrote his songs, the Negro question was uppermost, and the Northerner's sentimental reaction to the Negro echoes and vibrates in Foster's music. It could be said with equal validity that he was also a victim of his times. His was a period of enormous expansion, with men growing rich by striking out for new lands, or engaging in commerce and industry. Money-making was the greatest virtue of all, the single measure of success. In such a

scheme of things, music was a stepchild. The making of music
was consigned to young ladies who had no better way of
spending their time. It was then hardly to be expected that
young Stephen Foster be encouraged to develop his unmistakable talent. His father, Colonel William Barclay Foster, was
a pioneer who had settled near Pittsburgh when it was a
border settlement. He had acquired position and money
through his shrewdness as a trader and through his own industry. He believed that the country belonged to men unafraid
of work, men who had brains and initiative. Consequently, he
had little sympathy for culture, art, or book learning, nor was
he the man to look sympathetically on his son's musical striv-
ings.

It was also not to be expected that this was an age to give
just rewards to a creative artist. Compared to the popular
composers of a later age, Foster earned a pittance. His royalties amounted to about $1,000 a year for eight years; he sold
some of his songs outright for as little as $15.00. He was
usually in debt, nearly always living on advances from his
published or still unpublished (and at times unwritten) songs.
Just before his death he was a hopeless alcoholic, living alone
and in miserable penury in New York's Bowery.

Stephen Foster was born in Lawrenceville, near Pittsburgh,
on July 4, 1826. An early musical influence was the religious
song of the Negro. Stephen was only seven when he was taken
by his household slave to a Negro church. What he heard
there was so indelibly impressed on his malleable mind that
many years later he used some of these melodies in songs like
"Hard Times, Come Again No More" and "Oh! Boys, Carry
Me 'Long." He was an exceptionally gifted child and tried to
find satisfaction for his musical yearning in any instrument
that came within reach: a drum, a guitar, a flageolet. He used
to love imitating black-faced entertainers in songs and routines
like "Jump Jim Crow," "Zip Coon," and "Coal Black Rose."

His musical gifts, however, were completely ignored, and he received no formal instruction to speak of.

For his academic education he was sent to the Athens Academy at Tioga Point, Pennsylvania. To put it mildly, he was no scholar. Most of his time was spent in playing the flute or in daydreaming. It was during this period that he wrote his first piece of music to get a performance: "The Tioga Waltz," written for and introduced at an exhibition held by the school at the Presbyterian Church on April 1, 1841. He was soon transferred to another school in Pennsylvania, the Jefferson College at Canonsburg, where he remained only a few days. "I must regret," wrote father Foster to his brother, "that Stephen has not been able to . . . avail himself of the advantages of a college education. . . . His leisure hours are all devoted to music, for which he possesses a strange talent."

By the fall of 1841 he was through with all his schooling, and for a while he concentrated on music. In or about 1842 he wrote a song which became his first published piece, "Open thy Lattice, Love," lyrics by George P. Morris, and published in *The Mirror* in December 1844. Ironically, on the head of this, Foster's first published song, his name appears erroneously as "L. C. Foster," almost as an unhappy omen of a life and career that were never destined to go right. "Open thy Lattice, Love" was a sentimental melody, graceful, pleasing, though hardly original, and gave little indication of the composer's coming lyric powers. Other songs followed, some written for a club of young men which met twice weekly at Foster's home and whose meetings were enlivened with the singing of songs. Foster wrote a few of these in the style of the popular tunes then being sung by black-faced minstrels: "Lou'siana Belle," "Oh! Susanna," and his first sentimental song about the Negro, "Old Uncle Ned."

Since a career in music was not to be seriously considered, Stephen found employment as a bookkeeper in his brother's commission house in Cincinnati. This was either late in 1846 or early in 1847. Here he came into contact with the work songs of Negroes who loaded and unloaded the Mississippi river boats. Like the religious chants he had heard in child-hood, they left an unforgettable memory. Here, too, he found in W. C. Peters a publisher. "Lou'siana Belle" was issued in 1847, and "Old Uncle Ned" and "Oh! Susanna," one year after that. For the first two songs he received no payment whatso-ever, but "Oh! Susanna" brought him one hundred dollars. This song, with which Foster made his first bid for fame, was introduced publicly in an ice-cream parlor in Pittsburgh on September 11, 1847. As a novelty song with banjo accompani-ment, it was immediately taken over by leading black-faced minstrels who, by 1849, had made it so familiar that it became the theme song of the Forty-Niners en route to California.

Foster returned to Pittsburgh in 1849. He had had enough of business and intended henceforth to make his way in music. Two significant developments advanced his career. He had consummated a deal with the powerful New York pub-lishing house of Firth, Pond & Co., by which he received for each song a royalty of 8 per cent, thus insuring him some kind of income. Besides this, his principal songs were now being featured by the Ed Christy Minstrels, thereby guarantee-ing him an audience and an agency for the popularization of his music. He continued writing songs with renewed zest and fertility. One was "Camptown Races," originally entitled "Gwine to Run All Night," published in 1850. Another, in 1851, was his first masterpiece, and one of his most celebrated songs—"The Old Folks at Home," also known as "Swanee River."

When he first wrote "The Old Folks at Home," Foster had no intention of growing sentimental over the Suwanee River. It is doubtful that he even knew of its existence. His original choice was "Peedee River," but he soon came to the conclusion that this name was not euphonious. Needing a two-syllable name he began a hunt through the map of Florida. Thus he came upon the Suwanee River, whose source was in Fargo, Georgia, and which coursed into north Florida. The word "Suwanee"—which Foster contracted to "Swanee"—had a melodious ring to it, and it is for this reason that he picked upon an obscure and unimportant little river for his song.

He sent his manuscript to Ed Christy, who paid him fifteen dollars both for its use and for the privilege of using his own name as composer on the published sheet music. It is interesting to remark that the reason Foster agreed to this peculiar arrangement was not for the fee but because he felt that his Negro—or, as they were sometimes then known, "Ethiopian"—songs were inferior to his sentimental ballads, and he did not like having his name associated with what he regarded as a mere potboiler. As he wrote to Christy: "I had the intention of omitting my name on my Ethiopian songs, owing to the prejudice against them by some, which might injure my reputation as a writer of another style of music." But apparently he regretted this decision, for six months after "The Old Folks at Home" was published under Christy's name, he wrote to the minstrel: "I find that by my efforts I have done a great deal to build up a taste for Ethiopian songs among refined people. . . . Therefore, I have concluded to reinstate my name on my songs and to pursue the Ethiopian business without fear or shame and lend all my energies to making the business live, at the same time that I will wish to establish my name as the best Ethiopian song writer." The fifteen dollars Christy paid him was not all Foster earned from his masterpiece. He was also getting royalties from the publishers, which within six months accumulated over $1,500.

"The Old Folks at Home," introduced by Ed Christy, was such an immediate triumph that by 1852, less than a year after its first appearance, it was, according to the *Albany State Register*, "on everybody's tongue, and consequently in everybody's mouth. Pianos and guitars groan with it, night and day; sentimental young ladies sing it; sentimental young gentlemen warble it in midnight serenades; volatile young bucks hum it in the midst of their business and pleasures; boatmen roar it out stentorially at all times; all the bands play it; amateur flute players agonize over it every spare moment; the street organs grind it out at every hour; and singing stars carol it on the theatrical boards and at concerts; the chambermaid sweeps and dusts to the measured cadence of 'The Old Folks at Home'; the butcher boy treats you to a strain or two of it as he hands in his steaks for dinner; the milkman mixes it up strangely with the harsh ding-dong accompaniment of his tireless bell; there is not a 'live darkey,' young or old, but can whistle, sing, and play it."

The Musical World of 1852 also reported: "The publishers keep two presses running on it, and sometimes three; yet they cannot supply the demand."

Despite this remarkable acclaim, not all reactions were favorable. When the concert singer, Anna Zerr, included it on her program at a concert at Castle Garden in 1853, one music critic remarked: "One would as soon think of picking up an apple core on the street." And to John S. Dwight, the editor of *Dwight's Journal,* the song's charm was only "skin deep," and he compared it to a "morbid irritation of the skin."

Between 1852 and 1853, Foster continued to establish himself as "the best Ethiopian writer." Two gems appeared in that period: "Massa's in the Cold, Cold Ground" in 1852, and one year later, "My Old Kentucky Home," both introduced by the Ed Christy Minstrels. In a brief period, each song sold over 50,000 copies of sheet music—a considerable figure for that era—and earned for the composer about $2,000.

While Foster was writing his best songs, his private life was becoming complicated. On July 22, 1850 he married Jane Denny McDowell, who subsequently inspired him to write, "Jeanie With the Light Brown Hair." On April 18, 1851, they had a daughter, Marion. It was an unhappy marriage. Foster chafed under the restrictions of domesticity. Besides, he and his wife were worlds apart in outlook and personality. She was a Methodist who cared nothing about music, objected to his association with minstrels and the musical stage, and with greater justification was in horror of his pronounced predilection for alcohol. Practical to the point of being prosaic, down to earth, and coldly calculating, she had little sympathy for her husband's musical ambitions, and was impatient with his frequent flights into fancies and dreams. She nagged him continually to give up song writing as a profession and to settle down to some respectable business, incapable of realizing that a lark can neither be kept from melody nor be confined permanently to the ground.

Foster wrote his last great Negro song, "Old Black Joe," in 1860, inspired by a kindly slave belonging to his wife's household. But from 1860 on, Foster devoted himself principally to sentimental balladry, with songs like "Poor Drooping Maiden," "Under the Willow She's Sleeping," and "Beautiful Dreamer," the last completed in 1864, just a few days before his death. Here the old hot flame of melodic genius flickered only at infrequent intervals. It was at about this time, too, that he left Pittsburgh to settle in New York with his family, induced to do so by a new and profitable arrangement with his publishers. In New York, his physical and moral disintegration was rapid. He took more and more to writing potboilers for a pittance, and they were failures. His popularity, which once had made his name a household word, had become completely dissipated. As an escape from his mental anguish, from frustrations and disappointments, he turned to the bottle, for which he had always had a weakness. He fluctuated between excessive inebriation, which often left him in a stupor, to a penitence in which he groped savagely for any and every remedy that might liberate him from his vice. Finally, his family left him to his squalor and misery and returned to Pennsylvania. He lived in a little, sordid room in the American Hotel on the Bowery, a man broken in health and spirit.

"In January 1864," recalled Foster's brother, "he was taken with ague and fever. After two or three days he arose, and while washing himself he fainted and fell across the wash basin, which broke and cut a gash in his neck and face. He lay there insensible and bleeding until discovered by the chambermaid who was bringing the towels he had asked for to the room. She called for assistance and he was placed in bed again. On recovering his senses he asked that he be sent to a hospital. He was so much weakened by fever and loss of blood that he did not rally."

He died in Bellevue Hospital on January 13, 1864. After his death, there was found in the pocket of his frayed suit a sadly worn purse containing three pennies, thirty-five cents in scrip, and a slip of paper on which was scrawled, "dear friends and gentle hearts," probably the title of a song he did not live to write.

IV

While in New York, in 1863, Stephen Foster wrote music to eighteen lyrics by George Cooper, an impoverished New York poet whom he had met in the back room of an East Side grocery store. These songs were all potboilers, and none is remembered.

But other Cooper lyrics—and to music by other composers—had better luck. One was "Sweet Genevieve," which the poet wrote in 1869 as solace for losing the only woman he ever loved: his young wife, Genevieve, who died shortly after their marriage. Cooper sold this lyric for five dollars to Henry Tucker, a prolific composer, who then wrote for it a sentimental melody that made this one of America's best known ballads. The song was published in 1869 and was soon performed extensively in minstrel shows.

Another well-loved sentimental ballad to achieve its fame in the minstrel show was "Silver Threads Among the Gold," lyrics by Eben E. Rexford, and music by H. P. Danks. Rexford was the editor of a small farm journal in the West who enjoyed writing verses. One day he sold a batch for a few dollars to Danks, who had already gained some recognition with religious hymns and sentimental tunes. The lot included "Silver Threads Among the Gold." Danks wrote the music in 1873, an expression of hope that he and his beloved wife might live together to a ripe old age. (Ironically, Danks and his wife separated soon after the song was published.) "Silver Threads Among the Gold" was not an immediate success, and was forgotten soon after its publication. But in 1902, Richard José, a famous minstrel, revived it with the Primrose and West Minstrels and set into motion a two-million copy sheet-music sale. Danks, who died in Philadelphia late in 1903, lived long enough to enjoy this belated success.

Among the most important of Stephen Foster's successors in the writing of "Ethiopian" songs made famous in minstrel shows was James A. Bland, a Negro, born in Flushing, New York, in 1854. Bland used to call himself "the best Ethiopian song writer in the world," and was the proud author of about seven hundred songs, though he received credit for only a fraction of these. Bland's father, a one-time slave, became one of the first Negroes in America to receive a college education, and also one of the first Negroes to serve as examiner in the United States patent office. His son, James, also received a thorough academic education that included the study of law at Howard University. But his heart belonged to music, and his crowning ambition was to become the star of a minstrel show. As a boy, while working as a page in the House of Representatives, he often entertained prominent Washington politicians by singing and playing the banjo, usually in songs of his own composition. In 1875 he found a place in a colored company of minstrels, the Original Georgia Minstrels, and for the next few years played and sang on the minstrel-show stage. It was during this period that, inspired by the songs he performed and heard, he produced a handful of masterpieces by which he is best remembered: "Carry Me Back to Old Virginny," in 1878; "In the Evening by the Moonlight" and "Oh, Dem Golden Slippers," both in 1879, and "Hand Me Down My Walking Cane" in 1880. He had a personal way with a sentimental song that, at its best, reminds us of Stephen Foster.

With opportunities to appear in minstrel shows few and far between for a Negro (the preference was for white men in black-face rather than for the authentic product), Bland went to Europe in 1882. There he became a favorite of English royalty, and enjoyed considerable esteem and prosperity. But by the time he returned to the United States, in 1901, he had run through all of his savings, and found himself both forgotten and impoverished. He was saved from actual starvation by a friend who gave him a menial job. Bland died in Philadelphia in 1911 without ever regaining his lost fame. He was buried in an unmarked grave, his death and burial unnoticed by the newspapers. Recognition came posthumously, and in several ways besides the wide distribution of his greatest songs. In 1939, the American Society of Composers, Authors and Publishers, placed a headstone on his grave, and provided his neglected plot with fresh landscaping. And in 1940, the Virginia Legislature officially designated "Carry Me Back to Old Virginny" as the song of that state.

chapter five

FROM EXTRAVAGANZA
TO VAUDEVILLE

MUCH CLOSER than the minstrel show to the approach and methods of the later-day musical comedy was *The Black Crook,* the first American spectacle or extravaganza. This was the first musical production to establish some of the ritual to be followed by later musicals.

Accident and coincidence played important roles in the career of *The Black Crook.* In the 1860s, two New York impresarios—Henry C. Jarrett and Harry Palmer—imported some expensive stage sets from Europe and at the same time contracted a troupe of French dancers. Their intention was to produce an elaborate French ballet at the Academy of Music. Late one night, in 1865, the Academy burned down, and the projected French ballet lost its home. The two impresarios now decided to enter into negotiations with William Wheatley, owner of Niblo's Gardens, for the use of his theater.

So much for accident. Coincidence now appears through the fortuitous circumstance that when Wheatley was broached by Jarrett and Palmer, he had just received the rights to a melodrama by Charles M. Barras, *The Black Crook.* The play was a cornucopia of hokum. Its complicated plot involved magic

[79]

spells, transformations, and enchantments. Veteran showman that he was, Wheatley knew the full value of novelty, and he realized that a combination of Barras' drama with the scenery and French dancers of Jarrett and Palmer might create an attraction that "will certainly arouse curiosity."

As a co-producer, Wheatley began scheming along gargantuan lines to make his production the largest, the most lavish, and the most expensive ever mounted in New York up to then. He altered the stage of his theater to provide the space necessary for the elaborate sets and for the complicated apparatus needed for extravagant stage effects. He fitted out the girls of the ballet in expensive, and usually transparent, Parisian silks and laces. He spent what at that time was a fabulous figure—$55,000—before the curtain went up on the finished product, on September 12, 1866.

The Black Crook turned out to be a gilt-edged investment. It had a continuous run of sixteen months, up to 1866 the longest of any theatrical entertainment in New York. It earned for each of the three producers $600,000, and for its author, Barras, $60,000. It is not difficult to explain this unparalleled success. For five and a half hours, the audience was in turns dazed and thrilled by the sights: the extravagant display of scenic and female beauty; the breath-taking stage effects; the spectacular ballets.

But the tremendous audience appeal of the show came not only from its incomparable sights. No less important to its success was the publicity, widely circulated, that this was devil's brew. The production was bitterly attacked both in the newspapers and from the pulpit as an immoral and degrading spectacle. "The police should arrest all engaged in such a violation of public decency," wrote James Gordon Bennett editorially in *The Herald*. From a platform at the Cooper Institute, the Reverend Charles B. Smythe described "the immodest dress of the girls," apparently with the naïve expectation that this was a way of discouraging his listeners from seeing the play. He explained that the girls appeared "with thin, gauze-like material allowing the form of the figures to be discernible. The attitudes were exceedingly indelicate. . . . When a danseuse is assisted by a danseur, the attitudes assumed both in conjunction suggest to the imagination scenes which one may read, describing the ancient heathen orgies."

Such denunciations, intended to discourage attendance, succeeded only in arousing the curiosity of most New Yorkers, who came to the theater in droves. Everybody wanted to see this "degrading spectacle" for himself. Respectable women disguised themselves with veils—but they came. Many people saw the show several times.

Besides bringing to the American stage suggestive dances and undraped females, *The Black Crook* also introduced a new quality of sex insinuation into song. When Milly Cavendish stepped lightly in front of the footlights, wagged a provocative finger at the men in her audience, and sang in her high-pitched baby voice, "You Naughty, Naughty Men"—by T. Kennick and G. Bicknell—the American musical theater and the American popular song both started their long and active careers in sex exploitation.

II

Burlesque also made a contribution to musical comedy, through its emphasis on satire and parody. Burlesque was the logical evolution of the third part of the minstrel show in which earlier procedures were burlesqued with broad strokes. The burlesque of the early and middle 1800s is not to be confused with that of a later generation. In those early years it consisted primarily of caricature. It first became the rage in 1828 when John Poole presented a hilarious parody of *Hamlet*. Ten years later, William Mitchell introduced a new kind of burlesque entertainment in *La Mosquita*, a broad satire on Fanny Elssler, the famous ballerina, high-lighted by Mitchell's own grotesque take-off on the graceful Viennese dancer. In *Ixion*, in 1869, satire and parody were combined with feminine beauty: Lydia Thompson and her English Blondes introduced flesh-colored tights to the American stage.

In 1877, Weber and Fields began adapting the individual characteristics of burlesque to their own special thespian talents. At the Bowery Music Hall, they produced a series of burlesque extravaganzas which included *Twirly-Whirly*, *Whoop-dee-do*, and *Hoity Toity*. Rowdy humor and uninhibited horseplay surrounded their unique caricatures of Dutchmen. Out of these Weber and Fields' productions stepped a few of the most glamorous and acclaimed personalities of the nineteenth-century stage, among them being Lillian Russell, Ray Templeton, De Wolf Hopper, Sam Bernard, and David Warfield.

The music for the Weber and Fields shows was written by its musical director, John Stromberg, whose way with a simple easy-to-catch melody was his salient charm. Among his best songs, to lyrics by Robert B. Smith, were "When Chloe Sings a Song" (the first coon song sung by Lillian Russell, and heard in the first Weber and Fields show in which she was starred, *Whirl-i-gig*), "Dinah" (sometimes known as "Kiss Me Honey, Do"), "Ma Blushin' Rosie," and the song by which he is most often remembered and a song still associated with Lillian Russell who introduced it—"Come Down Ma Evenin' Star." The last number was introduced in *Twirly-Whirly* in 1902. Just before the opening of the show, John Stromberg was found dead in his hotel room, probably a victim of suicide. In his pocket was the manuscript of the song which he had written for Russell. When Lillian Russell tried singing it on opening night she broke down and wept, and was unable to continue. From then on, the song and the star became inextricably associated with each other.

Still another offshoot of burlesque was the series of Mulligan plays with music with Edward Harrigan and Tony Hart, which dominated the New York stage from 1879 until Hart's death in 1891. In 1873, Harrigan had introduced in a Variety theater in Chicago a song and sketch with an Irishman named Dan Mulligan as central figure. It was a hit. The song, "The Mulligan Guard"—a sardonic commentary on the amateur military groups then springing up in all parts of the country—became a potent weapon in destroying them through ridicule. This success led Harrigan to build an entire show around Dan Mulligan—the result being *The Mulligan Guard Ball,* in 1879. Other Mulligan shows followed in rapid succession. The *Mulligan Guard's Chowder* and *The Mulligan Guard's Christmas,* in 1879; *The Mulligan's Picnic, The Mulligan Guard's Nominee,* and *Mulligan's Silver Wedding* in 1880; and so on. In seventeen years, Harrigan wrote, produced and starred in about twenty-five such Mulligan shows. With broad satirical strokes he portrayed various familiar New York types: an Irish grocer, a German butcher, a Negro cook. He plunged these and other similar characters into complicated situations that yielded an earthy kind of humor. Several popular songs came out of these shows, all of them by the company's musical director, David Braham, with lyrics by Harrigan. The best were "Maggie Murphy's Home," "The Babies on Our Block," "Taking in the Town," "Hats Off to Me," "They Never Tell All What They Know," and "When Poverty's Tears Ebb and Flow."

The influence of Harrigan and Hart was reflected in several musicals of the same period. The most popular was Charley Hoyt's *A Trip to Chinatown,* in 1891, whose run of 656 performances smashed all existing American box-office records. Like Harrigan and Hart, Hoyt used recognizable American types, but he used them to poke fun at such contemporary subjects as woman's suffrage, the temperance crusade, and small-town politics. *A Trip to Chinatown* owed much of its appeal to its down-to-earth humor and stinging satire; much to its plethora of song hits. Indeed, the producers of *A Trip to Chinatown* were among the first to discover how much shining gold could be mined through the publication and sale of sheet music—particularly since this score contained such nuggets as "Reuben, Reuben," "Push Dem Clouds Away," and a song still remembered, "The Bowery," all three with music by Percy Gaunt and lyrics by Hoyt himself. And with these was Charles K. Harris' immortal ballad, "After the Ball"—about which more will be said later—which was interpolated into the production after the show had begun its run.

III

Another form of musical entertainment to emerge after the Civil War was Variety, subsequently renamed "Vaudeville."* If any single person can be credited with its creation, that man is Tony Pastor, a graduate from the minstrel show, and one of the most successful popular-song composers of his day.

Pastor was born in Greenwich Village, in New York City, in 1837; his father was a musician in the orchestra of the Park Avenue Theatre. "There is a divinity that shapes our ends," Pastor once philosophized. That divinity led him to the theater. At six he won prizes in elocution. Two years later he made a public appearance as a child singer at a Temperance Meeting at Old Day Street Church and emerged as an impresario by organizing a circus show in the backyard of his home. Within a short period he started a peep show for adults which went into bankruptcy when he was fined twenty dollars for conducting a performance without the proper license; he was engaged as a black-face minstrel on a steamboat sailing between New York and Staten Island; he worked as a water-carrier for a comedian appearing in Croton Hall; he appeared in a song-and-dance act with the Barnum and Bailey Circus, billed as "a talented child"; and he inaugurated social eve-

* The French term "Vaudeville" was used for Variety entertainment for the first time in the United States by H. J. Sargent, on February 23, 1871, at Weisiger's Hall in Louisville, Kentucky, where his troupe was billed as "Sargent's Great Vaudeville Company."

nings of stage entertainments in rural district town halls, court-houses, and school auditoriums. All this—mind!—before he reached his thirteenth birthday.

For four years, between 1851 and 1855, he was seen as a black-face minstrel and applauded both for his effective rendition of Negro songs and for his ready wit. After 1858 he abandoned burnt cork to appear as a white-faced song-and-dance man. It was during the latter period that he created a *genre* of popular song with which he was henceforth associated: the topical song. Accident rather than plan was responsible for its introduction. One day, on his way to Butler's American Theatre where he was then appearing, he learned that the Civil War had just broken out. During his act, he interrupted his regular performance to make a short patriotic speech and to sing "The Star Spangled Banner." The ovation he met gave him an idea for his act which from then on made him one of the top entertainers of his time. Henceforth he interpolated into his act songs of his own composition which commented on the news of the day, and while the news was still hot. During the war, principal battles and events were covered in such Tony Pastor songs as "The Monitor and the Merrimac," "The North and the South," and "Corcoran's Irish Brigade." After the war, Pastor continued to discourse musically on topical events, covering kidnapings, fires, elections, assassinations, political corruption, the invention of electricity, and current fashions. It is sometimes said that part of Abram S. Hewitt's success in being elected Mayor of New York City in 1886 was due to a Pastor song in which was born a catch phrase used throughout the campaign: "What's the matter with Hewitt? He's all right!"

The topical song made Pastor both an ace entertainer and a top-ranking song writer. But his greatest achievement in the theater came on March 21, 1865 when, with Sam Sharpley, he introduced a new kind of stage entertainment in Paterson,

New Jersey. He called it Variety. Pastor had long felt that the musical theater could attract a large, new clientele of women and children if smoking and drinking were forbidden in the auditorium and if the entertainment were clean and wholesome. His first adventure in this direction was not a success. Newspapers referred to him derisively as "the self-appointed pastor of the theater," and women and children were still hesitant about entering a precinct so long regarded as profane ground. But Pastor was not easily discouraged. In 1866 he brought his new type of entertainment to New York City at the Tony Pastor Opera House at 201 Broadway. In an effort to attract the new clientele for which he was reaching, he offered door prizes of dress patterns, pots, pans, half-barrels of flour, sewing materials. "I am quite serious in saying," wrote James L. Ford in *Forty Odd Years in the Literary Shop*, "that the most important moment in the history of the development of the theater in this country was that in which Tony Pastor first gave away his coal, flour, and dress patterns to secure the patronage of respectable women."

The women and children started coming, and Tony Pastor's theater was an outstanding success. In 1876 he opened a new and larger theater, this time further uptown at 585 Broadway. Five years later he opened the house that became one of the theatrical showplaces of the city, if not of the entire country: a cathedral of Vaudeville known as the Tony Pastor Music Hall, in Union Square. Upon its stage first appeared many who were soon to become the brightest lights on the theatrical marquee: Lillian Russell, née Helen Louise Leonard (it was Pastor himself who baptized her for the stage as Lillian Russell), first winning recognition at Pastor's playhouse for her poignant rendition of popular ballads; the four Cohans, one of whom was the incomparable George M.; Weber and Fields, and Harrigan and Hart, each pair appearing in skits which became the embryo for their later famous burlesque-extravaganzas; and Pat Rooney, Gus Williams, Eddie Foy,

Emma Carus, Nat Goodwin, May Irwin, and so many others. It was at Tony Pastor's that Maggie Cline brought down the house in the 1890s with her boisterous rendition of "Throw Him Down, McCloskey," words and music by J. W. Kelly, in which even the stagehands joined by throwing around the stage objects of all kinds; that Gus Williams first won the heart of his public with his "Kaiser Don't You Want to Buy a Dog?"; that Ben Harney first popularized piano rags and thus started a nationwide vogue for ragtime.

Tony Pastor's Music Hall was the first of several temples of Vaudeville where both stars and song hits were born. In 1893, the Colonial Theatre was opened by B. F. Keith. Five years after that, Oscar Hammerstein erected the Victoria Theatre on 42nd Street and Broadway, in New York, which (managed by his son William) became the leading center of Vaudeville entertainment for seventeen years. Its successor, the Palace Theatre, at 47th Street and Broadway, took over where the Victoria had left off, to become the Number One Vaudeville theater in America, for a period of nineteen years. The Majestic in Chicago and the Orpheum in San Francisco were two lesser shrines of Vaudeville entertainment.

Tony Pastor was not only the first to establish the popularity of Vaudeville in New York; he was also the first to send Vaudeville shows on tour. His successor in both efforts was B. F. Keith who, in 1883, founded his first Vaudeville theater, The Gaiety in Boston, in partnership with E. F. Albee. Here the practice was inaugurated of offering Vaudeville continuously through the day and evening. Here, too, was introduced one of the earliest motion pictures, *The Milk-White Flag*, in Edison's Vitascope. Keith became so successful that he eventually combined with F. Proctor in forming a chain of some four hundred Vaudeville theaters that extended from one end of America to the other, and became the route by which more than one performer, and popular song, traveled from obscurity to nationwide fame.

IV

One song writer can be said to have come out of Vaudeville: Gus Edwards. In the early 1890s, while working as a tobacco stripper, Edwards spent his evenings in Union Square trying to get a job. He soon found one as a boy song plugger, at a salary of five dollars a week. He would rise from his seat at Tony Pastor's, or Miner's Bowery Theatre, or Koster and Bial's, and repeat several times the refrain of a song that had just been sung on the stage. Before long he progressed from a seat in the audience to a place on the stage. He joined an act called "The Newsboy Quintet" in which the boys (like characters out of a Horatio Alger novel) appeared in rags and with dirty faces, singing the day's ballads. Gus Edwards' first original song was introduced in this act in 1898, "All I Want Is My Black Baby Back" (Tom Daly). Since he could not write a note of music, he had Charles Previn write down the melody for him. May Irwin liked the song so well that she included it in her Vaudeville act.

During the Spanish-American War, Edwards was sent to Camp Black to help entertain troops bound for Cuba. There he met Will Cobb, a lyricist, with whom he established a permanent working arrangement which came to be known as "Words and Music." They had their first major hit in 1900 with the ballad, "I Can't Tell Why I Love You, But I Do," first introduced in Vaudeville. One year later their very next song, "I'll Be With You When the Roses Bloom Again," brought them an advance of several thousand dollars, said to be the largest ever given by a publisher to a songwriter up to then. With "Good-bye, Little Girl, Good-bye" in 1904, "I Just Can't Make My Eyes Behave" and "Sunbonnet Sue" in 1906, and "School Days" in 1907, they happily extended their skein of successes.

"Tammany," which became the official song of New York's Tammany Society, was written for a party held by the National

Democratic Club of New York. Gus Edwards was the master-of-ceremonies, and one of the numbers on the program was his song, "In My Merry Oldsmobile" (Vincent P. Bryan). But, according to one version, on the way to the Tammany Club, Gus Edwards heard a hand organ in the street play some Indian songs (another version is that he heard these songs played by an orchestra in the Club prior to the entertainment). The idea came to him to write a new number for Tammany which would parody an Indian song. A half-hour or so before the program started, Edwards wrote down his melody to lyrics by Vincent Bryan. When the song was run through for some of the Democratic Party leaders, they were delighted with it and gave it their blessing. The song was then used as a replacement for "In My Merry Oldsmobile" and was hailed, even though some of the lines chuckled warmly at some of the less creditable methods of the political group. The popularity of the song was later enhanced when Lee Harrison sang it in a Broadway musical, *Fantana,* produced in the same year of 1905.

In 1907, Gus Edwards started a Vaudeville act which made him as famous a performer as he had been a songwriter. In one variation or another he continued to produce and appear in that act for the next two decades, touring the leading Vaudeville circuits. That first Vaudeville act of his was called "School Boys and Girls," with Edwards appearing in the role of a schoolteacher at the head of a classroom of young kids who sang and danced, many of the songs written expressly for the number. One of these songs was Edwards' own "School Days," which had a sensational three-million copy sale, and with which Gus Edwards launched his own publishing house at 44th Street and Broadway.

This school act was so popular that at intermittent periods Gus Edwards conceived new ones, similar in format, peopled with gifted youngsters. His emphasis on juvenile talent inspired a remark current on Broadway in his day: "Pull in your kids—here comes Gus Edwards." Through the years, the act became a nursery for future stars of Vaudeville and musical comedy. Even a partial list of these names discloses what a remarkable scent Edwards must have had for latent talent: Eddie Cantor, George Jessel, George Price, Ray Bolger, Eleanor Powell, Groucho Marx, Jack Pearl, Herman Timberg, Lila Lee, Charles King, Mae Murray, Eddie Buzzell, Bert Wheeler, Ann Dvorak, among many others. These acts also became the frame for several of Edwards song hits. The best known is "By the Light of the Silv'ry Moon," words by Edward Madden, introduced in the act in 1909 by Georgie Price. Though originally published by Edwards himself, the song was soon taken over by the house of Remick for the impressive sum of $20,000.

chapter six

UNION SQUARE—
Where the Popular Song
Becomes Big Business

BEFORE 1880, the most important song publishers were scattered throughout the country, mostly in New York, Chicago, Pittsburgh, Detroit, Milwaukee, and San Francisco. In those years, song publishing was much of a hit-and-miss process. Chance, rather than design, led to a hit. Since there was little awareness of the efficacy of good exploitation, hits in those days assumed comparatively modest proportions.

One man above others gave the first hint of some of the things that would happen to the publishing business in the 1890s and early 1900s. He was Charles K. Harris, master of the sentimental ballad, who was born in Poughkeepsie, New York, in 1867. As a boy, his interest in the songs of the minstrel show made him construct a banjo on which he could strum his favorite tunes. A Vaudeville performer then gave him a real banjo as a gift. In his boyhood, Harris earned his living in small Vaudeville theaters in Milwaukee accompanying himself in minstrel-show songs. While attending a performance of

The Skating Rink, a musical starring Nat C. Goodwin, Harris felt that he could write a far better skating song than the one used in the production. He went home, wrote his song, and then somehow managed to convince Goodwin to substitute it for the regularly scheduled number. After that, Harris wrote other songs, his eye always fixed on some performer of musical comedy or Vaudeville who might sing it. One or two of his songs were used. From all these creative efforts, Harris earned virtually nothing, but he did have the satisfaction of being a composer who was being performed.

He soon came to the decision that the only way to make money through his songs was to publish them. He opened a small office on Grand Avenue in Milwaukee. His rent was $7.50 a month, and running expenses amounted to another $2.50. Outside his office he hung up a sign reading: "Songs Written to Order." *Songs written to order!* . . . In the humble setting of Harris' cramped office, Tin Pan Alley was beginning to emerge as a factory for the production of songs.

In a few years' time, Harris brought the song business to another milestone—this time by writing and publishing the first popular song to sell several million copies of sheet music. That song was the famous "After the Ball," inspired by an incident personally witnessed by the composer during a brief visit to Chicago. At a dance there, Harris happened to notice a young couple quarrel and separate. The thought suddenly came to him: "Many a heart is aching after the ball." Harris knew at once that he had just come upon not only a felicitous line for a lyric but also a wonderful idea for a sentimental ballad. He wrote both the lyrics and the music of "After the Ball" immediately after returning to Milwaukee. He described his ballad as a "song story" because his lyric was a long and lachrymose tale of mistaken identity. An old man explains to his little niece why he never married: Many years ago at a ball he saw his sweetheart kiss a strange man. Convinced she was unfaithful, he left her for good, and only many, many years later did he discover that the stranger was his sweetheart's brother.

"After the Ball" was introduced in a Vaudeville theater in Milwaukee in 1892 by a singer named Sam Doctor. The song was a failure, largely because midway in his rendition Doctor forgot his words. But another performance, not long afterward, reversed the fortunes. When J. Aldrich Libby, the baritone, interpolated it in the Charley Hoyt extravaganza, *A Trip to Chinatown,* "not a sound was heard," as Harris recalled in his autobiography. "I was ready to sink through the floor. He then went through the second verse and the chorus, and again complete silence reigned. I was making ready to bolt, but my friends . . . held me tightly by the arm. Then came the third verse and the chorus. For a full minute the audience remained quiet, and then broke loose with applause. . . . The entire audience arose and, standing, wildly applauded for fully five minutes." A few days later Harris received from Oliver Ditson, a Boston music shop, an unprecedented order for 75,000 copies. The Harris presses started rolling, nor did they stop until about five million copies were sold. John Philip Sousa played the ballad at the World Exposition in 1893 where it became such a favorite that henceforth he had to include it in each of his programs. "After the Ball" laid the solid foundation for Harris' dual career as songwriter and publisher.

II

When "After the Ball" was published, Union Square was the entertainment center of the country. It was the locale for Tony Pastor's Music Hall, the Union Square Theatre, the Academy of Music, as well as for numerous restaurants, burlesque houses, dance halls, and saloons.

Realizing that such an amusement mecca provided almost limitless possibilities for the exploitation of songs, Harris decided to shift his firm from Milwaukee to Union Square. But he was not the first publisher to come there. As early as the beginning of the 1880s, Willis Woodward was situated in the Star Building on 13th Street and Broadway. In 1888, the then still young and struggling house of Witmark moved to 32 East 14th Street. Six years later, the new firm of Joseph W. Stern & Co. opened on 14th Street; and to a near-by street came another new house, that of Howley, Haviland. By the middle 1890s, Union Square contained the greatest concentration of song publishers in the country.

Many of the procedures that were later to make Tin Pan Alley a mighty trust of song were first introduced in Union Square. Most of the publishers in Union Square, particularly the newcomers, had no capital to speak of. Frequently their entire wealth consisted of a desk, a chair, and a handful of songs. But there neophytes had drive and initiative. Impatient with the haphazard processes by which, in preceding years, a song was written, published, and became successful, they decided that a song was no different from any other commodity on the market. It had to be manufactured to meet the prevailing taste; and it had to be sold to the public.

Consequently, these publishers devised formulas by which songs could be produced with speed and dispatch—formulas so efficacious that most often these songs were created by composers who did not know how to write a note of music. Songs were now to be produced from a serviceable matrix, and issued in large quantities: stereotypes for foreign songs, Negro songs, humorous ditties, and, most important of all, sentimental ballads.

The sentimental ballad grew more popular than ever before, largely as a result of the triumph of "After the Ball." Harris himself wrote and published three others that caught on: "Break the News to Mother" and "I've Come to Say Goodbye" in 1897, and "Hello, Central, Give Me Heaven" in 1901. But the most sensational ballads of this period came from other pens, and from the presses of other publishers.

When Edward B. Marks and Joseph W. Stern teamed up in 1894 to write "The Little Lost Child," each was more or less a novice at songwriting. Marks was a salesman of buttons, notions, and novelties; Stern, a necktie salesman who, as he said, "could play the piano with one hand and fake with the other." The idea to write "The Little Lost Child" came to Marks when he read in a newspaper that a child, lost in the city streets, was found by a policeman who turned out to be its long-lost father. Marks, who for some time had spent his leisure hours writing lyrics that had never been published, adapted this tale into suitable song verses, which Stern then set to music. The authors opened an office on 14th Street to publish and sell the song. One of the first customers to visit them was Della Fox, the star of the musical extravaganza, *Wang.* She took the song and made it a craze; and the song, in turn, made the house of Joseph W. Stern & Co.

Two years later, Stern and Marks went on to even greater prosperity with a second ballad, "My Mother Was a Lady." The subject, like that of "The Little Lost Child," came from life. The writers were in a German restaurant on 20th Street when they saw a waitress being insulted by some patrons. She burst into tears and exclaimed to her tormentors that they would not have dared treat her this way if her brother Jack were present. Then she added proudly: "My mother was a lady." In the Stern and Marks song, the man who insults the waitress is a drummer who turns out to be Jack's lifelong friend and who then and there offers marriage to the insulted woman. The song was introduced at Tony Pastor's Music Hall by Meyer Cohen, and later became a staple of Lottie Gilson's act at Tony Pastor's and other Vaudeville theaters. It sold over a million copies and made the phrase "my mother was a lady" an everyday slogan.

In the same year of 1896 when they issued their own "My Mother Was a Lady," Stern and Marks published another major ballad success, this time one from somebody else's pen.

Maude Nugent, a performer at Johnny Reilly's saloon on Eighth Avenue, sold the words and music of a song called "Sweet Rosie O'Grady" to the house of Joseph Stern for a flat fee of several hundred dollars. Since her husband, Billy Jerome, was an experienced hand in writing songs, and since she herself never again wrote a song worthy of attention, it has often been suggested, and probably not without justification, that "Sweet Rosie O'Grady" was Jerome's work and not Nugent's. In any event, Maude Nugent helped to make this gentle little waltz popular—one of the biggest hits published by Stern.

The sentimental ballad also proved the making of the publishing house of Witmark. Witmark's came into existence in 1886, when Isidore Witmark wrote a number called "President Grover Cleveland's Wedding March," which he and his brothers ran off on a toy printing press. To their amazement they made a *coup*. Nobody in the business had thought of capitalizing on the marriage of President Cleveland to Frances Folsom. When that event materialized, the demand for Witmark's number became nationwide.

The Witmarks were now in the song business. They set up their office at their home on West 40th Street, and continued publishing Isidore's songs. One of the earliest, "I'll Answer That Question Tomorrow" was taken by Mlle. René, an English music-hall star, for her first tour of the United States. (Mlle. René later became the wife of William A. Brady, the theatrical producer, and mother of the famous actress, Alice Brady.) The Witmarks also published songs of other writers. They soon had to seek new and larger quarters, and in 1894 found them in Union Square.

When success first came to the Witmarks it arrived with one of the best-loved sentimental ballads of the 1890s: Charles Graham's "The Picture That Is Turned Toward the Wall." Graham, an Englishman, was a prolific composer of ballads, one of which was "If the Waters Could Speak as They Flow," published by Willis Woodward. In 1891, Graham attended a play on 14th Street, *Blue Jeans,* in which a farmer turns the picture of his daughter toward the wall because she had just run away from home. This touching scene provided Graham with the idea for his ballad, which he sold to Witmark for fifteen dollars. The Witmarks put the song away in a file of unpublished numbers and forgot about it. One day, Andrew Mack, an Irish tenor, dropped into the Witmark office seeking a new song for his Vaudeville act. When nothing in the catalogue appealed to him, the Witmarks opened for him their file of unpublished music. Thus Mack came upon "The Picture," and recognized at once its potential appeal. He took it, and made it a hit. As Isidore Witmark says in his autobiography: " 'The Picture That Is Turned Toward the Wall' was more than a financial success for the Witmarks. It brought them a coveted prestige. Formerly they had sold sheet music by the hundred copies; now they knew sales in the thousands. . . . Jobbers who had scorned to deal with 'children' were camping on their doorstep for copies. Dealers who had refused them displays now buried other songs beneath the 'Picture.' Singers whom they had been obliged to chase now chased them."

One of Witmark's best-selling ballads was "Sweet Adeline." Though it was issued in 1903, after the Witmarks had moved out of Union Square to greener pastures uptown, its composition belongs to the 1890s. Harry Armstrong, who liked singing in vocal quartets, had written the melody in Boston in 1896 when he was only eighteen. For a time, his song had no lyrics. After Armstrong came to New York—first to play the piano in various saloons, and later to work for Witmark—he asked Richard H. Gerard to write a lyric for his melody. Now called "You're the Flower of My Heart, Sweet Rosalie," the song went from one publisher to another without finding a taker. Gerard finally suggested a change of title. By chance, the authors came upon a poster announcing the farewell tour of the prima donna, Adelina Patti, which provided the lyricist with an idea. "Let's call the girl in our song, Adeline," he suggested. The new title—contracted to a simple "Sweet Adeline"—apparently turned the trick, for Witmark accepted the song at once. For about a year after its publication, the sheet music failed to move. Then The Quaker City Four, a Vaudeville quartet, came to the Witmarks looking for a new number. When they turned down everything that was offered, "Sweet Adeline" was played for them. "That's what we've been looking for," the manager of the quartet exclaimed. The Quartet introduced the song the following week at the Victoria Theatre on 42nd Street and saw it acclaimed. Before long it became a favorite of barbershop quartets everywhere; the theme song for two successful mayoralty campaigns for John J. Fitzgerald of Boston; and, many years later, the title of a musical comedy by Jerome Kern and Oscar Hammerstein II.

III

The richest contributor of sentimental ballads to Union Square was a huge hulk of a man as famous for his generosity, sentimentality, and extravagance as for his melodic gift. He was Paul Dresser, the brother of the novelist, Theodore Dreiser. Less disposed toward clichés than so many of his rivals, less inclined to stretch an emotion to the point of a maudlin and cloying sentimentality, Dresser was a composer whose finest ballads have a winning charm and a lingering fragrance.

"He was," wrote brother Theodore in the introduction to *The Songs of Paul Dresser,* "ever full of melodies of a tender . . . nature—that of a ballad-maker of a nation. . . . He seemed to have a peculiar fondness for the twilight hour, at which time most often he might be found thrumming over one or another strain, until at last some particular one might capture his fancy and presently he might be in tears. The sighings over home and mother and lost sweethearts and dead heroes that were here! Yet with something in the completed song or mood which gave it the wide appeal which most of his songs enjoyed. They bespoke . . . a wistful seeking . . . tender and illusioned, with no practical knowledge of any side of life, yet full of true poetic feeling for the mystery and pathos of life and death, and wonder of waters, the stars, the flowers, accidents of life, success and failure."

Paul Dresser was born in 1857 in Terre Haute, Indiana, by the banks of the Wabash which he glorified in his best-known song. When he was sixteen he ran away from home and joined a traveling medicine show where he sang parodies of popular songs; later on, billed as "Paul Dresser, the Sensational Comique," he appeared with various theatrical troupes. In 1885 he joined the Billy Rice Minstrels as an end man. For this troupe he wrote the words and music for his first sentimental ballad, "The Letter That Never Came," its inspiration being one of his own unhappy love affairs. T. B. Harms published it in 1886 and it was moderately successful. He wrote other sentimental songs for the house of Willis Woodward which increased his reputation in Union Square. Among them was his greatest hit up to then, "The Pardon Came Too Late," in 1891. Three years later, he became a partner in the publishing firm of Howley, Haviland, which began issuing his songs. Some of these had a tremendous vogue and made a fortune both for the publisher and the author: "The Blue and the Gray," "Just Tell Them That You Saw Me," "The Curse of the Dreamer," "My Mother Told Me So," and his gem, "On the Banks of the Wabash."

There are several versions of how Dresser came to write "On the Banks of the Wabash." Theodore Dreiser has written that he suggested the subject to his brother because rivers always did well in popular songs; Dreiser further insisted that he himself provided the lyric. But what is probably a more authoritative and accurate account comes form Max Hoffman, the orchestrator of the Witmark firm. He is quoted by Isidore

Witmark as saying: "I went to his room at the Auditorium Hotel where instead of a piano there was a small folding camp organ, always carried with him. It was summer. All the windows were open and Paul was mulling over a melody that was practically in finished form. But he did not have the words. So he had me play the full chorus over and over again at least for two or three hours, while he was writing down the words, changing a line here and a phrase there until the lyric suited him. . . . When Paul came to the line, 'through the sycamores the candlelights are gleaming," I was tremendously impressed. . . . I have always felt that Paul got the idea from glancing out of the window now and again as he wrote, and seeing the lights glimmering on Lake Michigan. . . . The song was published precisely as I arranged it. . . . During the whole evening we spent together, Paul made no mention of anyone's having helped him with the song."

Though Dresser earned huge sums from his songs (in the neighborhood of half a million dollars in less than two decades) he kept very little of it. He always lived in the grand manner, spent money recklessly, and was generous to a fault. By the time he was fifty, he was totally penniless, and deserted by friends whom he had so long feasted, wined, and at times even supported. His spirit cracked in the face of adversity. But he still had a winning card up his sleeve. His last song, "My Gal Sal," one of his triumphs, was published by himself late in 1905. Soon after that, on January 30, 1906, he died suddenly in Brooklyn, New York, probably of a broken heart. He did not live to see "My Gal Sal" reinstate him among the foremost writers of sentimental ballads of his generation.

IV

While sentimental ballads reigned supreme in Union Square, other and more virile kinds of songs also made a strong bid for popularity. There were such rough-and-tumble songs as "Drill Ye Tarriers," published in 1888, "Down Went McGinty," in 1889, and "Throw Him Down, McCloskey," in 1890. The first is believed to have been written by Thomas F. Casey, who had been an unskilled laborer before going on the stage. He drew to good advantage from his own experiences with rock-drilling in writing his hit song, which was successfully interpolated in *A Brass Monkey,* a musical extravaganza by Charley Hoyt. "Down Went McGinty" was a humorous ditty by Joseph Flynn about an Irishman who was so accident-prone that he was always falling in the strangest of places, finally in the river. Flynn introduced the song with his partner, Frank B. Sheridan, at Hyde and Behman's theater in Brooklyn, where it scored, and started a long and successful career in Vaudeville. "Throw Him Down, McCloskey," by J. W. Kelly, was a vigorous ballad about a boxing match also made famous in Vaudeville by Maggie Cline.

"Coon Songs" (with which ragtime first entered the song business) also flourished in Union Square. The "coon song" emerged from the shell of the more energetic Negro dialect song of the minstrel show, acquiring verve and electricity through the assimilation of ragtime rhythm. The first "coon song" to command attention was "New Coon in Town," by Paul Allen, which he himself introduced in the Vaudeville act of Lester and Allen in 1883. One of the first major hits in this *genre* was actually written by a Negro, even though that race deeply and rightly resented the term "coon song" and some of the expressions and sentiments found in the lyrics. He was Ernest Hogan, a popular vaudevillian of the 1890s, who wrote "All Coons Look Alike to Me" in 1896 and himself made it successful. Witmark, who published the song, said that Hogan later regretted having written it, and was heartily ashamed of it. Nevertheless, he had succeeded in writing one of the most dynamic examples of this kind of popular Negro song. Two other familiar "coon songs" appeared in the same year of 1896. One was "The Bully Song," or "The New Bully." It had been a favorite at Babe Connors' night spot in

St. Louis where it was heard by Charles E. Trevathan, a sportswriter, who in turn taught it to May Irwin. May Irwin, who is sometimes credited with being its author, introduced the song in *The Widow Jones* at the Bijou Theatre in New York, and later made it the crowning number of her Vaudeville act. The other, "My Gal Is a Highborn Lady," was written by Barney Fagan, a graduate of the minstrel show, and subsequently a Vaudeville buck-and-wing performer. Fagan disclosed how he came to write his song. He was bicycling along Lake Michigan in Chicago when a pedal broke. Its persistent click against the wheel suggested to him a ragtime melody, and he wrote it the same day. Witmark bought it for $100 and published it in 1896 in an arrangement by Gustave Luders.

A Union Square classic, "Ta-ra-ra-bom-der-é" was in the abandoned and rhythmically vital vein of the "coon song." Henry J. Sayers, a press agent, heard it in the same St. Louis cabaret where "The Bully Song" first became popular—at Babe Connors'. Sayers substituted more or less gibberish verses for the more ribald ones used at Babe Connors' and sold his song to Willis Woodward, who published it in 1891. "Ta-ra-ra-bom-der-é" traveled out of Union Square and half way around the world, after being given a sensational treatment on the London stage by Lottie Collins. Since the 1890s, the song has been intermittently revived in this country.

Two other Union Square gems are still remembered—less abandoned and more reserved than the "coon song." They are "The Sidewalks of New York" and "The Band Played On." The first was written by Charles B. Lawlor, a vaudevillian, in collaboration with James W. Blake, a hat salesman, and was issued by Howley, Haviland in 1894. Lottie Gilson first sang it at the London Theatre in the Bowery. Later on, Lawlor himself plugged the song in the leading New York Vaudeville theaters. "The Band Played On," words by John E. Palmer and music by Charles B. Ward, appeared in 1895. It deserves a special footnote in the history of our popular music as the first song hit ever promoted by a newspaper—the *New York World.*

V

Union Square publishers not only devised a successful methodology for producing songs but also for "plugging" them—that is, selling them to the public.

Before the 1890s, and outside Union Square, Will Rossiter, an enterprising Chicago publisher, became one of the first to go out himself and market the songs he published. He would invade local retail stores and sing his tunes as a spur to sheet-music sales. He was also the first to advertise his products in theatrical trade journals. He pointed a direction toward which all Union Square publishers later headed. Many of these publishers served as song pluggers for their own firms, among them being Julie Witmark, Patrick Howley, Edward B. Marks, and Joseph W. Stern. "In the 'Nineties," recalled Edward B. Marks in his autobiography, "a publisher had to know his way about the night spots. It was important to get his wares before the bibulous public; so he had to spend a large part of his time making the rounds for plugs and more plugs. In his wanderings he saw as broad a cross section of New York as any man—even broader than a wine agent, because the song plugger hit spots where champagne would have been considered an effeminate affectation. Sixty joints a week I used to make. Joe Stern, my partner, covered about forty. What's more we did it every week." These pluggers would induce performers in Vaudeville, musicals and burlesque, singing waiters and orchestra leaders—anybody who could bring a song to an audience—to interpolate their latest publications in their acts or on their programs. They would invade the local shops selling sheet music and play the tunes of their firm on the piano, all day long. They would also travel by truck through populated city streets singing their songs through megaphones to the passing crowds, and even use such well-attended events as six-day bicycle races as a means to bring their songs to the people.

Union Square was also a conservatory, training specialized song pluggers, whose only responsibility was to place songs and get them played. Upon the personal charm, contacts, and sales persuasion of these pluggers rested the fate of a song. The best pluggers were able to lift a song from obscurity to nationwide acceptance. Meyer Cohen, who worked for Stern and Marks, was single-handedly responsible for the sensation created by "My Mother Was a Lady." Besides introducing it at Tony Pastor's, he was able to convince Lottie Gilson to use it in her act. Mose Gumble, employed by Shapiro, Bernstein & Co., was a powerful influence in placing his firm's songs with stars like George M. Cohan, Weber and Fields, Nora Bayes, and many others; Gumble made Jean Schwartz's "Bedelia" a nationwide fad in 1903.

In Union Square, song pluggers devised new ways of supplementing old ones in getting songs played. One new method was to place the plugger in the audience. When his firm's song was featured on the bill, the plugger would rise, as if spontaneously. The limelight pointing a finger at him, he would sing several choruses of a song until it became indelibly engraved on the consciousness of the audience. It is believed that this procedure began at a Hurtig and Seamon Theatre in New York in 1893, and that the first such performer was twelve-year-old Gus Edwards. The boy Edwards was so well liked, and he had to repeat the refrain of his song so many times, that the trick of placing a plugger in the audience henceforth became standard operating practice. Irving Berlin, as a boy, plugged the songs of the Harry von Tilzer firm from a seat at Tony Pastor's Music Hall in the early 1900s.

Another method of plugging songs came with "The Little Lost Child." A Brooklyn electrician originated slides which could throw a series of pictures on the motion-picture screen.

These slides were able to dramatize a new song pictorially; at the same time, the words of the lyric were flashed with each picture. A set of these slides was manufactured for "The Little Lost Child" and, with the co-operation of William Fox, later the motion-picture producer, was used in a Union Square motion-picture theater. This community sing so delighted the audience that other publishers soon followed suit and used slides to promote their new songs. Thus a new and powerful medium for getting audiences to hear and learn new songs came into existence. This method was used in motion-picture theaters for over two decades. Eddie Cantor and George Jessel served their stage apprenticeships in their boyhood by appearing on the stages of New York movie houses and singing the songs dramatized by these slides.

chapter seven

FROM OPERETTA TO
MUSICAL COMEDY

THE AMERICAN operetta was a logical outgrowth of the ex-travaganza and burlesque. But it did not crystallize until the 1880s, after New York had for some time been inundated by a wave of musical entertainment from Europe: the *opéra bouffes* of Offenbach, operettas of Suppé and Johann Strauss II, and, most influential of all, the comic operas of Gilbert and Sullivan, which encouraged many Americans to write works in a similar vein. In 1879, one year after *Pinafore* was triumphantly introduced at the Boston Museum, John Philip Sousa wrote his first comic opera, *The Smugglers*. It was a failure, a fact that did not dissuade him from writing nineteen others, the best of these being *El Capitan,* in 1896, and *The Bride Elect,* in 1897. But a major success by an American was not slow in appearing. In 1886, *The Little Tycoon*—book and music by Willard Spencer—began a five-hundred-performance run which established a box-office record that stood for five years. This travesty on the weakness of Americans for foreign titles was truly the first American operetta. The songs by Spencer became popular, particularly "On the Sea," "Love

Comes Like a Summer Night," and "Sad Heart of Mine."

The first successful operetta by an American inevitably induced others to emulation. In 1891, Reginald de Koven came closer than anyone of his time to anticipate the spacious musical writing of Victor Herbert. De Koven was born in Middletown, Connecticut, in 1859, and received a comprehensive musical training in Europe as preparation for a career in serious music. After returning to the United States in 1882, he settled in Chicago where he worked first in a bank and then in a stockbrokerage house. Marriage to an heiress, followed by fortunate investments in Texas real estate, brought him wealth. Now possessing the means to return to music he divided his activity between musical criticism and composition. In his creative work he preferred working for the popular theater. He wrote his first operetta in 1887, a Hindu opus obviously modeled after *The Mikado,* and called *The Begum.* His librettist was Harry B. Smith with whom, three years later, he wrote his major success, *Robin Hood.* It is remembered not because either the book or the score had particular vitality; spasmodic revivals have long ago proved that this work is little better than a museum piece, too slight for an opera, too stuffy and pretentious for comic opera. *Robin Hood* lives because one of its songs—"Oh Promise Me"—has become a permanent fixture at American weddings. "Oh Promise Me" was not in the original score. Right after the opening night of the opera in Chicago, on June 9, 1890, Jessie Bartlett Davis who played the role of Allan-a-Dale, insisted that she be given an aria to showcase her effective contralto voice. To placate her, De Koven introduced into his score "Oh Promise Me," a song he had written three years earlier to lyrics by Clement Scott, and which had been published as an art song by Schirmer in 1889. There is good reason to believe that Davis did not like the song when De Koven played it to her. However, she grew more sympathetic to it on witnessing the audience response when she introduced it on the second night. It at once became the hit of the production, and completely threw all the other De Koven numbers into the shade.

Before Victor Herbert appeared on the scene, two other important operettas were written by Americans: *Wang*, in 1891, and *The Isle of Champagne*, a year later. The first was an elaborate Siamese spectacle in which De Wolf Hopper played the title role of the Regent of Siam. The musical score by Woolson Morse included "A Pretty Girl" and "Every Rose Must Have Its Thorn" (J. Cheever Goodwin). The second was set in a happy kingdom where the only known beverages were wine and champagne; the importation of water creates a sensation. Its ingratiating musical score, by William Wallace Furst, had such pleasing items as "Fly Little Bird," "There's a Land in the Silvery Shimmery Moon," and a topical number entitled "Old King Mumm Could Make Things Hum" (Charles A. Byrne).

During the 1890s another branch sprouted out of the trunk of the musical theater—the revue. More extended in concept and design than Vaudeville, the revue (like Vaudeville) came from the minstrel show where, in the middle fantasia section, each member of the company was allowed to perform his specialty. This new kind of musical entertainment was first seen at the Casino Theatre, in New York, in 1894. There and then Charles W. Lederer produced *The Passing Show*, an extravaganza containing basic elements of Vaudeville, burlesque, and comic opera. Lederer shared no expense in providing a sumptuous setting for his potpourri of diversified entertainment. For the next few years several imitations were seen on Broadway: *The Merry World*, in 1895; *In Gay New York*, in 1896; and *In Gotham*, in 1898, among others. The name of "The Passing Show" was not used again for a Broadway revue until 1912 when it was revived by the Shuberts for an annual production at the Winter Garden; but by that time the revue had become an established Broadway fixture.

II

On November 20, 1894, *Prince Ananias* introduced a new name to the American musical theater, that of Victor Herbert. This operetta did not attract much attention, but its composer was destined soon to become the most successful that the American stage had thus far produced. The story of the contemporary American musical theater begins with Victor Herbert. He was the first composer for the popular theater whose best work has survived; whose best operettas are still revived intermittently on stage and screen; whose songs are still great favorites.

Like its European equivalent, the American operetta of the 1890s escaped from reality into story-book make-believe. Saber-rattling officers, princes, princesses, fine-plumed ladies and elegant gentlemen moved within picturesque, exotic, or mythical kingdom settings. These characters became enmeshed in intrigues out of which the virtuous emerged triumphant, where evildoers met their just punishment, and where the hero always won the heroine. Sentimental romance was the thread on which to bead the pearls of song, usually in three-quarter time, and swirling dances.

Victor Herbert, America's first major composer of operettas, was content to conform to existing patterns and established conventions. He was not an innovator; he did nothing to inaugurate a new era. Actually he was the culmination of an old epoch, the summation of things that had already for several decades been said and done on our stage.

Music came easily to him. He once confessed that ideas crowded his head all the time; he had no difficulty in syphoning them into his scores. His music could be fresh and vital even when intended for shopworn ideas and synthetic sentiment.

Someone once said that Herbert's songs sound better outside

the theater than in it. It should also be pointed out that most of his songs sound better without their lyrics. These observations probably point up Herbert's essential weakness as a writer for the stage. He was first and foremost a composer—his primary concern, the writing of graceful, spontaneous, easy-flowing, charming melodies echoing a past age. That these melodies were written for the theater is mere coincidence. They derive nothing from the dramatic context for which they were intended.

He was amazingly facile and prolific. This is both his strength and weakness: strength, because his finest melodies convey a feeling of the spontaneity and ease with which they were written; weakness, because so much of his other music betrays haste and lack of discrimination. In less than forty years he completed fifty operettas, besides numerous independent numbers for other productions, and a library of serious works for the concert hall and opera house. He could finish an operetta score in a single month, even while engaged in sundry other activities during the same period. "He would come in and work out a new scene in my office," Florenz Ziegfeld once recalled, "and the next morning appear with the full orchestration." There were times when he worked on as many as three or four scores simultaneously.

He was always in a hurry in his work, always laboring at fever pitch; deadlines were merciless and he was most meticulous about meeting them. If only his concentration, dedication, and attention to detail had been the equal of his native talent! He was that enviable miracle: a born melodist, even as Stephen Foster had been, and he could produce a fresh and pliant melody as naturally as speech. But unlike Foster he also had a sound instinct for interesting harmonies and he was a gifted orchestrator. He had, in short, both the equipment and the native gifts with which to reach heights in the musical theater. He might have been the equal, if not the superior, of men like Sir Arthur Sullivan and Johann Strauss II and Offenbach. As it was, Herbert produced much that was pedestrian and third-rate, much that betrayed the casualness and haste with which it had been created. Only a fraction of his voluminous output had the robustness to survive, and the vitality to remain young.

But that fraction is as treasurable a contribution as anybody has made to American popular music. Its place there is secure. There is a world of ingratiating sentiment and sweetness, gaiety and tenderness in songs like "Kiss Me Again," "Ah, Sweet Mystery of Life," "I'm Falling in Love With Someone," "Because You're You," "A Kiss in the Dark," "Sweethearts," "Thine Alone," "Italian Street Song," and "Gypsy Love Song." Gems like these are responsible for the periodic revivals of Herbert's best operettas. When seen on the present-day stage, these plays—though often doctored and revamped—are hardly better than period pieces. The humor falls lamely; the stage business is often confused; the emotion is unconvincing. But the music never fails to elevate us into a world of encompassing graciousness.

His success was in the large design: it came early, and he never really knew struggle. He was born in Dublin, Ireland, in 1859, and received a thorough musical education at the Stuttgart Conservatory in Germany, and cello lessons from Bernhardt Cossmann in Baden-Baden. In 1886 he married Theresa Foerster, a prima donna. When that same year she was engaged by the Metropolitan Opera of New York, Victor Herbert came with her to the United States and joined the cello section of the Metropolitan Opera orchestra. He took out his first citizenship papers without delay. From then on his newly adopted country became his own. He never again set foot either on Irish or German soil, and except for a single hurried visit to England he never even left America.

In the years that followed his arrival in this country, Herbert became famous as a conductor of various festivals, of the Pittsburgh Symphony Orchestra, and of Patrick Gilmore's 22nd Regiment Band. He also became known as a composer of concertos, varied orchestral pieces, and grand operas. All this has earned for him a place of honor in American music. Yet such achievements are virtually obscured by his greatest contribution to American life: the music he wrote for our popular theater.

He wrote his first operetta, *Prince Ananias,* on a suggestion of the director of a Boston light-opera company, which introduced it in 1894. It was a failure. But Herbert did not have to wait long for recognition. One year later came *The Wizard of the Nile,* book and lyrics by Harry B. Smith, a production built around and for the comedy talent of Frank Daniels, who appeared in the leading role of Kibosh, a fake magician in Egypt. *The Wizard of the Nile* had a fruitful run at the Casino Theatre. Before that run ended, the whole country was whistling Herbert's lilting melodies, particularly "My Angeline," and an infectious waltz called "Starlight, Star Bright." And the country was also repeating *ad nauseam* a slang phrase popularized by Kibosh: "Am I *a wiz?*"

The next Herbert operetta, in 1897, was also a success— *The Serenade,* in which a serenade, "I Love Thee, I Adore Thee" (Harry B. Smith), is the pivot on which the plot revolves. A new stage star emerges here—the winning, winsome Alice Nielsen, whom Mrs. Victor Herbert discovered at the Murray Hill Theatre. Now an established star, Alice Nielsen won the privilege of having Herbert write for her a new operetta—*The Fortune Teller,* in 1898. A Hungarian setting, and some gyspy characters, provided Herbert with the opportunity to write music generously sprinkled with paprika, to lyrics by Harry B. Smith. Songs like "Romany Life" and "The Hussars' Chorus" may be only an Irish-German-American idea of what authentic Romany music is like; they are, nevertheless, soundly musical, skillful in their choral writing, rich-blooded in melody, with gypsy verve and passion. The most celebrated song in the score is a sentimental melody made popular by Eugene Cowles in his portrayal of the gypsy role of Sandor:

"The Gypsy Love Song" ("Slumber On, My Little Gypsy Sweetheart").

Herbert's greatest stage successes, and his best music, were still to come. On October 13, 1903, *Babes in Toyland*, a musical extravaganza, opened at the Majestic Theatre. This was an unashamed effort on the part of librettist-lyricist Glen Mac-Donough to capitalize on the popularity of *The Wizard of Oz* which had opened in New York in January of the same year. In Herbert's operetta, Oz became Toyland, where colorful and elaborately costumed characters stepped out of the pages of fairy tales and Mother Goose rhymes. The most celebrated musical number was an instrumental piece in the second act: the pert "March of the Toys," which opens with a piquant fanfare for toy trumpet. Equally appealing is "I Can't Do This Sum," sung by the schoolchildren as they tap out the rhythm with chalk on their slates, and "Toyland."

Before the year of 1903 ended, Herbert had another operetta on Broadway—*Babette*, whose only claim to interest rests in the fact that it consummated the transfer of Fritzi Scheff from opera to operetta. Since *Babette* was a failure, Fritzi Scheff had good reason to regret her decision to abandon the Metropolitan Opera for the musical-comedy stage. But two years later, on December 25, 1905, she was crowned queen of the operetta in a new work, *Mlle. Modiste*, written just for her by Herbert. Cast as Fifi, a milliner who becomes a concert singer, Fritzi Scheff gave such a winning performance that she and the role henceforth became synonymous. The song triumph of this operetta was, to be sure, the immortal waltz, "Kiss Me Again" (Henry Blossom). As originally planned for *Mlle. Modiste*, "Kiss Me Again" was meant to be satiric, rather than sentimental. It was one of several refrains for a number entitled "If I Were On the Stage" in which Fritzi Scheff as Fifi demonstrated her versatility by singing various types of songs, including a gavotte, polonaise, and waltz. Each type was actually a caricature of the *genre*. But the audience acclaimed

"Kiss Me Again" on opening night, and before long the melody was sung and played throughout the country not as a travesty of a waltz but as a waltz that was sentimental. Bowing to public judgment, Herbert eventually wrote a new introductory verse for the waltz and presented it in the form that is now known and loved.

In 1906 *The Red Mill,* starring David Montgomery and Fred Stone, had one of Herbert's best scores, including as it did such happy melodic inspirations as "The Isle of Our Dreams," "Because You're You," "Moonbeams" and—in a much lighter vein—"Every Day Is Ladies' Day With Me" and "Good-a-bye, John," all lyrics by Blossom.

Like *Mlle. Modiste, Naughty Marietta* in 1910 was written with a specific opera star in mind, this time Emma Trentini, a member of the Oscar Hammerstein Opera Company in New York. The frame for her operetta debut was eighteenth century New Orleans, where, as a spirited French countess, she falls in love with Captain Dick Warrington. There are three Herbert song classics here, lyrics by Rida Johnson Young: "Italian Street Song," "I'm Falling in Love With Someone," and most famous of all, "Ah, Sweet Mystery of Life." In the original stage production, "Ah, Sweet Mystery of Life" was an instrumental intermezzo repeated at the end of the show. But Orville Harrold, who appeared as Dick Warrington, recognized its potential appeal as a song and urged Herbert to have a lyric written for it. Rida Johnson Young complied, and the song was published by Witmark. Though never officially interpolated into the original run of the play, it ultimately became its most famous piece of music. It was also one of Herbert's greatest song hits. When the song was published, the house of Witmark was in such financial difficulties that for a time it looked as if operations would have to be suspended. But the sheet-music sale of "Ah, Sweet Mystery of Life" provided the salvation of Witmark.

After *Naughty Marietta,* Herbert seemed incapable of recapturing the formula that had made him so successful. He himself felt that the finest score he ever wrote was that for *Eileen,* produced in 1917, which included one of his most beautiful songs, "Thine Alone." "Thine Alone" became so popular that of all Herbert's songs its sale on sheet music and records has been rivaled only by those of "Ah, Sweet Mystery of Life." Yet *Eileen* had only sixty-four performances.

His operettas kept on appearing on Broadway up to the end of his life. He also wrote music for special productions, including the *Ziegfeld Follies* for various editions between 1918 and 1923. He was still in demand, still regarded with veneration by his associates. More than that, he still had a gift for appealing, sentimental songs, as in "Thine Alone," and "A Kiss in the Dark," the latter heard in *Orange Blossoms* in 1922. But his day was over. He had belonged to the age of the waltz; he was uncomfortable in an era glorifying the fox trot and the Charleston. His music was for a placid, sentimental era that died during World War I. In the newer and more frenetic period after the war his music sounded almost like an anachronism. This was the new day of ragtime and jazz—and new styles found new composers. "My day is over," he told a friend. "They are forgetting poor old Herbert."

In 1924, while working on special numbers for a new edition of the *Ziegfeld Follies,* Herbert felt suddenly ill, and collapsed in his doctor's office. He died there of a heart attack on May 26, 1924.

His death came a few years too soon. Had he lived another decade he would have heard his music played more often (and through that new medium, the radio) than that of any other American composer, living or dead. Had he lived another dozen years, he would have witnessed revivals on Broadway of *Babes in Toyland* and *Mlle. Modiste,* whose music inspired new accolades from the critics. Had he lived another two decades he would have seen some of his best operettas transferred to the talking screen, and he would have witnessed his own career glorified in song and dance in the motion-picture musical, *The Great Victor Herbert.*

Victor Herbert died thinking of himself as a has-been. But he had actually become a classic.

III

While Herbert was in his heyday, the Broadway musical stage was enriched with the music of several other important operetta composers. The best of these were Gustave Kerker, Karl Hoschna, Gustave Luders, and Rudolf Friml.

Kerker was born in Germany in 1857 and came to this country when he was ten years old. Before writing his first operetta—*The Cadets,* in 1879—he played in and led several theater orchestras. His first stage success was *Castles in the Air,* in 1890—De Wolf Hopper and Della Fox played the leads—after he had been appointed the conductor of the Casino Theatre in New York. It was in that theater, in 1898, that Kerker's greatest stage success was produced: *The Belle of New York,* in which Edna May became an overnight star as a Salvation Army lass who falls in love with the son of a New York vice crusader. *The Belle of New York* actually was only moderately successful in the United States. But in London it was a sensation, playing at the Shaftesbury Theatre for almost seven hundred performances. The score, like the play, is now forgotten. In their day the musical numbers that helped make Edna May famous were widely heard both in this country and abroad: "The Belle of New York" and "They All Follow Me," lyrics by Hugh Morton.

Gustave Luders, who wrote the score for *The Prince of Pilsen,* was also one of America's leading operetta composers in the first decade of the 1900s. Like Kerker he was of German birth, and was born in Bremen in 1866. He received a thorough musical training in Germany, then, in 1889, came to the United States, settling in Milwaukee, where he worked as director of several theater and light-opera company orchestras.

Charles K. Harris induced him to go to Chicago, where he found employment at Witmark's branch office as an arranger and orchestrator; in this capacity, Luders made a piano arrangement of Barney Fagan's classic ragtime tune, "My Gal is a Highborn Lady," when it was first published.

Luders' first comic opera, *Little Robinson Crusoe*, was produced in 1899. Henry W. Savage next engaged him to write the music for *The Burgomaster*, book by Frank Pixley. This was such a success when it opened in Chicago in 1900 that it made permanent the collaboration of Pixley and Luders and encouraged some critics to describe the composer as "another Victor Herbert." Its hit song was "The Tale of the Kangaroo." The Pixley-Luders-Savage combination next created *King Dodo* in 1901, which starred Raymond Hitchcock, and had two significant songs, "Look in the Book and See" and "The Tale of the Bumble Bee." In 1902 came their crowning achievement, *The Prince of Pilsen*, its story revolving around a Cincinnati brewer who is mistaken for a prince on the French Riviera. Its principal songs were "The Heidelberg Stein Song," a waltz, "The Message of the Violet," and "The Tale of the Seashell."

By 1913, Luders had written the scores for thirteen operettas. The number thirteen proved fatal for the composer. *Somewhere Else*, produced in 1913, closed after three performances because of the hostile reaction of the critics. Luders literally took his defeat to heart, becoming a victim of a heart attack one day after the operetta closed.

Karl Hoschna's triumph was *Madame Sherry*, in 1910. A native of Bohemia, where he was born in 1877, Hoschna arrived in the United States in 1896 after receiving his musical training at the Vienna Conservatory. For two years he played the oboe in an orchestra conducted by Victor Herbert, then went to work for Witmark as an arranger and orchestrator. In the early part of the new century he wrote three operettas, but none of these reached Broadway.

In 1908, Charles Dickson, an actor and playwright, acquired the rights to a farce, *Incog,* which he planned to make into an operetta. He asked Isidore Witmark to recommend a composer and writer. Karl Hoschna was suggested for the music. For the book and lyrics, Witmark recommended Otto Hauerbach, a young man with a literary bent who was then employed as copywriter for an advertising firm. (Later, Hauerbach contracted his name to Harbach and became one of Broadway's most distinguished writers of musical-comedy books.) Each was paid a flat fee of one hundred dollars for his job. Now called *The Three Twins,* the production opened on June 15, 1908 with Bessie McCoy. Her rendition of "Cuddle Up a Little Closer" and "Yama-Yama Man" (the latter with lyrics not by Harbach but by George Collin) made her the toast of the town; from this time on she became known as the "Yama-Yama Girl." Curiously, neither of these two songs was originally meant for this play. Hoschna wrote "Cuddle Up a Little Closer" for a Vaudeville sketch, while "Yama-Yama Man" was hurriedly introduced into the show while it was in rehearsal.

During the next three years, Hoschna and Harbach wrote eight operettas produced on Broadway. *Madame Sherry* was their best, opening at the New Amsterdam Theatre on August 30, 1910. The story concerned a man-about-town who hoodwinks his rich uncle into believing that an Irish landlady is the glamorous Madame Sherry. The tuneful score had a resounding hit in "Every Little Movement Has a Meaning Of Its Own," and a lesser success in a languorous waltz called "The Birth of Passion." Hoschna died a little over a year after the première of this operetta, at the height of his career.

IV

The composer who inherited Victor Herbert's mantle as Broadway's leading composer of operettas was Rudolf Friml. Appropriately, it was Herbert who—at least indirectly—was responsible for Friml's appearance on Broadway. Arthur Hammerstein, the producer, was planning a new Victor Herbert operetta for Emma Trentini following her triumph in *Naughty Marietta*. Since star and composer were no longer on speaking terms, each refused to work with the other. When Herbert definitely withdrew, a new composer had to be found. The publishers, Rudolph Schirmer and Max Dreyfus, came up with a name new not only to Broadway but also to Tin Pan Alley— that of Rudolf Friml. Thus far, Friml had written only some serious pieces for the piano and some art songs. The publishers, however, persuaded Hammerstein to take a chance on the new man, since he had shown a marked gift for writing vocal music. To engage an inexperienced and unknown composer for a major Broadway production was a gamble. How that gamble paid off can be judged by the fact that Friml's first operetta was *The Firefly*.

In writing his music for *The Firefly*, Friml (like Herbert) was faithful to the traditions of the European musical theater. Once again like Herbert, he was to remain loyal to those traditions for the rest of his career, even while the musical theater around him was experiencing a dramatic change. As long as foreign traditions prevailed in New York, Friml was productive and successful. Between 1912 and 1926 he wrote the scores for four of the best and most highly acclaimed operettas produced in New York: *The Firefly*, *The Vagabond King*, *Rose Marie*, and *The Three Musketeers*. But when the European traditions passed for good, Friml was also through. After 1930 he contributed only two shows to Broadway, neither well received. After 1924 he was comparatively silent. When he concentrated his activity in Hollywood, he was engaged not on new, modern productions, but mostly on adaptations of his old operettas.

It is perhaps understandable that he should work best within European patterns, since he had been steeped in European music before he wrote his first operetta. Born in Prague in 1881, he attended the Prague Conservatory, after which he toured Europe as pianist in joint recitals with the violin virtuoso, Jan Kubelik. When the violinist was engaged to tour America, Friml came with him, in 1901. After a second American tour, in 1906, Kubelik and Friml parted ways; the pianist had by now decided to stay in America and pursue here his own career. During the next few years he appeared as a concert pianist, and wrote music—mostly piano pieces, art songs, and shorter instrumental numbers. He might have remained permanently in the position acquired by 1910—as an industrious, competent, respected, but not particularly brilliant or successful serious musician—if chance had not thrown the book of *The Firefly* in his lap in 1912.

The Firefly, book and lyrics by Otto Harbach, was custom-built for Trentini. She appeared as a street singer who, disguised as a boy, stowed away on a Bermuda-bound ship, to meet the man of her heart. The score was also made for Trentini. Friml knew how to write for the voice as few others on Broadway could. He knew how to make an ingratiating, ear-caressing melody emphasize the best qualities of a large operatic voice. Singer and song became one, and it is difficult to say which won the audiences more completely—melodies like "Giannina Mia," "Love is Like a Firefly," "The Dawn of Love," and "When a Maid Comes Knocking at Your Heart," or the beguiling way Trentini sang them. The score had an additional winner in one of Friml's most appealing songs, "Sympathy."

Now a composer in demand, Friml found many assignments awaiting him. But he did not come up with another major stage success until over a decade after *The Firefly*—with *Rose Marie*, in 1924. Its setting, the primitive and awesome Canadian Rockies, served as the background for the fabled exploits of the Mounted Police and the amatory adventure of Rose Marie and Jim Kenyon. The program of *Rose Marie* carried the following explanatory note: "The musical numbers of this play are such an integral part of the action that we do not think we should list them as separate numbers." Yet, in spite of the noble intentions of the authors—Otto Harbach and Oscar Hammerstein II—the score and book were not an inextricable entity. Two songs, lyrics by Harbach and Hammerstein, stood out prominently from the musical texture, and they still do so whenever the operetta is revived: "Indian Love Call" and "Rose Marie."

Rose Marie had the substantial run of 557 performances. Only one year later, Friml wrote another operetta which passed the 500-performance mark. It was *The Vagabond King*, adapted by Brian Hooker and W. H. Post from J. H. McCarthy's story, *If I Were King*. The central character was the fifteenth-century French vagabond poet, François Villon (magnificently played by Dennis King). The rousing "Song of the Vagabonds" (Brian Hooker), sung by Villon's followers, caught the spirit of the play. It was, in the words of Alexander Woollcott, "a great roaring chorus that cut loose magnificently." It lifted the audience out of its seats. But there was also a welcome change of pace in music gentler in mood, all of it to Hooker's words: songs like "Only a Rose," "Some Day," and "The Waltz Huguette."

Another swashbuckling play with a French setting represented Friml's last major Broadway success—*The Three Musketeers*, in 1928—the Dumas romance transformed into an operetta by William Anthony McGuire, lyrics by Clifford Grey and P. G. Wodehouse. The now familiar alternation of Friml bravura and Friml sentiment once again distinguished the score. There was rich blood in the stirring "All For One, And One For All," the "March of the Musketeers," and the drinking song, "With Red Wine." And there were tenderness and poignancy in "Ma Belle," "Heart of Mine," and "Queen of My Heart."

The ingredients Friml had used in 1912 for a successful stage broth were still a good recipe in 1928—but not for much longer. The theater was changing. Friml was discovering he was getting out of touch with his audiences. After writing music for two failures in the early 1930s, he decided to make a discreet bow out of Broadway. He went on to Hollywood, where he wrote a few songs for several productions during the next few years. But his creative output, once a geyser eruption, was reduced to a trickle. Today Friml is essentially a memory of past achievements, a voice of a bygone epoch.

V

Sigmund Romberg was the next, and the last, giant of American operetta. When he died in 1951, a dynasty in the theater came to an end.

Romberg's musical versatility ran the gamut from inoffensive sentimentality and at times a delicate sweetness to gaiety, froth, and light-hearted irresponsibility; from grace and refinement to vigor and robustness. It is hard to say which was his best vein. Are *"Auf Wiedersehen"* and "When I Grow Too Old to Dream" more characteristically Romberg in their gentle loveliness and effeminate allure than such sterner items as "Stout-Hearted Men" or the drinking song from *The Student Prince?* Are the Schubertian mobility of melody in songs like "Lover, Come Back to Me" and "One Alone" a better measure of his gifts than such insouciant trifles as "Three Little Maids" from *Blossom Time* or "Jump, Jim Crow" from *Maytime?* It is hard to say. To whatever vein or style or mood he turned, Romberg was able to bring a charm uniquely his.

Romberg's best music is essentially Viennese. He never forgot, nor did he ever tire of recalling nostalgically, the gay times spent in Viennese cafés, *Heuriger,* salons, and theaters. The world he knew as a young man was the one he loved to write about in his music.

It is quite true that he produced literally a carload of songs in an American style and tempo. The first two songs he wrote and published were American one-steps: "Some Smoke" and "Leg of Mutton." He manufactured hundreds of songs for

the forty-six musicals and revues produced by the Shuberts;
they were typical Tin Pan Alley products, no better or worse
than most of the run-of-the-mill items turned out by the Alley
for Broadway consumption. Yet when he wrote with his
heart, what emerged was invariably Viennese in personality.

It was that way when he wrote the score for his first operetta, *The Blue Paradise,* an adaptation of a Viennese musical;
and it was that way when he wrote the music for such subsequent operettas as *Blossom Time* (the Vienna of Franz
Schubert), *May Wine* (psychoanalysis in a latter-day Vienna),
and *The Student Prince* (Heidelberg—but in Viennese tempo).
It was also that way when he fashioned such unmistakably
Viennese waltzes, in the style of Strauss and Lehar, as "Blue
Heaven" or "Will You Remember?" or "One Kiss"—songs
which appeared in plays with American settings. Finally, it
was still that way when he wrote his first original score for
the talking screen: *Viennese Nights,* whose hit song was appropriately called "I Will Remember Vienna."

He knew only too well how strong his ties were to Vienna.
Toward the end of his life he told his wife: "I'm two wars
away from my time. My time was pre-World War I. I've got
to get away from Vienna. That's all passé. I've got myself
stranded in Europe, and I've got to get out of it. I think I'll
refuse anything from now on without an American background." In line with such thinking he wrote music for the
screen adaptation of *The Girl of the Golden West,* in 1938;
the score for a resounding Broadway success, *Up in Central
Park,* in 1945; another score for Broadway, *The Girl in Pink
Tights,* produced posthumously in 1954. But the sad truth was
that he was never completely at ease as a musician, nor happy
as a man, when he worked in any manner other than Viennese.

He was born, not in Vienna, but in a small Hungarian
border town in 1887. Intended for engineering, he was sent to
various preparatory and engineering schools in Hungary and
Vienna. In Vienna he also studied music. After eighteen

months of service in the 19th Hungarian Infantry Regiment, he gave up all thoughts of engineering. Coming to the United States, he played the piano in several New York cafés and restaurants, and in 1912 was made conductor of his own orchestra at Bustanoby's Restaurant. One year later, Joseph W. Stern published his first songs, and soon after this J. J. Shubert, the renowned Broadway producer, hired him to succeed Louis Hirsch as composer of music for the varied musical enterprises of the Shubert combine.

Romberg's initiation to Broadway came in 1914 with *The Whirl of the World,* a Winter Garden extravaganza starring Eugene and Willie Howard. After that, the Shuberts placed the full burden of their musical needs squarely on the young man's shoulders. Since that burden consisted in writing all the music for about four productions a year, the wonder is not that Romberg failed for so long a time to rise above the level of mediocrity then prevailing in the musical theater, but that he was able to function without collapsing under the pressure of his assignments. Between 1914 and 1917, Romberg wrote 175 numbers for 17 Shubert musicals, 15 of these productions coming within a 22-month period. The music for all these musicals, save one, was the kind of functional commodity Tin Pan Alley was then producing with more despatch and speed than originality.

Romberg took stock of himself and was dissatisfied with the inventory. He had approached only one assignment with exhilaration, and this was *The Blue Paradise,* in 1915, an adaptation of a Viennese operetta with a Viennese background. It was for this production that Romberg wrote *"Auf Wiedersehen,"* lyrics by Herbert Reynolds (pen-name of Michael E. Rourke), the first of his songs with a nostalgic old-world flavor, and the first of his outstanding song successes.

Romberg suddenly decided that, to save his soul, he must break with the Shuberts and venture on his own with the kind of musical play able to provide him with larger scope for his talent. When Romberg explained to Shubert what was bothering him, the producer urged him to reconsider his decision, promising to find for him a book capable of testing and proving his musical powers.

Shubert was as good as his word. In 1917 he turned over to the composer a text which Rida Johnson Young had adapted from a German operetta and which now bore the title of *Maytime*. This was the first time that Romberg had a play in which music was intended as a basic element, in which it had to carry the responsibility for the play's success or failure. He worked with an excitement he rarely brought to an assignment. *Maytime,* opening in 1917, was such a box office bonanza that to accommodate the demand for seats a second company had to open in a near-by theater—the first time in Broadway history that two productions of the same musical ran simultaneously. There was no question in the minds of either critics or audiences that it was Romberg's music—particularly his unforgettable waltz, "Will You Remember?" (Rida Johnson Young)—that was responsible for this triumph.

Maytime notwithstanding, Shubert sent Romberg back to writing the more routine assignments that crowded his office: musicals like *Sinbad,* in which Al Jolson starred at the Winter Garden; revues like *Over the Top,* with Fred and Adele Astaire. Romberg himself was increasingly restive with such chores, impatient to test his wings again in more ambitious flights. But he had to wait. The year was 1918—and Romberg had to serve in the United States Army, writing music for army shows and going from camp to camp entertaining the troops. When the war ended, he finally broke with Shubert and set up his own producing firm to present the kind of shows he had faith in. The two shows he gave were both box office disasters. Now heavily in debt, Romberg returned meekly to Shubert to resume his old duties.

Happily, the first new assignment Shubert gave him was not a run-of-the-mill production for the Winter Garden, but a play with music in the style of *Maytime*. The Shuberts had acquired the American rights for a resounding European success, *Das Dreimädlerhaus,* whose central character was Franz Schubert, the Viennese composer of immortal *Lieder*. The score for the European production was judged unsuitable for America, and Romberg was called to write new music. This was an assignment into which Romberg could put both his heart and his teeth: a musical with Vienna as a background, the irresistibly gay Vienna of Franz Schubert. This, too, was a musical whose principal character was one of the world's geniuses of song. From the treasure-house of Schubert's music Romberg picked up the most familiar and characteristic jewels and gave them new settings within the more formal patterns of the American popular song. Thus he produced such charming items as "The Song of Love," which he had adapted from the beautiful cello melody in the first movement of *The Unfinished Symphony;* also "Three Little Maids," "Tell Me Daisy," "Lonely Heart," and "My Springtime Thou Art," all with lyrics by Dorothy Donnelly. *Blossom Time,* produced in 1921, was such a tremendous success that within a few months four road companies were organized to take the show throughout the country.

In *Blossom Time,* Romberg had adapted the music of a famous composer of the past. What he wanted to write now was an operetta with musical materials all his own. He had to wait three years for that chance. Meanwhile he wrote the scores for fourteen Shubert productions, including several starring Al Jolson.

In 1924, after prolonged and complicated negotiations, the Shuberts acquired the American rights to *Old Heidelberg,* a famous European operetta, set in the old German university town, and concerned with the frustrated love of a prince and a waitress. With the book adapted by Dorothy Donnelly, who also wrote all the lyrics, and renamed *The Student Prince,* it became Romberg's new—and, as he knew at once, his most ambitious—assignment. The Shuberts might consider the kind of music he was writing for it as too highbrow for Broadway, and often told him so. Nevertheless, Romberg insisted on doing numbers like "Serenade," "Golden Days," and "Deep in My Heart," which were expansive in melodic design and rich in harmonic texture. Romberg demanded the innovation of an all-male chorus of forty voices for his spacious choral pieces like the "Drinking Song." And he fought stubbornly, against the advice and opposition of the Shuberts, to retain the tragic ending of the European play. The Shuberts grumbled that all this was well and good for sophisticated Europe, but such procedures spelled doom on commercial Broadway. But since Romberg was intransigeant, he had to get his way.

The Student Prince opened at the Jolson Theatre on December 2, 1924, where it played to capacity houses for over a year. It was equally successful outside New York, with nine different companies touring simultaneously.

From 1924 on, Romberg devoted himself principally to the writing of operettas in the European style. The locale of the various books might shift out of Vienna or Germany to French Morocco, or eighteenth-century New Orleans, but the music never lost its Continental manners.

In 1926 came another Romberg triumph and another of Romberg's operetta classics—*The Desert Song,* in which he worked for the first time with the then up-and-coming lyricist, Oscar Hammerstein II. New York warmly welcomed this colorful, atmospheric, and melodious romance of a bandit chief in French Morocco. In the words of the critic of the New York *Sun,* the operetta combined "pageantry, romance, ringing music, vitality, and humor." The title song was only one of several jewels in a sparkling score; others including the poignant "One Alone," and the more stirring "Riff Song" and "Saber Song." All lyrics were the joint effort of Hammerstein and Otto Harbach.

The next time Romberg and Oscar Hammerstein II worked

together they realized Romberg's greatest box office triumph. *The New Moon,* in 1928—set in eighteenth-century New Orleans, and based on the life of the French aristocrat, Robert Mission—had the longest run on Broadway of any Romberg operetta (509 performances). Later on, when bought by Hollywood, it received the highest price paid up to that time for screen rights to a Broadway musical. The critics rivaled one another in using superlatives. The usually reserved St. John Ervine, a visiting English critic writing for the New York *World,* remarked that it was "the most charming and fragrant entertainment of its sort that I have seen for a long time." The song hit of the show was "Lover, Come Back to Me," which sold over a million copies of sheet music. (Its middle section made more than a passing reference to Tchaikovsky's "June Barcarolle.") But its tremendous audience-appeal did not completely obscure other delightful songs, including "Softly, As in a Morning Sunrise," "One Kiss," "Wanting You," and the virile "Stout-Hearted Men."

Now the most successful operetta composer in America, Romberg became logical prey for Hollywood with the advent of talking pictures. He settled permanently in Beverly Hills and produced the music for several new motion pictures, and helped transfer some of his most famous stage operettas to the new medium.

Soon after Pearl Harbor, he left Hollywood to undertake the first of several concert tours with his orchestra, which continued till the end of his life. "An Evening with Sigmund Romberg," as these concerts of Romberg and Viennese music were billed, became an assured success wherever they were given.

But Romberg had not withdrawn permanently from his main activity of writing music for the theater. In the last years of his life, he enjoyed his second best box office return in *Up In Central Park* (1945), which had a fourteen-month run. Few of his preceding stage successes brought him the personal satisfaction that this one did. For some years now, whispers had been circulating around Broadway and Hollywood that Romberg was through as a composer, that he simply could not adapt himself to new times and the demands made by the new musical theater. A few failures in the early 1940s appeared to confirm these suspicions. Yet when Romberg was called upon to write music for a thoroughly American musical comedy, and to a book entirely different from his past achievements, he once again put down a winning hand. The background of *Up in Central Park* was New York in the 1870s during the infamous reign of the Tweed Ring. To the play Romberg contributed a score with five aces: "Close as Pages in a Book," "Carousel in the Park," "It Doesn't Cost You Anything to Dream," and "April Snow," (all with lyrics by Dorothy Fields), and the background music for a spellbinding ice-skating ballet in a Currier and Ives setting.

Romberg's valedictory to the stage, *The Girl in Pink Tights*, also to a thoroughly American book, was produced post-humously in 1954. (He died in New York City on November 10, 1951.) Unfortunately, *The Girl in Pink Tights* was neither good nor successful. As Richard Watts, Jr. complained, "a curious air of heaviness hung over the proceedings." Romberg's score contained a few fetching moments—as in the songs "Lost in Loveliness" and "Up in the Elevated Railway" (Leo Robin), but it did not rise above the prevailing level of mediocrity. To Brooks Atkinson, Romberg's score overflowed with "mechanical melodies out of a departed era." Note well the phrase "departed era"! To the very last days of his life, Romberg was living in the past, and writing for the past.

VI

Something fresh and novel entered the American musical theater with the explosive personality of George M. Cohan. At the turn of the twentieth century, he was the living, vibrant present; he was the new era. Brash, cocksure, egocentric, chauvinistic, energetic, gigantic in scheming and planning, he was, in his own way, the symbol of a new day in this country.

With the boisterous self-assurance, bulging ego, and feeling of inward power that marked the era, George M. Cohan was virtually a one-man trust of the musical theater. He wrote his own plays, and the words and music of its songs. He devised his own dances, and staged, directed, and produced his own shows. Frequently he was also the star. He was not equally gifted in every department, nor was he ever profound or particularly imaginative. But he *did* know the theater; he was a born song-and-dance man, whose long presence on the stage, from childhood on, had taught him how to make an immediate contact with his audience. He was a showman second to none, not only as a performer but as a creator, and everything he said and did had the showman's flair. And it was as a show-man, rather than a creative force, that he injected such a vital spark into our theater.

The blood of the theater was in his veins. He was born in Providence, Rhode Island, on July 3, 1878, the third child of two veteran vaudevillians. In his ninth year, George made his bow as actor when, billed as "Master Georgie," he spoke some lines in a sketch presented by his parents in Haverstraw, New York. In 1888, at the B. F. Keith Bijou in Boston, the husband-and-wife team, the boy George, and his sister Josephine first became known as "The Four Cohans." George played the violin; Josephine performed skirt dances; the older Cohans enacted one of the father's facile sketches.

It was not long before George began playing an increasingly significant role in the stage affairs of the Cohans. He started doing a specialty of his own, appearing as a bootblack; he combined this routine with sentimental recitations and per-formances of buck-and-wing dances. When he was eleven, he wrote a sketch used in the act. From then on he always had a hand in the writing of new material. He was only thirteen when he began writing songs, words as well as music, as was henceforth to be his practice. In his sixteenth year, "Why Did Nellie Leave Home?" was bought by Witmark for $25.00 and published. A year later came "Hot Tamale Alley," effectively introduced by May Irwin. By the time he was twenty he had a substantial hit in "I Guess I'll Have to Telegraph My Baby."

It was not long before The Four Cohans became headliners across the country, from the Orpheum in San Francisco to the Tony Pastor Music Hall in New York. By the time the century ended, there was a fifth Cohan in the act. In the summer of 1899, George married the singing comedienne, Ethel Levey, a star in her own right, who from then on would speak George's lines, sing his songs, and live more or less in the reflected glory of his fame.

The vaudeville sketch could no more contain the varied gifts and irresistible drive of George M. Cohan than a drawing-room could a hurricane. He needed more *Lebensraum.* In 1901 he expanded one of his sketches into a full-length musical comedy, calling it *The Governor's Son.* With all the Cohans in the cast, it opened in New York in 1901—Cohan's first invasion of the musical-comedy world. The show folded up after only thirty-two performances. Two years later, the Cohans appeared in another extended vaudeville sketch, *Running for Office,* also a failure.

In 1904, Cohan joined forces with the producer Sam H. Harris. Their first collaboration as producers was on the new Cohan musical, *Little Johnny Jones,* the first time Cohan wrote a complete original book, as well as the songs, for the Broadway stage. George M. Cohan himself appeared in the title role, the prototype of Tod Sloan, the American jockey who had gone to England in 1903 to ride for King George. Three of the four Cohans were also in the cast; Josephine, now married to Fred Niblo, preferred for the time being to go on her own.

There were many things in *Little Johnny Jones* that the

audiences and critics liked. There was George's little sentimental recitation, "Life's a Funny Proposition," which injected
some homely philosophy into the gay proceedings. There were
two Cohan hit songs by which he would henceforth be remembered—"Yankee Doodle Boy" and "Give My Regards to Broadway"—and a third, "Goodbye Flo," which was no less appealing. There was his breezy portrayal of the jockey. But,
apparently, audiences liked Cohan himself better than his
play, for it closed after only two months. This time Cohan was
convinced that he, and not his public, was right. He kept on
playing *Little Johnny Jones* on the road until it caught on
there, then brought it back to New York in 1905 to establish
it finally as a definite hit.

Transforming *Little Johnny Jones* from a failure to a success
was the turning point. From this time on, Cohan was Mr. Big
on Broadway. For the next two decades he dominated the
musical theater so completely that his biographer, Ward More-
house, could say that he "*was* Broadway in the years just after
the turn of the century."

One of the triumphs of his career as a musical playwright
came the first day in 1906 with *Forty-Five Minutes from
Broadway*—the locale referred to in the title being the New
York suburb of New Rochelle. Fay Templeton, a burlesque
star for more than twenty years, here made her first appearance in "a clean play." She enchanted her audiences with
homespun renditions of "Mary's a Grand Old Name" and "So
Long Mary," and in doing so set into motion for herself a new
career on the Broadway stage. The cast also included a young
comedian, Victor Moore, who as Kid Burns managed to steal
some of the thunder from the leading performers and to assert
his right to stardom.

As if to emphasize Cohan's unique position on Broadway at
this time, the most serious rival to *Forty-Five Minutes from
Broadway* for the patronage of theater-goers was another
Cohan musical, *George Washington Jr.* Here Cohan starred

himself as a super-patriotic American boy whose chauvinism leads him to assume the name of America's first President. This characterization enabled Cohan to drape the American flag around himself and strut with it up and down the stage chanting, "You're a Grand Old Flag"—a routine that, in one variation or another, was to become a part of many of his later musicals.

It would appear that there was nothing in either the song or the routine to arouse tempers. Nevertheless tempers *were* aroused, and something of a minor scandal developed. Cohan got his idea for the song from a G.A.R. veteran who once told him of having been the color-bearer during Pickett's charge on Gettysburg. Pointing to the American flag, the veteran exclaimed: "She's a grand old rag." As introduced in his play, Cohan called his song "You're a Grand Old Rag." But the day after the première several patriotic societies protested that Cohan was insulting the American flag by referring to it as a "rag." (Cohan himself always suspected that the storm had been unleashed by a drama critic who had been denied seats for opening night.) Cohan changed the provocative word "rag" to "flag," and the protests subsided.

When *George Washington Jr.* returned to New York after a road tour, the role formerly assumed by his wife, Ethel, was taken over by Vinnie Daly. The change of casting gave proof to a rumor long circulating along Broadway that Cohan and his wife were splitting. After his divorce decree became final, Cohan married Agnes Nolan in 1907. They both lived to celebrate thirty-five years of a happy marriage.

Not yet thirty-two in 1910, Cohan was already one of the richest and most powerful figures on Broadway—not only by virtue of his own plays and songs, but also through the successful plays of other writers which he produced through the years with Sam H. Harris. It did not seem that there were any more avenues in the theater through which he might travel to new triumphs. Yet there were. He wrote comedies without songs or dances which were numbered among the leaders of the Broadway theater before World War I: *Get Rich Quick Wallingford, Broadway Jones,* and *Seven Keys to Baldpate.* And in 1917 he wrote the most stirring song to come out of World War I, "Over There," about which much has already been said.

He had reached the pinnacle in his profession when his zest and excitement for the theater was smothered by an unforeseen development. On August 7, 1919, the Actors Equity Association called a strike to compel theater managers to recognize it as a bargaining representative for its members and to remedy some of the more flagrant abuses victimizing actors then existing in the theater. Twelve Broadway shows had to close, and in four weeks' time that number doubled. Cohan, like every other producer, was seriously affected. But unlike most other producers he came to regard this strike not as a managerial-employee problem but as a personal attack upon him. For in the vanguard of the Equity forces stood many actors whom Cohan had helped time and again, some of whom he had lifted to stardom, others whom he had provided with funds. To see them line up solidly against him seemed to him a betrayal of friendship. From that moment on, he refused stubbornly to recognize the validity of the issues involved in the strike, insisting that the theater had no place for unionism, and that performers had no just cause for grievance. He promised to throw every dollar he owned to defeat Equity. And he threatened to leave the theater for good if he failed in the struggle.

The war between Equity and George M. Cohan was of brief duration, but while it lasted it was acrimonious. Cohan became the outspoken enemy of many who had been his closest friends for years; and they rejected him just as fiercely as he did them. He withdrew his membership from both the Friars and Lambs clubs. He organized the short-lived Actors

Fidelity League as a rival to Equity, for actors who believed as he did.

By the time a new season got under way, right after Labor Day, the Actors Equity had won a complete victory. But Cohan fought on long after the war was over. He kept on using his immense popularity and influence to discredit or undermine Equity; he continued with his threats to withdraw from the American theater. He was only shadow-boxing, since the position of Equity had become unassailable. In spite of everything he had done on Broadway, and everything he had accomplished, he just could not turn back the clock.

He did not retire from the Broadway theater, but he did seem to lose interest in the affairs of the stage. In 1920 he dissolved the still prosperous firm of Cohan and Harris. He traveled and rested more, wrote and acted less. And while Cohan hits did not completely disappear from Broadway, they grew increasingly rare compared to the earlier harvest. In 1920, Cohan produced his non-musical *The Tavern,* in 1923 *The Song and Dance Man* also without a score, and in 1927 the musical *The Merry Malones.* But the Cohan name was beginning to lose its magic. Nobody realized this better than Cohan himself, who told a friend sadly: "I guess people don't understand me any more and I don't understand them. It's got so that an evening's entertainment just won't do. Give an audience an evening of what they call realism, and you've got a hit. It's getting too much for me, kid."

His defeat was accentuated by some rather unfortunate incidents during his single excursion to Hollywood, in 1932. He was starred with Jimmy Durante and Claudette Colbert in a Rodgers and Hart musical film, *The Phantom President.* He was not long in Hollywood before discovering that he, once a legend on Broadway, was just one more actor in the movie capital. Strange to say, some people there knew only vaguely what he had accomplished; others mistook him for somebody else. A gatekeeper would not allow him to park his car on the lot because he insisted Cohan was not a star. A junior executive took him severely to task for daring to submit some ideas for the picture in pencil and on yellow paper. Even those who remembered him could not forget that he was stepping into a new medium about which he knew nothing. Cohan learned that he would have no control over the lines he spoke or the songs he sang. Only one old Cohan routine was interpolated, "You're a Grand Old Flag," but even here the director insisted on teaching him how to do the number. He regarded this Hollywood adventure as "the most miserable I have ever had in my life." When he returned from California he said: "If I had my choice between Hollywood and Atlanta, I'd take Leavenworth."

Yet there still remained for him enough glory to suffice other men for a lifetime. In May, 1940 he received a gold medal from President Franklin D. Roosevelt. In 1942 he saw Hollywood finally giving him a true measure through a screen dramatization of his life starring James Cagney—*Yankee Doodle Dandy*. In less than six months the picture grossed over a million dollars, and the same fall the picture was acclaimed in London. There was no question but that the personality of George M. Cohan, and the golden aura of his fabulous career in the theater, made this picture so attractive to so many. Mayor La Guardia recognized this fact when he declared July 3, 1942 to be George M. Cohan Day in New York.

Another resounding triumph came to him, at the dusk of his career, for his acting. In 1933, a new generation of theatergoers and critics hailed him as one of the leading performers on the American stage for his poignant, nostalgic interpretation of a small-town editor in *Ah, Wilderness*, Eugene O'Neill's comedy of American life in the early 1900s. And once again in 1937 the public and the press acclaimed him, this time for his vigorous and subtly etched portrait of President Franklin D.

Roosevelt in the Rodgers and Hart stage musical, *I'd Rather Be Right.*

But as far as Cohan was concerned there was a hollow ring to these triumphs. In *Ah, Wilderness* he was speaking lines that were not his. And, final irony, in *I'd Rather Be Right,* he was singing and capering to music that somebody else had to write for him. When, in 1940, he did appear in one of his own plays—*The Return of the Vagabond*—it closed after seven performances. "They don't want me no more," he remarked bitterly the night the show closed. And he never again appeared in public. About two years later, on October 5, 1942, he died in New York City.

He left behind him a record of achievement probably unique in our musical theater. All but eight of his sixty-four years had been spent on the stage. He wrote forty plays, collaborated in writing about forty others, and had had a hand in the production of still another hundred and fifty. He published over five hundred songs, and one of them was one of the most popular American war songs ever written. Besides all this, he made between five and ten thousand appearances as an actor. No wonder, then, that Gene Buck could call him "the greatest single figure the American theater has produced."

There is sufficient ammunition with which to attack Cohan's musicals if one is inclined to do so. His stories were always trite; his characters, synthetic; his philosophy, cliché-ridden; his songs, simple and ingenuous. James S. Metcalf in *Life,* like so many other critics of Cohan's day, recognized the less pleasing qualities of Cohan's dramatic art. He described Cohan as a "vulgar, cheap, blatant, ill-mannered, flashily dressed, insolent, smart alec who, for some reason unexplainable on any basis of commonsense, good taste, or ordinary decency, appeals to the imagination and approval of large American audiences." But what so many critics failed to realize at the time—but what audiences sensed with a sure instinct—was that Cohan's musicals struck a completely new and vital note. They

brought an invigorating new tempo, spirit, impudence, exuberance, and brashness into both text and song. With Cohan's
informality, racy language, and bulging ego, the American
musical approached the threshold of modernity. Indeed, an
historian of our theater can hardly resist the temptation of
saying that the American musical comedy, as it was known
in the 1920s and 1930s, was born with George M. Cohan.

chapter eight

RAGTIME, BLUES, JAZZ

ANOTHER branch of popular music was growing in New Orleans. Compared to the hothouse product of New York, this music was a wild growth. It derived its identifying characteristics from the songs of the Negro. In New Orleans this music was known as ragtime, but actually it was jazz—"real jazz" or "hot jazz"—though the term "jazz" came into existence in a later day and in another city. Many of the later varieties of jazz music came from seeds fertilized in New Orleans.

There is good reason why this music should have bloomed in New Orleans. The receptivity of the city to the febrile rhythms of jazz music had long been prepared through its contact with the African bamboula, danced on Sundays in Place Congo to the accompaniment of throbbing drums. Besides this, the emotional climate was favorable to music as sensual and undisciplined as jazz in the only city in America in which prostitution was licensed. After 1897, prostitution in New Orleans was confined by a city ordinance to a specific locality known as Storyville. Cradle of vice, Storyville became also the cradle in which jazz spent its infancy.

After Emancipation, many Negroes tried earning a living by singing their songs, to banjo or guitar accompaniments, in the streets. Some of these street singers made for New Orleans, a free-and-easy city where they knew they would be accepted with less reservations than elsewhere in the South. For in New Orleans—where it was part of the social pattern for white gentlemen to have affairs with quadroons, the fair-skinned daughters of natives—there was a high degree of tolerance to dark-skinned people.

The Negro discovered new musical instruments in New Orleans, since for many years that city had been a manufacturing center for wind instruments. These were plentiful and comparatively cheap—particularly since secondhand ones were available—coming within the price range of any Negro hungry to make music. The ready access to these wind instruments led to the formation of numerous bands. Band music flourished in the streets of New Orleans, accompanying funerals, processions, patriotic parades, weddings, lodge parties, excursions, carnivals. Band music served as entertainment on the river boats ploughing up and down the Mississippi River. It was used to advertise bargain sales in the stores and prize fights.

Wind instruments provided the Negro with a greater musical satisfaction than he had heretofore acquired from either singing or playing his banjo or guitar. He took to them eagerly. Since these novices did not receive formal instruction, but had to learn to play by a continual process of experimentation, they evolved not only a new technique of performance but also unorthodox sounds and timbres not found in formal exercise books. Even after they had to learn to play well, most of the Negroes could not read a note of music. Compelled to depend upon ear rather than eye, they took the known popular melodies and allowed free play to their native musical intelligence and imagination. Through spontaneous improvisations, guided only by intuition and the emotional impact of the moment, these musicians brought to their music new color combinations, dissonances, unusual figurations of melody, disjointed counterpoints. They also brought to their music techniques, qualities, and devices found in their folk songs. The new music—jazz—abounded with marked syncopations, strong accentuations, deviating pitch, curious intonations, and often febrile emotions found in spirituals, "Shouts," and work songs. Naturally, too—since this was a singing people—they tried to emulate in their playing the harsh, guttural, throaty sounds which they used in their singing; in doing this they created a new kind of instrumental tone which has since been described as "dirty."

Thus these Negro musicians helped evolve a new kind of popular music—blatant, abandoned, vulgar, hyperthyroid, with an animal kind of energy. This was music to which the clients of the pleasure domes of Storyville could respond. Such a music would, at that time, have shocked and been violently rejected by most other cities. But in New Orleans it flourished —in such sporting-houses, saloons, gambling joints and honky-tonks as *The 101 Ranch, The Tuxedo Dance Hall, Lulu White's Mahogany Hall,* and *Pete Lala's Café.* Haunts such as these, on or near Basin Street, provided the Negro musician with opportunities for employment no other city, or district, could match at the time. He was not well paid for his services. The best of them received only about two dollars a night, and many had to double during the day as barbers, waiters, day laborers, in order to make a living. But they were encouraged, and at times idolized. In Storyville, these musicians were given the necessary stimulation to develop their highly personal art in a highly personal manner. For in Storyville, the jazz-musician was king.

II

The two basic elements of New Orleans jazz were ragtime and the blues.

The word "ragtime" was probably derived from the clog-dancing of the Negroes, often referred to as "ragging." Ragtime was marked by strong syncopations in the treble—that is, making a weak beat strong, or conversely, making an expected strong beat weak—while the bass maintains a rigidly even rhythm. Syncopation had appeared in such early minstrel-show tunes as "Zip Coon" and "Old Dan Tucker"; was a characteristic of the cakewalk, a Negro dance made popular in the minstrel show and in Vaudeville in the early 1880s; and was found in the northern "coon songs" of the same period.

But the application of syncopation against a steady bass rhythm does not make its first official appearance until the middle 1890s. The first published "rag" was Kerry Mills' "Georgia Camp Meetin'" in 1897. Two years later, Scott Joplin's "Maple Leaf Rag" once and for all established and popularized ragtime style. Joplin was a Negro pianist who played in the honky-tonks of St. Louis. It was there that he developed his piano rag style. While playing his music at the Maple Leaf Club in Sedalia, Missouri, he was discovered by a local music publisher who issued Joplin's first composition, "Original Rag" in 1899, and in the same year followed it with Joplin's most famous piece, "The Maple Leaf Rag." Other rag tunes, an instruction book called *School of Ragtime,* and a ragtime opera in 1903 called *A Guest of Honor,* brought Joplin the title of "king of ragtime" in the early 1900s.

But even before Scott Joplin wrote and published his piano rags, ragtime had been in the process of evolution in New Orleans. The bands in the streets, and the jazz performers in saloons and bawdy-houses, would often "rag" familiar melodies—in so many different ways, and for such a prolonged period of time, that the listeners would be left limp with emotional fatigue.

The "blues," the poignant lament of a lonely man or woman, were an outgrowth of the earlier "sorrow song" in which the Negro race bewailed its sad fate. In the blues, the singer voices his personal woes in a world of harsh reality: a lost love, the cruelty of police officers, oppression at the hands of white folk, hard times. The blues came into being after the Civil War, when wandering Negro minstrels sang these laments on street corners or in saloons, improvising their own lyrics as they sang. The word "blues" was to be coined later as the official name for this type of song; but already in the latter part of the 1880s there were crystallized some of the stylistic qualities with which this type of song is identified. The lyric would usually be constructed out of three-line stanzas, the second line always repeating the first as if to emphasize the woe of the singer; these lines were often in classical iambic pentameter. The melody itself spread over twelve bars, made up of three four-bar phrases. In time, other distinguishing traits were evolved: the flatting of the third and seventh steps of the diatonic major scale, henceforth called the "blue-note"; the astringent dissonances that entered when the accompaniment provided a harmony devoid of blue notes; "breaks" in the melody, which originally allowed the singer to utter such exclamations as "Oh Lawdy" or "Oh Baby" and in New Orleans permitted the jazz musician to embellish his melody with intriguing figurations.

W. C. Handy was the one who christened this kind of song "the blues," who was the author of the first *published* blues. But this happened long after the blues became an established song style among Negro singers and musicians—and it happened out of New Orleans. Handy, the son of a pastor, was born in Florence, Alabama, in 1873. The urge to make music was born in him. He was only a child when, despite parental objections to all musical avocations, he saved his pennies and bought a guitar. In boyhood he became proficient with a trumpet bought for a dollar from a visiting circus musician. "My son," his father once told him sternly, "I would rather see you in a hearse than have you become a musician." Since his musical urges would not be denied, young William ran away from home and joined a traveling minstrel troupe. When the show was left stranded on the road, William, penniless, made his way as best he could on freight trains. Sobered by his recent experiences, he renounced music as a profession and found a job as a foundry hand. At last, he decided to make a second attempt at becoming a professional musician. He went to St. Louis where, for a while, he suffered intense poverty. Then in 1896 he became a cornetist for Mahara's Minstrels, remaining with this outfit for seven years, many of those years as a bandmaster. After that for a period he led a band of his own in performances of ragtime and jazz in various smaller cities in Mississippi.

Handy wrote his first blues in 1909. The impetus was a mayoralty campaign in Memphis, Tennessee, where a candidate named Crump was running on a reform ticket. To help advance Crump's campaign, Handy decided to write a song which would rally the votes of Negro citizens of Beale Street to the reform candidate; and the melody he used was the blues, a style these people could best understand and respond to. Under the title, "Mr. Crump," the song remained popular long after its namesake was swept into office. In 1912, Handy published "Mr. Crump" in Memphis as a piano piece and called it "The Memphis Blues." A shrewd New York publisher bought all the rights to the song for fifty dollars and re-issued it in 1913 with new lyrics by George A. Norton. It became a sensation. As the first published blues, "The Memphis Blues" helped popularize this *genre* of Negro song throughout the country.

Since he had sold "The Memphis Blues" outright, Handy did not profit from its phenomenal sale. He decided, then, to write another song in a similar style to capitalize on the success of his first blues. He rented a room in Beale Street and went to work. In his autobiography, *Father of the Blues,* he described how the successor to "The Memphis Blues" came into being:

"A flood of memories filled my mind. First there was a picture I had of myself, broke, unshaven, wanting even a decent meal, and standing before the lighted saloon in St. Louis without a shirt under my frayed coat. There was also from that same period a curious and dramatic little fragment that till now seemed to have little or no importance. While occupied with my own miseries during the sojourn, I had seen a woman whose pain seemed even greater. She had tried to take the edge off her grief by heavy drinking, but it hadn't worked. Stumbling along the poorly lighted street, she muttered as she walked, 'My man's got a heart like a rock cast in the sea.' . . . By the time I had finished all this heavy thinking and remembering, I figured it was time to get something down on paper, so I wrote 'I hate to see de evenin' sun go down.' If you ever had to sleep on the cobbles down by the river in St. Louis you'll understand the complaint."

And so Handy wrote the words and music of "The St. Louis Blues," his classic—certainly the best known blues ever played or written. Strange to say, in view of the widespread popularity of its immediate predecessor, "The St. Louis Blues" was turned down by every publisher to whom Handy submitted it. Finally, in partnership with Harry Pace, Handy formed his own company, and printed the song in Memphis in 1914. The sheet music started moving after Handy transferred his company to New York, when Sophie Tucker began singing the song in theaters, and Victor issued a highly successful recording. It was not long before every recording company and manufacturer of piano rolls had some version of "The St. Louis Blues." In time, the song was destined to sell more phonograph records than any other popular or serious piece of music. It was used in a Broadway revue, was the inspiration for a motion picture, and lent its title to three other movies. Forty years after its publication, its commercial value was still so great that it was even then earning for its composer an annual royalty of about $25,000.

It has become an American classic, almost as much a favorite abroad as in this country. It was the piece of music that King Edward VIII asked the pipers of Scotland to play for him, and one of the favorites of Queen Elizabeth. It was played at the wedding feast of Prince George of England and Princess Marina of Greece, who danced to its strains. It became the battle hymn of the Ethiopians when that land was invaded by Italy in the 1930s.

Handy wrote other blues after 1914, the most famous being "The Beale Street Blues," "The John Henry Blues," "The Harlem Blues," and "The Joe Turner Blues." But "The St. Louis Blues" is his masterpiece, the one piece of music to immortalize his name. It is because of this one blues that Handy has become something of a hero in Memphis, with a public park named after him; that he was listed at the New York World's Fair as one of the leading contributors to American culture; that, on the occasion of his sixty-fifth birthday, he was the recipient of an eloquent and unforgettable tribute on the stage of Carnegie Hall.

The blues became popular not only in Handy's compositions but also in the performances of such eloquent blues singers as Ma Rainey, and her protégé, Bessie Smith, both of whom were in their heyday in the 1920s. Against the throbbing background of the trumpets, trombones, and clarinets of some of New Orleans' greatest men of jazz, Ma Rainey and Bessie Smith began making phonograph records in 1923 which made both of them something of a cult among their many admirers. Carl van Vechten once described Bessie Smith as "a woman cutting her heart open with a knife until it was exposed for us all to see, so that we suffered, as she suffered." In her first year of recording, Bessie Smith sold over two million records and was a star in Vaudeville. As long as she held the limelight, up to about 1930, she was spoken of as "the empress of the blues." She, in turn, became the inspiration and the model for the great singers of blues to follow her—among them being Ethel Waters, Ella Fitzgerald, and Billie Holiday.

III

But we have traveled far afield from New Orleans of the early 1900s where the blues was a basic style with the great jazz men; and we must retrace our steps.

In New Orleans, jazz was a performing as well as a creative art. Jazz musicians brought colorations to ragtime and the blues never before realized on their instruments by others, and through personal and unique methods of performance. These New Orleans musicians further opened new horizons for their music through their fabled gift of improvisation. One man would provocatively throw out an idea; it would be seized and embellished by another. The two would join forces, each proceeding in his own direction without losing sight of the other. A third would suddenly intrude with a fanciful cadenza, then still others would join in the ritual. Improvisation, then, became not only an art for the solo instrument, but for combinations of instruments, in which different rhythms were daringly combined, conflicting tonalities assembled, dissonant sounds blended. So it would go—sometimes for hours at a stretch—as the musical imagination would be given full freedom of movement.

There were some excellent hot bands in New Orleans in the 1880s. Several of these were led by the drummer, John Robechaux; another, the St. Joseph Brass Band, by the cornetist, Claiborne Williams. But the person generally credited with being the first of the great jazz figures of New Orleans came early in the 1890s: Buddy Bolden, a cornetist who was also a barber and the publisher and editor of a scandal sheet. Tall, slender, strikingly handsome—a hellion with the women— Buddy was indeed a king in New Orleans, after he organized his own band in the middle 1890s. He was according to Louis Armstrong, "a one-man genius that was way ahead of 'em all." It was said that on a clear day you could hear the sound of his cornet miles away, while his ability at embroidering a melody with all kinds of strange and irresistible filigree was a stunning aural experience. Buddy improvising on a blues like "Make Me a Pallet on the Floor" or a rag like "The Idaho Rag" could hold his listeners spellbound for hours. Buddy set and established the organization of a hot-jazz ensemble that became more or less standard in New Orleans—comprising six or seven men, with one or two cornets (the spine of the ensemble), clarinet, trombone, double bass, guitar, and drums. Bolden went insane in or about 1907 while playing his cornet in a street parade and had to be consigned to an asylum where he remained up to the time of his death, in 1931.

He had brought into existence an era in jazz. That era saw the emergence of a long succession of jazz artists who helped make New Orleans the capital of jazz up to about 1917.

There were Joe "King" Oliver and Freddie Keppard, trumpets, and Alphonse Picou, clarinetist, all three of whom played with the Olympia Band at Pete Lala's, one of the best jazz groups in Storyville before World War I. King Oliver also played at the *101 Ranch* in a group that included such other greats as Sidney Bechet (clarinetist and later soprano saxophone) and Emanuel Perez (cornetist). In 1915, the trombonist, "Kid" Ory took over the band at Pete Lala's and in this ensemble were found King Oliver, "Miff" Mole (trombone), and later on Louis Armstrong (trumpet). The Tuxedo Band, which played at the *Tuxedo Hall,* had for a while Keppard, and later on, Johnny Dodds at the clarinet and Zutty Singleton at the drums. The Eagle Band had, at various times, Johnny Dodds, Keppard, Bechet, and such famous trumpets as "Bunk" Johnson and "Papa Mutt" Carey. In 1911, Bill Johnson—the bass player who devised the technique of slapping the strings with open palm because he broke his bow during a performance —joined the Original Creole Band, organized by Freddie Keppard, and comprising several members of the Olympia Band.

Several others enriched the history of New Orleans jazz.

There was Stale Bread, a zither player, who toward the end of the 1890s devised a "spasm" band made up of harmonica, zither, a bass made out of half a barrel with clothesline wire for strings, a guitar constructed out of a cheesebox, a banjo derived from a soapbox, and tin cans and barrels as drums. And, though jazz pianists were not a New Orleans specialty, there was Jelly Roll Morton, credited with making "Tiger Rag" out of a French quadrille. Jelly Roll's barrelhouse music in Storyville's brothels made these places temples of jazz to his many devotees.

White musicians were definitely in the minority, but one of these should be mentioned: Jack "Papa" Laine, often described as the "father of white jazz." Laine, a disciple of Buddy Bolden, formed several bands of his own which achieved renown in New Orleans, principally the Reliance Brass Band and, after that, Jack Laine's Ragtime Band.

Competition was keen among bands and among individuals. Sometimes two bands crossed each other in the streets, each followed by its own admirers. The bands would soon engage in a free-for-all in which each tried to outdo the other in timbre and sonority. "Bands in those days fighting all the time," recalls Bunk Johnson. "During Mardi Gras and parades, bands got taken around in wagons, and they'd back them, tail gate to tail gate, and play each other down." Kid Ory has written: "They used to have 'cutting contests' every time you'd get on the streets. Freddie Keppard's band whipped us good because he was a stronger trumpet player than we had at first. Then we started whipping everybody. The public was on my side. When the other band finished, they'd tie the wagons together. The crowd tied them to keep them from running away from us." A successful revival in 1955 of "When the Saints Come Marching In" brought the present generation a reminder of the kind of music played in New Orleans streets at the turn of the century.

Rivalry between different jazz kings was equally keen. When

a competitor appeared and tried to steal Buddy Bolden's followers, Buddy took a stand in Lincoln Park (a spot near where
his rival was performing) and played the blues and rags with
all his heart and soul. The crowds began flowing back to listen
to Buddy's fanciful improvisations. After his performance, in a
state of exhaustion, Buddy remarked with gratification: "My
chilluns' come home." Joe Oliver first became famous when he
used his cornet to challenge his superiors. He took a stand on
Iberville Street, pointed to Pete Lala's where Freddie Keppard
held sway, and began playing a blues. "There," he said, "that'll
show 'em." Then he walked further down the street, pointed
his cornet to the place where Emanuel Perez was hero, and repeated his performance. After that he returned to his own
stamping grounds, the *Aberdeen Cabaret*, bringing back with
him a new army of followers ready to accept him as their new
king.

IV

Just before America's entry into World War I, Storyville was
closed down by an order from Washington, D. C. With jazz losing its happy hunting grounds, it had to look for pasture elsewhere.

But New Orleans jazz had been moving north even before
Storyville's doom. In 1911, the Creole Band, with Freddie
Keppard as its mainstay, toured the Vaudeville circuit, the first
opportunity the rest of the country had to hear real jazz. In
1914, a vaudevillian named Gorham asked trombonist Tom
Brown to organize the Brown Band from Dixieland, made up
of white players; one year later it settled at the Lambs Café
in Chicago. This group is sometimes credited with pioneering
jazz performances in Chicago. Certainly, its popularity led
other Chicago cafés to seek out New Orleans musicians for
their own establishments. Another white group, the Original
Dixieland Band, found a haven at Schiller's Café while, in
1915, Alcide "Yellow" Nunez, the gifted clarinetist who had

played with Laine's Reliance Band, came to the Athenia Café. Negroes were also welcome in Chicago. In 1916, Emanuel Perez formed for the De Luxe Café a five-piece ensemble that included Sidney Bechet.

With the decline and fall of the Storyville empire, the flow of Negro jazz players out of New Orleans and into Chicago became a veritable exodus. Freddie Keppard established himself in Chicago in 1917 and worked with Sidney Bechet at the De Luxe Café. King Oliver appeared at the Dreamland Café, and after that at the Royal Gardens, where, in 1918, Bill Johnson's Original Creole Band took over. The New Orleans Rhythm Kings, headed by Paul Mares at the trumpet, and including the clarinetist Leon Rappolo and trombonist George Brunies held sway at the Friar's Inn beginning with 1922. Jelly Roll Morton appeared in Chicago between 1923 and 1928, organizing the Red Hot Peppers, one of Chicago's most distinguished jazz ensembles, which included Kid Ory and the guitarist, Johnny St. Cyr. When Louis Armstrong formed a band of his own at the Dreamland Café in 1924, and began making his first phonograph recordings with a group called The Hot Five, Chicago became the unquestioned capital of jazz—just as New Orleans had been before the war.

It was in Chicago that the word "jazz" came into existence. No one can really say where the word comes from. Some think it was derived from the French word *jaser* meaning "to prattle." Some believe it was derived from the minstrel-show term "jasbo." Some pundits insist it is a corruption of "jass," an Elizabethan term used in bawdy-houses. There is also a belief that there was in New Orleans a musician by the name of Charles; the contraction of his name to "Chas" or "Jas" may have given his music the name of jazz. The most popular usage of the word, however, was in the gutters where it had a sexual connotation; and it is for this reason that for a long time officials of the musician's union were violently opposed to applying the word to popular music.

The word "jazz" as applied to New Orleans and Chicago popular music, makes its first appearance with the Original Dixieland Band in Chicago. This group was performing at the Boosters Club in Chicago when the patrons kept calling out to it to play "more jazz." This inspired the manager of the band to change the name of his organization to "Original Dixieland Jass (*sic*) Band." Before long the Tom Brown group also called itself a "jass band." By 1917, the term "jass" or "jazz" was in such general usage in Chicago that *Variety* reported on January 5 of that year: "The most popular attractions in Chicago cabarets are the jazz bands or orchestras, and every cabaret, regardless of its size, has a jazz aggregation."

Chicago appears not only to have established the term "jazz" but also "jam session." Jazz musicians had always gathered on their own to make music for each other's and their own delight: contests in feats of virtuosity and improvisation that came to be known as "cutting contests." In Chicago, these musicians often gathered after hours in The Three Deuces, a basement dive, and it was there that cutting contests first came to be known as jam sessions.

During the 1920s, Chicago produced jazz men of its own, who not only kept alive New Orleans jazz, but helped to produce a tradition. Some of these newer personalities had the popularity and the importance of their distinguished New Orleans predecessors.

First and foremost there was Bix Beiderbecke, whose cornet playing combined sweetness and strength, and whose clear, pure tone and artistic phrasing made him one of jazz's true aristocrats. "His continual searching for some sort of ultimate," once wrote Paul Whiteman, "created almost a mystic halo about him—it gave you the feeling that here was a genius who knew of something beautiful to strive for, and that, even though he might never reach it, he was far above you merely because he could sense that beauty for which he was reaching." Bix began playing in small Chicago joints in 1922. One year later he organized and played with The Wolverines, one of the major jazz organizations to come out of Chicago; with this outfit he made some historic recordings. He later transferred his activity to New York where he played with several outfits, including Paul Whiteman's Orchestra, and where he came to an unhappy end in 1931, a victim of broken health and excessive drinking. After his death he became a legend in jazz circles. An excellent novel was written about him by Dorothy Baker, *Young Man With a Horn,* which in 1950 was made into a motion picture with Kirk Douglas playing the part of Bix.

Others also contributed generously to Chicago jazz. A number of jazz-crazy kids from Austin High School became inflamed with a passion for jazz after hearing the records King Oliver made in 1923. These youngsters included Jimmy Mc-Partland, trumpet; Frank Teschemacher, clarinet and the saxes; and Bud Freeman, tenor sax. They became the spine of the second of Chicago's brilliant jazz groups, The Blue Friars.

Among the individual performers who came to prominence in Chicago were: Muggsy Spanier (cornet); Coleman Hawkins (tenor sax); Earl Hines and Jess Stacey (piano); Eddie Condon (guitar); Gene Krupa (drums); and Mezz Mezzrow (clarinet and the saxes). They played in various small ensembles, the most celebrated being the Chicago Rhythm Kings, led by Teschemacher, and The Chicagoans founded by Eddie Condon. Among the better known larger jazz ensembles in Chicago was the one led by Erskine Tate at the Vendome Theatre between 1918 and 1929; its roster included Louis Armstrong, Freddie Keppard, Earl Hines, and the pianist, Fats Waller.

Though Louis Armstrong was born in New Orleans and received there his first musical experiences, it was in Chicago that he achieved full maturity as a jazz artist. There his virtuosity with trumpet became a thing to inspire awe among his followers; there, too, he first developed that personal and somewhat exhibitionistic style of playing his instrument and his

"scat" singing. He came to Chicago in 1922 on an invitation
by King Oliver to join his band. Two years later, Armstrong
married Lillian Hardin, a pianist, who had studied music seriously at Fisk University, but who turned from the classics to
jazz soon after her appearance in Chicago. After his marriage
to Lillian, Armstrong formed his first band—for the Dreamland Café. His appearances there and in other Chicago hot
spots—and his recordings with the Hot Five, the Hot Seven,
and the Quintet, in which he played with such pre-eminent
jazz artists as Kid Ory, Johnny Dodds, St. Cyr, Babby Dodds,
Earl Hines, Zutty Singleton, Ma Rainey, and Bessie Smith—
made him a giant figure in Chicago's world of jazz. Then, in
1929, he went on to New York for still greater triumphs.

Chicago was not only the birthplace of many new jazz performers but also of some new jazz styles. Boogie-woogie came
to being in Chicago's South Side in the 1920s. It was first
heard at the monthly parties sometimes called "pitchin' boogie,"
given to raise the rent. The music heard at these affairs consisted of exciting piano improvisations which soon came to be
known as boogie-music or boogie-woogie. The term itself first
comes into general usage in pieces by Pine Top Smith, a pioneer of piano blues, and the composer of one of the best of
these numbers, "The Pinetop Boogie-Woogie." The style itself,
an outgrowth of the blues, placed emphasis not on melody but
on rhythm. A blues melody was set against an accompanying
brief rhythmic figure, usually eight beats to the bar, which was
repeated without variations throughout the piece, thus creating
a powerful rhythmic momentum. Outstanding exponents of
boogie-woogie, after Pine Top Smith, were Jim Yancey, composer of "Yancey Stomp," "State Street Special," and "Eternal
Blues"; Albert Ammons, who just before his death was invited
to perform at the inauguration ceremonies of President
Harry S. Truman; and, probably the most important of all,
Meade Lux Lewis, composer of such boogie-woogie favorites as

"Honky Tonk Train," "Blues Whistle," "Chicago Flyer," and "Bear Cat Crawl." Boogie-woogie first came to national attention at a concert entitled "From Spirituals to Swing" which presented Meade Lux Lewis and Albert Ammons in Carnegie Hall on December 23, 1938. After that these same pianists, and boogie-woogie, attracted enthusiasts to the Greenwich Village cabaret, Café Society.

"Swing" first received recognition as a definite jazz style in Chicago. The date was November 6, 1935, the place, Congress Hotel. It was then and there that Benny Goodman and his band started a sensational Chicago engagement that first made the country "swing" conscious.

Goodman, a native of Chicago, had been raised on New Orleans and Chicago jazz by listening to records and by visiting hot spots, where he studied at first hand the styles of King Oliver, Freddie Keppard, and Louis Armstrong. Further, as a friend of such jazz enthusiasts as Jimmy McPartland, Frank Teschemacher, and Bud Freeman, Goodman—who had already learned to play the clarinet—often joined them in improvised jam sessions.

He was only sixteen when he joined a white-jazz band ensemble led by Ben Pollack, formerly a member of the New Orleans Rhythm Kings. Goodman played the clarinet in this ensemble for several years, and with it made his first recording, "He's the Last Word," in 1926. During this appearance, Goodman quarreled with Pollack, left his band, and went on his own, performing in various theater orchestras, on records, and over the radio. In 1934, he organized a group of hot musicians who made some excellent records for Columbia, and soon after this he acquired a sponsored radio program. After appearing with his band at the Billy Rose Music Hall and the Roosevelt Hotel, both in New York, Goodman went on a coast-to-coast tour. As an adjunct to this ensemble he formed a small group of hot-jazz performers: first the Benny Goodman

Trio, with Gene Krupa at the drums and Teddy Wilson, pianist, one of the earliest interracial jazz groups; after that a Quartet, with Lionel Hampton joining the other three; subsequently, a Sextet, adding Charlie Christian at the guitar, and Arthur Bernstein, bass.

During his nationwide tour with his orchestra, Goodman found audiences generally indifferent both to his hot numbers and to his sweet music. In Palomar, California, he told his men to get as hot as they wished. They went to town in numbers like "Sugar Foot Stomp," "King Porter Stomp," and "Sometimes I'm Happy," and brought down the house. The booking at the Congress Hotel in Chicago followed. It was there that Goodman's hot music received the official label of "swing"—in an advertisement announcing the engagement. In reporting Goodman's performance, *Time* referred to Goodman as "the king of swing."

Swing, either as a word or as a style, was nothing new. Jazz musicians had often used the term to designate improvisations of melodic rhythm, and in 1932 Duke Ellington wrote a song called "It Don't Mean a Thing if It Ain't Got That Swing" (Irving Mills). The style itself also was not new. It was a variation of New Orleans improvisation, with this difference: group-notated improvisation usurped the prominent role once occupied by solo improvisation, and the melodic line retained a definite and clearly enunciated beat while the harmony was sprinkled with highly-spiced dissonances. Some of the performances of Fletcher Henderson's orchestra in New York in the 1920s had an unmistakable "swing" character; and it must be remembered that it was with Henderson's arrangements that Goodman and his band first became prominent. But it was Benny Goodman who, in Chicago, brought both the word and style to national acceptance. And it was Goodman who was to play a dominating role in "swing" music during the next decade in New York.

V

New Orleans jazz first became familiar to New York on the Vaudeville stage in the middle 1910s through appearances by Tom Brown's Band from Dixieland. As early as 1915, a hot-jazz unit, the Louisiana Five, led by Yellow Nunez, played at Bustanoby's Restaurant in New York. About two years later, on January 16, 1917, Nick La Rocca's Original Dixieland Band started an engagement at Reisenweber's Restaurant on Columbus Circle, featuring such all-time jazz favorites as "Tiger Rag," "Sensation Rag," and "The Livery Stable Blues." The loud, nervous, seemingly disordered music so puzzled the clientele of this restaurant that for a time nobody made a move to dance to its febrile strains. Finally, only after the proprietor announced that this was jazz and meant for dancing, did the patrons move out to the dance floor.

Several members of this group made the first hot-jazz records. In 1917, the Victor Company tried to induce Freddie Keppard to make some recordings. Keppard refused, fearing that then everybody would be able to steal his stuff. As a substitute for Keppard, Victor gathered some of La Rocca's men from Reisenweber's, named them the Original Dixieland Jazz Band, and produced in 1917 several disks, including "The Livery Stable Blues" and "Tiger Rag." Thus it was a white group that made the first jazz records. In 1921, Kid Ory made his first disks for a small company and James P. Johnson recorded for Okeh the first jazz piano solo; a year later, the Gennett Company engaged King Oliver and some of his men for a recording session in Richmond, Indiana. In New York, the first Negro outfit to make records was the Fletcher Henderson Orchestra, which produced some disks with orchestra alone, and several others with Ma Rainey and Bessie Smith.

The jazz empire in Chicago was breaking up in the 1920s. Many of the leading jazz personalities now made a move to

New York. Louis Armstrong came in 1924 to join the Fletcher Henderson Orchestra, and in the same year Bix Beiderbecke arrived to play in a Times Square dance hall. (In the next few years Bix played with the Jean Goldkette Orchestra and with Paul Whiteman.) Sidney Bechet came in 1926, Jelly Roll Morton in 1928. In 1928, too, Jimmy McPartland, Gene Krupa, Eddie Condon, Bud Freeman, and Frank Teschemacher formed an ensemble to play in New York for the Vaudeville singer, Bea Palmer.

Benny Goodman began appearing in New York, at the Hotel Roosevelt, in 1937. But before his arrival, "swing" was given official recognition at a concert on May 24, 1936 at the Imperial Theatre. The performers included a "swing" orchestra conducted by Bob Crosby; the Clambake Seven, led by Tommy Dorsey; and several other groups, including the Artie Shaw String Ensemble consisting of Artie Shaw's clarinet supplemented by a string quartet. Artie Shaw stole that show. It was this performance that led him to form a "swing" ensemble of his own and become one of the most formidable of Goodman's rivals.

But Benny Goodman was king. When, in 1937, he started an engagement at Paramount Theatre, the house was mobbed by "swing"-happy youngsters who had to be kept in check by the police and fire departments. On the first day of the engagement, over 20,000 passed the box office. Once Goodman started playing, pandemonium broke loose. The true-believers shouted their approval; some of them started dancing in the aisles. In January, 1938, Benny Goodman rocked the staid Carnegie Hall with a "swing" concert, the first time that that style was heard in a serious concert auditorium. Olin Downes, the music critic of the *New York Times,* reported: "When Mr. Goodman entered, he received a real Toscanini send-off from the excited throng. It took some minutes to establish quiet. There was some quivering excitement in the air, an almost electrical effect. . . . The audience broke out before the music stopped, in crashing applause and special salvos, as one or another of the heroes of the orchestra rose in his place to give his special and ornate contribution to the occasion."

"Swing" now became a national disease. On May 29, 1938, a Carnival of Swing was held at Randall's Island, in East River, New York, in which 23,400 jitterbugs danced for almost six hours to the music of twenty-five "swing" bands. New "swing" ensembles came into existence and found eager followers. Besides the one founded and led by Artie Shaw, there were, in the ensuing years, "swing" groups conducted by Tommy Dorsey, Woody Herman, Chick Webb, Cab Calloway, Count Basie, Jimmie Lunceford, Glenn Miller, Erskine Hawkins, among others.

A convincing testimony to the popularity and influence of "swing" is found in the way it was denounced in certain quarters. The head of the New York School of Music prepared a bill to make the performance of all "swing" music illegal. A *New York Times* headline on May 30, 1938 read: "Pastor Scores Swing as Debasing Youth. Declares It Shows an Obvious Degeneracy in Our Culture and Frothiness of Age." In an editorial in the Emporia *Gazette,* William Allen White indignantly described this new music as something that "squawked and shrieked and roared and bellowed in syncopated savagery."

New jazz ensembles, other than those dedicated to "swing," flourished in New York. One of the first major jazz groups formed in New York was Fletcher Henderson's Orchestra, organized in 1919 for Roseland, a dance hall. An excellent pianist and a remarkable arranger, Henderson introduced a jazz more formal than that formerly heard in New Orleans and Chicago: carefully prepared orchestrations replaced ad lib solos and group improvisations. From time to time, many outstanding jazz artists found a place in the Henderson Orchestra, including Coleman Hawkins and Don Redman (saxes), Buster Bailey (clarinet), and Louis Armstrong.

Henderson's prepared orchestrations used some of the techniques, colors, and nuances of real jazz, but to these were contributed a new richness of harmonic coloring, a lush sonority, and some beautiful solo writing. The orchestra broke up in 1924. After that Henderson devoted himself to arranging. His arrangements for the Benny Goodman group were a major factor in the early success of that ensemble.

Truer to the spirit and character of New Orleans and Chicago jazz was the band created and led by Duke Ellington. At one time or another, the Ellington group embraced such all-time greats of jazz as the trombonist Joe Nanton, the clarinetist Barney Bigard, the trumpeter Cootie Williams, the alto sax Johnny Hodges, and the drummer Sonny Greer.

The Duke, who was born in Washington, D. C. in 1899, had been playing the piano from the time he was seven, and participating in jazz-band performances from his seventeenth year on. Before coming to New York in 1923 he had not only organized his own jazz band but had also written his first popular tune, "The Soda Fountain Rag." After playing for a while in various New York groups, notably the Wilbur Sweatman Jazz Band in Harlem, he formed a five-piece ensemble for the Kentucky Club. It was with this group that he first stepped forward as a major spokesman for jazz. One of his admirers was Irving Mills, the music publisher, who signed him to a contract. With a band expanded to fourteen men, Duke Ellington made some excellent recordings and started a historic engagement at the Cotton Club in Harlem where he first became famous. "We came in with a new style," Ellington later reminisced to an interviewer. "Our playing was stark and wild and tense. . . . We tried new effects. . . . We put the Negro feeling and spirit in our music."

From then on, Ellington was a leading figure in New York jazz. In live performances in night clubs, theaters, and musical comedies, on the radio, in motion pictures, on records, he reached out to larger audiences than possibly any other jazz musician. Wherever he was heard he was acclaimed. During one of his triumphant European tours he gave a command performance at Buckingham Palace and was acclaimed "the most original musical mind in America" by Constant Lambert, a leading English serious composer and critic. In 1940 *Swing* Magazine picked seventeen of his records among the twenty-eight best of the year. In 1942, in a national poll conducted by *Downbeat* for the country's most popular musician, Ellington led a field of 15,000.

Ellington not only leads his band and plays the piano, but he has also prepared most of his orchestrations. (Since 1939, many of Ellington's excellent arrangements have been prepared by his disciple, Billy Strayhorn.) In addition, since 1933, Ellington has occupied a leading position among America's popular composers when "Sophisticated Lady" and "Solitude" became hits, the latter winning an ASCAP prize of $2,500 as the best popular song of the year. A year later came one of his best known songs, "Mood Indigo." His instrumental works include "East St. Louis Toodle-Oo," written in 1927, and after that known as his identifying radio theme song. He has also written numerous jazz instrumental works in more spacious forms introduced in Carnegie Hall and the Metropolitan Opera House auditorium.

In time, New York produced not only new jazz groups but also new jazz styles. In or about 1945 Be-bop—or Re-bop—became a fad. Its high priest was the trumpeter, Dizzy Gillespie, who led a small outfit in a night club on 52nd Street. Be-bop was an exciting kind of whirlwind music that avoids a definitely articulated melody; where, despite the velocity, the notes are clearly articulated; where the accentuation usually falls on the upbeat; and where the harmony changes frequently, sometimes several times in a single bar. As Rudi Blesh described it in the *Herald Tribune*, December

14, 1947: "Be-bop is a fantastic music that produces a peculiar nervous excitement. This excitement, deriving far more from manner than from matter, tends after repeated objective hearings to recede, leaving operative only an unnerving effect. Phrased in incoherently broken rhythms, successive and disparate instrumental solos are projected against short 'modern' chordal sequences. . . . Be-bop offers no coherent development of idea. A capricious and neurotically rhapsodic sequence of effects for their own sake, it comes perilously close to complete nonsense as a musical expression." This music was often wedded to lyrics filled with double-talk and nonsense lyrics.

When Be-bop first became a vogue, youngsters started imitating Gillespie's favorite head dress (a beret), his goatee (if they could raise one), and his heavy spectacles (even if they did not need them). Gillespie's most significant successor, and one of the most imaginative jazz men of the 1940s, was Charlie Parker, performer on the alto sax, and one of the most original talents in the art of improvisation produced by the new era of jazz.

VI

In other parts of the country, other jazz styles were introduced in the 1940s and 1950s. "Cool jazz"—that is, jazz music that is soft-spoken and relaxed—came as a reaction to Be-bop and its principal voices were men like Lennie Tristano, pianist, and Miles Davis, trumpeter. Progressive Jazz was in a somewhat different vein. The Progressives, led by Stan Kenton and later David Brubeck, both pianists, departed sharply from the uninhibited jazz performances and the spontaneous creation of New Orleans and Chicago. Progressive Jazz combined technical and stylistic features of real jazz with the harmonic, instrumental, and contrapuntal techniques of serious contemporary music. As Stan Kenton explained: "We are trying to present a progressive form of jazz. . . . Modern musicians will use every conceivable method. . . . My band has gone beyond my own technical knowledge in its use of the complexities of modern orchestration."

chapter nine

TIN PAN ALLEY—
Yesterday and Today

BEFORE the nineteenth century ended, the monopoly of Union Square in the song publishing industry was broken. With the center of theatrical activity moving further uptown, the song publishers of Union Square began one by one to follow the trend. In the first years of the new century, the industry had found a new center of activity: 28th Street between Fifth and Sixth Avenues became the nation's street of song. Most of the Union Square publishers were now in this new location, and they were joined by such neophytes as Leo Feist, Harry von Tilzer, and Gus Edwards. For the next quarter of a century, 28th Street remained the street where the tunes of the country were manufactured; where the pianos banged all day; to which an endless stream of performers and musicians flowed in search of new material. This was the street where the song plugger was king. All the techniques and methods for making hits that had originated downtown were here brought to their ultimate development. The million-copy sale of sheet music, a phenomenon in Union Square, became an almost habitual event. Between 1900 and 1910 there were almost a hundred songs that sold in excess of a million copies. Harry von Tilzer's "A Bird in a Gilded Cage," which Shapiro, Bernstein and von Tilzer published in 1900, sold two million copies. In 1910, "Let Me Call You Sweetheart," words and music by Beth Slater Wilson and Leo Friedman sold eight million copies, and "Down By the Old Mill Stream," by Tell Taylor, four million. Midway in the decade, in 1905, "In the Shade of the Old Apple Tree" by Egbert van Alstyne (Harry Williams) sold two and a half million copies in its first year of publication.

This street of song was baptized Tin Pan Alley in or about 1903 by Monroe Rosenfeld, a journalist, bon vivant, and writer of sentimental ballads. He was preparing an article on popular music for the New York *Herald* when he went to 28th Street for material. While at the offices of Harry von Tilzer he heard an upright piano into which von Tilzer had stuffed strips of paper through the piano strings to produce a tinny effect that von Tilzer favored. These sounds gave Rosenfeld an idea for the title of his article: Tin Pan Alley. From the time his piece was published, 28th Street and the American popular-music industry came to be known as Tin Pan Alley.

II

In Tin Pan Alley's first decade some of its most successful songwriters were those whose talents were discovered and nurtured by the Broadway musical theater—men like Victor Herbert, George M. Cohan, Rudolf Friml, Sigmund Romberg among others, who have already been discussed. Other composers, however, were the children of the Alley, born and bred there. It was in the Alley that these children learned their musical trade, and it was the Alley that first brought them fame and fortune.

The house of Harry von Tilzer, which came into existence in 1902 on 28th Street, had the solid foundation of hits by Harry von Tilzer himself—one of the Alley's most prolific and successful songwriters. Toward the end of his life he often told interviewers that he had written over eight thousand

songs, and that three thousand of these came before he had his
first hit. It is known that he published over two thousand
songs. But he had quality as well as quantity. Some of the
Alley's best sentimental ballads and most cogent "coon
songs" came from his busy pen.

He was born in Detroit in 1872, his name originally being
Harry Gumm. The lure of the stage made him run away from
home when he was fourteen. He first joined a circus. Then he
became a member of a theatrical troupe where he sang,
played the piano, and wrote songs. It was at this point that
he discarded the uneuphonious name with which he was born
and adopted his mother's maiden name of Tilzer, preceding it
with a flamboyant "von" to give it added distinction. While
playing in a burlesque theater in Chicago, he met Lottie
Gilson, the beloved star of Vaudeville, who in 1892 induced
him to come to New York and find a place for himself as a
songwriter.

His first song success came in 1898—"My Old New Hampshire Home" (Andrew B. Sterling), bought for $15.00 by the
firm of William C. Dunn, but soon taken over by Shapiro,
Bernstein & Co. After being introduced in Vaudeville, "My
Old New Hampshire Home" sold about two million copies.
Maurice Shapiro now offered von Tilzer a cash sum of $4,000
to leave the stage and concentrate on writing songs; an additional bait was a partnership in the publishing firm of Shapiro, Bernstein & Co. This move proved a gilt-edged investment
for the wily publisher. In less than two years von Tilzer produced another two-million copy smash in "A Bird in a Gilded
Cage" (Arthur J. Lamb). It is believed that von Tilzer agreed
to write the music to this lyric on the condition that the verse
made it perfectly clear that the unhappy girl in the song was
the millionaire's wife, and not his mistress. Sigmund Spaeth
points up the amusing paradox of von Tilzer's moral upright-
ness by noting that the composer actually wrote his melody in
a brothel. When von Tilzer tried out his song before some of

the girls and saw them burst into tears he exclaimed: "If *these* ladies weep real tears over my song, I have composed a hit."

In 1902, von Tilzer left Shapiro, Bernstein and von Tilzer to found a publishing house of his own bearing his name exclusively. He started the firm of Harry von Tilzer on 28th Street with a veritable blaze of fireworks, producing seven major hits in the first four years, four of them among his most famous songs, and three appearing in his firm's initial season. "The Mansion of Aching Hearts" (Arthur J. Lamb) preached the sermon that gold, diamonds, and a mansion cannot buy a happy heart. "Down Where the Wurzburger Flows" (Vincent P. Bryan) was written to order as a drinking song for the musical production, *Wild Rose*, but was never used there. The composer then induced Nora Bayes, still a comparative newcomer to the stage, to try it out in Vaudeville. She did, at the Brooklyn Orpheum Theatre; the composer sat in a box and, following sound song-plugging practice, rose to sing several refrains of the song when Nora Bayes finished her own rendition. Bayes subsequently performed the song so frequently that she soon became labeled "the Wurzburger Girl."

"On a Sunday Afternoon" occurred to the composer one Sunday afternoon at the beach when, lying lazily in the sun, the line "they work hard on Monday, but one day that's fun day" came to him. He asked Andrew B. Sterling to write a lyric on the subject, and when it was done produced an appropriate melody. "Wait Till the Sun Shines, Nellie" (Sterling), in 1905, was inspired—so some say—by a newspaper item about an impoverished family which prophesied that after the storm the sun would shine for the victims. Others have written that von Tilzer completed the melody after hearing a casual remark, "wait till the sun shines, Nellie," in a hotel lobby.

In the decade that followed "Wait Till the Sun Shines, Nellie," Harry von Tilzer wrote another ballad that has not been forgotten: "I Want a Girl Just Like the Girl That Married Dear Old Dad" (William Dillon).

Harry von Tilzer was not only a master of sentimental ballads but also of "coon songs," a style so popular in the late 1800s, and carried by von Tilzer into the twentieth century. One of his best was "Alexander, Don't You Love Your Baby No More?" (Sterling) in 1904. Von Tilzer wrote this "coon song" after watching the black-face Vaudeville act of McIntyre and Heath. A moment in the act that always provoked laughter was when McIntyre called Heath "Alexander." Von Tilzer has said that the entire song came to him the same day when, standing in the theater lobby after the show, he waited for a rainstorm to subside.

A remark by a Negro woman at the Miami railroad station gave von Tilzer the theme for another "coon song." She was upbraiding her gentleman friend for his lack of ambition when she added angrily: "What you goin' to do when de rent comes 'round?" Sterling wrote the lyric for him, and von Tilzer completed his song "What You Goin' to Do When the Rent Comes 'Round?" in 1905.

III

Among other leading writers of ballads in Tin Pan Alley in the early 1900s was Ernest R. Ball, about whom the beloved Irish tenor, John McCormack, once said: "He will live forever in his songs." Ball was a melodist in the grand tradition, a melodist who knew how to write "honestly and sincerely of the things I knew about and that folks generally knew about and were interested in." He was born in Cleveland, Ohio, in 1878. Showing aptitude for music he was given a thorough training at the Cleveland Conservatory. He was fifteen when he wrote his first piece of music, a march. In the early 1890s he came to New York and for a while worked as a pianist at the Union Square Theatre. A few years after that he was hired as pianist at Witmark's for twenty dollars a week. "At

Witmark's," he told an interviewer, "when I was not busy demonstrating songs, I used to play over any that came to me; and it was here, in odd moments, that I did my first adult composing. My first serious effort was a flop. A little later I wrote 'In the Shadow of the Pyramids.' It went over when sung on the stage by May Irwin, but it never became a widely-sold favorite. So it was with a number of others I tried."

One night, in the spring of 1903, he met James J. Walker, at that time a State Senator and many years later the Mayor of New York. Walker gave him a crumpled sheet of paper on which were scrawled the words of a song lyric. "I put the paper in my pocket, and for the next two months carried the scribbled lines around with me," Ball recalled many years later. "Bit by bit, I worked out a tune that somehow seemed to fit and, finally, I wrote the music to the words. The result was 'Will You Love Me in December As You Do in May?' I awoke one morning to find that I had written a piece of music that was being sung from one end of the country to the other." The song made so much money that Witmark's at once signed Ball to a twenty-year contract. Walker earned over $10,000 from his lyrics; he was still receiving royalties for it thirty years after publication.

The success of "Will You Love Me in December" convinced Ball that his talent lay with songs that came from the heart and appealed to the heart. "If the sentiment is straight and true," he said, "the song has a chance. . . . Talk to a man about his home, his wife, his mother, or his children, and you get his attention." In line with this thinking he wrote, in 1906, "Love Me and the World is Mine" (Dave Reed, Jr.), one of the decade's leading hits, which duplicated its American popularity in foreign lands in many different translations. It was some years before Ball produced anything else as good. But, in 1910, he got his second wind and in co-operation with Chauncey Olcott, star of Irish musicals, wrote a ballad that

Olcott used in *Barry of Ballymore*. It was "Mother Machree," lyrics by Rida Johnson Young, destined to enter the permanent repertory of Irish tenors and a favorite at John McCormack's concerts. Later ballads kept Ball in the front rank of Tin Pan Alley's composers. The best were: "Till the Sands of the Desert Grow Cold" (George Graff, Jr.); "When Irish Eyes Are Smiling" (Chauncey Olcott and George Graff, Jr.); and to lyrics by J. Keirn Brennan, "A Little Bit of Heaven," "Turn Back the Universe and Give Me Yesterday," and "Let the Rest of the World Go By."

IV

In the second decade of the 1900s, three composers helped to emancipate the popular song in Tin Pan Alley from its bondage to clichés and formulas. All three started their professional careers by working in the Alley; all three profited immeasurably from their experiences there. They were as formidable a trio of composers as our popular music has thus far produced: Jerome Kern, Irving Berlin, and George Gershwin.

Jerome Kern's association with the Alley began in 1905 when he was twenty years old. Only after he had undergone a rigorous apprenticeship there did he attain success in the musical theater where he earned his greatest triumphs. He was born in New York City in 1885 to a comparatively well-off family. When he was graduated from Newark (New Jersey) High School, he entered the New York College of Music. There was no question of his enthusiasm for music, nor of his industry and over-all ability. But he was no blazing flame. His level-headed father, consequently, refused to give his consent for Jerome to go to Europe for more music study as the boy had wished. Instead, Jerome had to enter his father's business, a fairly prosperous merchandising house in Newark.

Jerome joined his father in 1902, but his business career was brief. One day, sent to New York City to buy two pianos, he became so spellbound by the persuasive arguments of a super-salesman, that he purchased not two but two hundred pianos. With that single stroke he almost ruined his father financially. Now convinced that the world of business was alien to the boy, and probably guided by a healthy instinct for self-preservation, the father decided to send his son to Europe after all. (Actually this affair with the pianos did not turn out so disastrously as had first been feared. After Jerome went to Europe, the father—faced with the necessity of disposing of the two hundred pianos—evolved an attractive installment plan project which netted him a handsome profit for the whole deal.)

Jerome Kern went to Europe in the fall of 1903. He traveled about, listened to a great deal of music, and did some studying with private teachers. In London, faced with the necessity of replenishing his sadly depleted funds, he took a job in the office of Charles K. Frohman, an American producer then presenting musical shows in London. Kern's duties consisted in writing little songs and musical pieces as opening numbers —an inconsequential and poorly paid assignment, since London theater-goers came habitually late and never heard the opening music.

Humble though this task was, it gave Kern the direction he needed. He now permanently discarded his one-time ambition to write symphonies and concertos, and instead turned to popular music. During this period he wrote several songs, the lyrics provided by a young writer then also employed by Frohman and later famous both in literature and in the American musical theater—P. G. Wodehouse.

Early in 1905, Kern returned to America. Since he wanted to make his way in popular music he decided to learn everything he could about the song business. For the next two years he worked in Tin Pan Alley for various publishers, accepting any assignment that came his way. Sometimes he worked as a song plugger: within the publishing house he played the latest publications for performers and entertainers;

outside, in department stores and large shops, he spurred on
the sale of sheet music by plugging his publisher's current
tunes at the piano. He also adapted the songs of other composers for his firm's catalogue, and at times wrote stock numbers of his own.

He became a salesman for the house of Harms, where he
attracted the attention of Max Dreyfus. Dreyfus, recognizing
Kern's possibilities, had him write songs for the firm, some of
which were published. (Kern was subsequently published
exclusively by Harms, and in time became its vice-president.)
Dreyfus procured a job for Kern to accompany Marie Dressler
on the piano. She was then a popular vaudevillian but later a
character actress of the screen. He also helped open for Kern
doors that led to the Broadway theater.

Kern received his first important stage assignment in 1910
when he was called upon to revise the music of *Mr. Wix of
Wickham*. Kern's score was so completely his own, so fresh in
melodic and harmonic approaches, that at least one New York
critic sat up and took notice. "Who is this Jerome Kern," inquired Alan Dale in the *American*, "whose music towers in
an Eiffel way above the average primitive hurdy-gurdy accompaniment of the present-day musical comedy?"

After *Mr. Wix of Wickham*, Kern moved swiftly upward in
his profession. In 1911, the Shuberts signed him to collaborate
with Frank Tours in writing the music for *La Belle Paree*, an
extravaganza which, as part of a dual bill, opened the Winter
Garden. One year later came Kern's first complete original
score for Broadway, *The Red Petticoat*. In 1914, Kern had his
first Broadway success in *The Girl from Utah*, and his first
song to attain a million-copy sale in "They Didn't Believe Me"
(Herbert Reynolds). From this point on, his story belongs
with that of the musical theater and will be detailed in a later
chapter.

Like Kern, Irving Berlin received his first song experiences
in Tin Pan Alley; unlike Kern, he had no musical training

to speak of. He could play the piano with only one finger. (Later on, as a successful composer, he could employ all ten digits; but even then he could perform only in a single key.) He could not read or write a note of music. But what he did have, and what so many others in Tin Pan Alley lacked, was the creative power to arrive at new and fresh ways of expressing threadbare sentiments.

He was born as Israel Baline in Russia in 1888. Four years later his family fled from Russia in the wake of a pogrom and settled in New York's East Side. On its streets, Irving spent his boyhood, in a setting of extreme poverty. When he was fourteen he ran away from home. For a while he earned about fifty cents a day as a street busker by singing in saloons and on street corners such ballads as "The Mansion of Aching Hearts." He graduated to a regular Saturday night job at Callahan's saloon in Chinatown and The Chatham in Doyer Street. Occasionally, he also worked for the publishing house of Harry von Tilzer as a plugger at Tony Pastor's Music Hall.

In 1906 he found a full-time job at Pelham's Café. From dusk to dawn he served at tables, swept the floors, and entertained the clientele by singing popular songs. It was at this time that he wrote his first popular song—but only the lyric. Two waiters of a rival café had written and published a song. The proprietor of Pelham's insisted that his men do likewise. The café pianist, Nick Nicholson, was recruited to write the song, which a neighborhood violinist helped him to put down on paper. Since Berlin had already proved glib at making up parodies of current songs, he was asked to prepare the lyric. Together they wrote "Marie from Sunny Italy," which was published by Joseph W. Stern. Berlin's income from his share in the collaboration was thirty-seven cents. Incidentally, it was on this publication that the boy who had been born as Israel Baline appeared for the first time as Irving Berlin.

Union Square was Berlin's next stop. For a while he worked

as a singing waiter at Jimmy Kelly's restaurant, a few steps from Tony Pastor's Music Hall. Then he filled a job as song plugger for Leo Feist. He continued writing lyrics which various musicians set to music. One was "Sadie Salome, Go Home," music by Edgar Leslie, which was published by Ted Snyder and had the respectable sale of 200,000 copies. "Sadie Salome" led Snyder to engage Berlin as a staff lyricist with a drawing account of $25.00 a week. Berlin soon became such an ace in this field that in 1910 the New York *Journal* asked him to write a string of parodies to one of his own lyrics; and J. J. Shubert signed him and Ted Snyder to appear in a revue, *Up and Down Broadway*, singing two of their hits, "Oh, You Beautiful Rag" and "Sweet Italian Song."

It was accident that led Berlin to write his first melody. Before he had become a successful lyricist, Berlin wrote "Dorando," a verse about an Italian marathon runner for a vaudevillian scheduled to appear at Tony Pastor's. The performer decided not to use it in his act. Berlin now tried marketing it to Ted Snyder, whose general manager consented to buy it for $25.00 if the lyric had a melody. Rather than lose the sale, Berlin dictated an improvised melody to the arranger, and his maiden effort was bought and published. This was in 1909. For a while, Berlin concentrated on writing words to the music of other composers, principally to that of his publisher, Ted Snyder. But once in a while he tried going on his own, as in "That Mesmerizing Mendelssohn Tune" (Mendelssohn's *Spring Song* with a dash of ragtime) and "Yiddle On Your Fiddle," both in 1909. The former was a modest hit, and both were the kind of ditties that delighted Vaudeville audiences of that day and that Tin Pan Alley delivered by the carload.

But Berlin nursed a creative spark that soon burst into hot flame. It was only two years after he had dictated his first melody to one of Ted Snyder's arrangers that he wrote a song that made him a national figure in American popular music,

indeed a song that made both musical and social history—
"Alexander's Ragtime Band." Here, as in all future Berlin
songs, the composer wrote his own lyrics and music.

Ragtime was, of course, nothing new in Tin Pan Alley.
Ben Harney, a ragtime pianist, helped to popularize ragtime
style in New York toward the closing years of the nineteenth
century, by playing rags at Tony Pastor's, by editing *The
Ragtime Instructor* which Witmark's published in 1897, and
by writing such song hits in 1896 and 1897 as "Mister Johnson,
Turn Me Loose" and "You've Been a Good Old Wagon," the
former introduced by May Irwin in *Courted into Court*. May
Irwin's "coon song," "The Bully" was in ragtime, and so was
"At a Georgia Camp Meeting," which Kerry Mills wrote in
1897 in protest against "coon songs." Indeed, ragtime had
grown so popular by 1899 that the *Musical Courier* found it
necessary to attack it editorially that year: "A wave of vulgar,
filthy, and suggestive music has inundated the land. The
pabulum of theater and summer-hotel music is 'coon music.'
Nothing but ragtime prevails." In 1901, the American Federa-
tion of Musicians passed a resolution pledging that its members "make every effort to suppress and discourage the playing
and publishing of such musical trash." On the other hand
there were those who spoke up for ragtime. Rupert Hughes
wrote in the *Musical Record* of April 1, 1899: "If ragtime
were called *tempo di raga* . . . it might win honors more
speedily." Then he went on to prophesy: "Ragtime will find its
way gradually into the works of some great genius and will
thereafter be canonized." And the celebrated prima donna,
Emma Nevada, told an interviewer for the Boston *Herald* in
1901 that she liked ragtime and hoped "they will not squelch
the new fad."

But if Irving Berlin uncovered no new trend in "Alexander,"
he did succeed in endowing an existing and already familiar
style with such a personal touch, and to invest it with such
vitality and freshness, that momentarily it almost seemed as if

he had been its inventor. For years after "Alexander" had become popular, many believed that it was Berlin who had started the ragtime craze, and a few even ventured the guess that he had created the idiom. When in the years just before World War I Berlin appeared in New York and London theaters billed as "The Ragtime King" there were many in the audience who thought that every ragtime tune in existence had been written by him.

"Alexander's Ragtime Band" started out as a piano rag in 1910, possibly inspired by Harry von Tilzer's "coon song," "Alexander, Don't You Love Your Baby No More?" In 1911, the Friars Club of New York elected Berlin as a member and invited him to appear as a performer in the *Friars Frolics* at the New Amsterdam Theatre. For this occasion Berlin wanted to write and introduce a new song. He finally decided to take his piano rag out of his trunk, add a lyric to it, and introduce it. It was favorably received, but soon forgotten.

A few months later, the dynamic vaudevillian, Emma Carus, revived the song in Chicago. She scored so definitely with it that in a few days' time she had everybody in the city humming the tune. One Chicago newspaperman wrote: "If we were John D. Rockefeller or the Bank of England we should engage the Coliseum and get together a sextet including Caruso. . . . After the sextet sang it ["Alexander's Ragtime Band"] about ten times we should, as a finale, have Sousa's Band march about the building tearing the melody to pieces with all kinds of variations."

"Alexander's Ragtime Band" was now on its way to conquer the nation. Within a few months it sold a million copies, was the most frequently performed popular song in the country. It helped ragtime temporarily displace the sentimental ballad, the dialect song, and the Vaudeville ditty in the affections of Americans everywhere. Ragtime consequently received top priority in Tin Pan Alley. With seemingly everybody trying to write ragtime tunes, the one-time emphasis placed by songwriters on formal, evenly balanced melodies and rhythms was shifted to the comparatively less formal rhythms and accentuations of ragtime. This change of emphasis permitted a new vitality to enter the writing of popular music.

"Alexander's Ragtime Band" had another far-reaching influence—on our social rather than musical life—by inducing a new vogue for social dancing. Before 1911, social dances like the polka, the waltz, and the schottische taxed physical endurance. Consequently only the young danced, and even they required rest periods between numbers. But the 2/4 and 4/4 rhythm of ragtime made dancing a simpler process. Anybody who could walk could now also dance. Even older people joined in the fun. With "Alexander" a national passion, quickening the pulse and heartbeat and making feet restless, people suddenly became dance crazy. For the first time dancing was introduced into restaurants and hotels during meal hours. Special tea-time dancing was inaugurated. The demand for after-theater dancing resulted in the opening of New York's first night clubs: Lee Shubert's Palais de Danse and William Morris' Jardin de Danse. Everybody was getting into the dancing act. Business men slipped away from work late in the afternoon for an hour of such diversion; some factories introduced it during the lunch period. The newspapers disclosed that Mrs. John D. Rockefeller was taking private lessons; that Mrs. Stuyvesant Fish had commissioned the Castles to create "The Innovation" for her social functions, so that the dancing might be more polite and discreet than that inspired by the prevailing one-step, two-step, fox trot, turkey trot, bunny hug, or grizzly bear.

After "Alexander" Berlin wrote many other successful ragtime tunes. Among the best were "Ragtime Violin," "Everybody's Doin' It," and "That Mysterious Rag."

Now the recognized king of ragtime, Berlin was soon destined to send the American popular song back to an old and well-beaten path: the sentimental ballad. In 1912, he was married to Dorothy Goetz. Returning from a Cuba honeymoon to their new home on Riverside Drive, they settled down to a happy marital existence which was suddenly and tragically shattered. Dorothy succumbed to typhoid, contracted in Cuba. This major tragedy led Berlin, in 1912, to write the first of his great personal ballads, "When I Lost You." Once again a truly vital creative force enabled Berlin to bring to a long-existing style such a personal charm that it seemed reborn and revitalized.

"When I Lost You" was a success second only to "Alexander." Henceforth, Berlin was to write many ballads, some of them autobiographical in subject matter, in which a potent melodic gift capable of evoking varied moods and feelings was combined with simplicity, directness, and a caressing charm. Between 1921 and 1924, he wrote "All By Myself," "What'll I Do?" and "All Alone"—to this day among the most beautiful love songs to come out of Tin Pan Alley. Two of his greatest love ballads came in 1925, during his stormy courtship of Ellin Mackay, daughter of the tycoon who was the head of Postal Telegraph. It is now a familiar story how the father renounced Berlin as a possible son-in-law, how he did everything in his power to break up the love affair. "Always" and "Remember" were testaments of his love for Ellin during a period when they were forcibly kept apart. On January 4, 1926 they were secretly married, and went off for a European honeymoon. It was some years before Ellin's father became reconciled to what has since proved to be one of the most durable and happy marriages on Broadway. This romance, that broke down social and religious barriers, inspired Jimmy McHugh of Tin Pan Alley to write to Al Dubin's lyrics a song called "When a Kid Who Came From the East Side Found a Sweet Society Rose."

The years following Berlin's marriage brought still more imperishable ballads: "How Deep Is the Ocean?," "I've Got My Love to Keep Me Warm," "The Song is Ended," and two which have almost acquired the status of folk music, "Easter Parade" and "White Christmas." The Berlin ballad might trace its genealogy to the sentimental tune of Union Square. But from that origin there arose, through Berlin, an American song so personal in melodic character, so haunting in its expression of lyrical beauty that it is as different from the hothouse product of the 1880s and 1890s as a Schubert *Lied* is from the Viennese popular tune.

In 1919, Berlin intruded more boldly into Tin Pan Alley by leaving the firm of Waterson, Berlin and Snyder, with which he had been connected for about a dozen years, and organizing his own publishing house, that of Irving Berlin, Inc. This event was commemorated throughout the country with an Irving Berlin Week. The Loew Vaudeville circuit had two current Berlin songs on every program at each of its theaters; Irving Berlin himself appeared that week on the New York Vaudeville stage; music stores had special displays of his best-known songs. From 1919 on, Berlin had a monopoly on the choicest property in Tin Pan Alley—the songs of Berlin himself. But he would also publish the music of others. Within eighteen months, Berlin realized from his firm a profit of almost $200,000. Three decades later, the Berlin house was earning for him over a million dollars a year.

For half a century, and up to the present moment, Berlin has retained the golden touch of writing songs that are hits, and some which become classics. (More will be said about him and his songs in later chapters on the musical theater and motion pictures.) With his gifts and equally formidable achievements, Berlin has helped prepare the way for other strongly-endowed creative figures in Tin Pan Alley. Many of them would bring to the popular song some of the melodic, rhythmic, and harmonic science of classical music.

One of those who was most strongly influenced, even inspired, by Berlin was George Gershwin.

In his early adolescence, Gershwin had been tireless in his

attempts to convince his piano teacher, Charles Hambitzer, that there was artistic validity to the Tin Pan Alley song.
Gershwin was thinking particularly of "Alexander's Ragtime
Band." His profound admiration for Berlin continued through
the years. Berlin's songs continually provided him with in-
contestable proof that a composer could reach greatness
through the popular-song medium. "Irving Berlin is the greatest American song composer," Gershwin wrote after he had become famous. "He is America's Franz Schubert."

Like the man whom he admired so deeply, Gershwin was a
son of Tin Pan Alley. He was born in Brooklyn, New York,
in 1898. His childhood and early boyhood were spent, like
Berlin's, in the city streets, mostly in New York's East
Side. His talent at first lay mainly in the pastimes of the
streets: roller-skating, punch ball, fights. However, a sensitivity
for music was latent within him, and every once in a while
something happened to bring it to the surface. He was about
six when he heard Anton Rubinstein's *Melody in F* in a penny
arcade. That melody, he later recalled, "held me rooted . . .
standing there barefoot and in overalls, drinking it all in avidly." About a year later, he would sit for hours at a time on
the street curb outside the Baron Wilkins night club in Harlem, drinking in the intoxicating sounds of Jim Europe's jazz
music. He was about ten when, playing ball outside his public
school, he heard the strains of Dvořák's *Humoresque* played by
a violinist. He stopped to listen. This music was, in his own
words, "a flashing revelation." The violinist was one of
George's schoolmates—a gifted young musician named Maxie
Rosenzweig who subsequently became famous on the concert
stage as Max Rosen. George sought out Maxie and became his
friend. Maxie often played the violin for George and told him
about the world of great music. Once when George invented a
melody of his own, he hurriedly brought it to his friend for
criticism. Maxie told him with brutal frankness: "I'm sorry,

George. You'd better forget about music. You just haven't the talent for it."

A piano came into the Gershwin household when George was twelve years old. From then on, the boy was tireless in attempting to evoke from the keyboard the popular melodies he knew and loved, and in making up some of his own. He began to study with local teachers. His first important one was Charles Hambitzer, an association that marked the actual beginning of George's awareness that music was henceforth to be a major preoccupation. Hambitzer, a musician of remarkable perception, background, and intuition, recognized George's talent immediately, and knew how to nurse it. He introduced Gershwin to what up to then had been for the boy *terra incognita*: the piano classics from Bach and Chopin to Debussy and Ravel. He fired the boy with his own intense ardor, and transmitted to him some of his own flaming enthusiasms. He soon encouraged Gershwin to supplement piano study with some badly needed instruction in harmony and theory with Edward Kilenyi.

Gershwin responded enthusiastically to this instruction. He worked hard, absorbed a great deal. But the boy also had a mind of his own. He was—as Hambitzer once wrote to his sister—"crazy about jazz and ragtime" and was convinced that in the hands of a gifted composer these popular idioms could become important music; slowly he acquired the assurance that this was the kind of music he wanted to write. "The boy is a genius without a doubt," Hambitzer told his sister in the same letter. "He wants to go in for this modern stuff, jazz and what not. But I'm not going to let him for a while. I'll see that he gets a firm foundation in standard music first."

Determined to learn all he could about American popular music, and at its source, Gershwin sought a job in Tin Pan Alley. He found a place as staff pianist at a salary of $15.00 a week at Remick's, under its ace song plugger, Mose

Gumble. Gershwin's duties consisted in playing Remick tunes all day for potential clients, and occasionally going out to plug these songs in five-and-ten-cent stores and other establishments selling sheet music. "I still recall George's earnestness, his intense enthusiasm for his work, his passionate interest in every phase of the popular-music business," recalls Harry Ruby, in those days also a song plugger, but since become a major popular-song writer. "Sometimes when he spoke of the artistic mission of popular music, we thought he was going highfalutin'. The height of artistic achievement to us was a 'pop' song that sold lots of copies, and we just didn't understand what he was talking about."

Gershwin was learning the song business from the inside: the subtle and complex mechanism that produced a song hit. He was put into direct contact with the best popular tunes of the day; those by Irving Berlin and Jerome Kern stimulated and inspired him. Before long he was writing his own songs, in which he unashamedly imitated his favorite composers. His serious approach to songwriting is best illustrated by an incident. A fellow song plugger at Remick's found him one day practicing Bach's *Well-Tempered Clavier*. "Are you practicing to become a concert pianist?" the plugger inquired. Gershwin answered: "No, I'm studying to be a great popular-song composer."

By 1916 he had entered professional ranks. One of his songs, "When You Want 'Em, You Can't Get 'Em" (Murray Roth) was published by Harry von Tilzer. Another, "The Making of a Girl," (Harold Atteridge) was introduced in a Broadway revue, *The Passing Show of 1916*, the rest of whose score was by Sigmund Romberg.

Gershwin was outgrowing his cramped cubicle at Remick's. He left his job and held several others, none of which advanced him in his songwriting career. Irving Berlin, one day, gave him an attractive offer as a musical secretary. "But," Berlin added, "I hope you don't take the job. You're too talented to be anybody's secretary." Gershwin followed Berlin's advice and turned down the position. Then came an opening that promised much more for his future. Max Dreyfus of Harms offered him a weekly salary of $35.00 to write songs. There were no set duties or hours. All Gershwin had to do was to show Dreyfus everything he wrote, and to listen to the older man's counsel.

With Dreyfus behind him, Gershwin began to advance quickly. In 1918, he wrote the complete score for a revue, *Half-Past Eight,* which opened and closed in Syracuse, New York, in the same week. He had songs in three other Broadway productions. In 1919, Alex A. Aarons, a young man engaged in theatrical producing for the first time, signed him to write his first full score for a musical comedy, *La, La Lucille.* One of its songs was "Nobody But You" (Arthur Jackson), whose melody had a Jerome Kernish charm. In the same year, Gershwin was the proud father of his first song hit, "Swanee," that sold over two million records and a million copies of sheet music.

"Swanee" was born in Dinty Moore's restaurant in New York. Gershwin and his lyricist, Irving Caesar, were having lunch there to discuss song ideas when they decided to write a one-step in the style of the then popular "Hindustan." They would choose an American setting, "something like Stephen Foster's 'Swanee'," as Gershwin suggested. The idea jelled further atop a Fifth Avenue bus, and by the time they reached Gershwin's apartment on Washington Heights, they clearly had in mind the song they wanted to write. They completed it in Gershwin's living room the same afternoon, while a poker game was in progress in the adjoining dining room. That game was temporarily interrupted as Gershwin and Caesar tried out their song for the first time, with Papa Gershwin providing an obbligato by whistling into a comb in which tissue paper was stuffed.

Ned Wayburn accepted "Swanee" for a lavish stage production with which the then newly-built movie palace in New York, the Capitol Theatre, was opened on October 24, 1919. Sixty chorus girls, electric lights glowing on their slippers, danced to its rhythms on an otherwise dark stage. The song did not at first go over, and the sale of the sheet music was anemic. But one day Gershwin played it for Al Jolson who took it for one of his Winter Garden shows. Jolson first introduced "Swanee" at a Sunday night concert at the Winter Garden and made such a hit that he decided to interpolate it into the musical extravaganza, *Sinbad*, in which he was then appearing. Jolson spelled the difference. "Swanee" swept the country, and lifted its young composer to a position of prominence.

By 1920, Gershwin's place on Broadway and in Tin Pan Alley was further solidified when George White engaged him to write the music for the *Scandals*, a lavish revue which White had launched one year earlier to compete with the *Ziegfeld Follies*. For five editions, Gershwin wrote all the music for the *Scandals*. In that time he passed from a composer of promise to one who fulfilled some of the high hopes expected of him.

V

The firmament of Tin Pan Alley, in the 1910s and 1920s, had satellites as well as planets. Seven shone with particular radiance: Walter Donaldson, George W. Meyer, Milton Ager, Richard A. Whiting, Harry Ruby, Con Conrad, and Sammy Fain.

Berlin, Jolson, and Gumble who appeared so prominently in Gershwin's early career also play a part in the history of Walter Donaldson. A native of Brooklyn, New York, where he was born in 1893, Donaldson tried to make his way in a Wall Street brokerage firm before deciding to make popular music his life work. Once this decision was reached, he went to Tin Pan Alley for a job, and found one for $15.00 a week as staff pianist and song plugger. He was fired when found writ-

ing songs on company time. One of these, his first published
piece, was "Back Home in Tennessee" (Billy Jerome), written in 1915 and since become a favorite song of that state.

During World War I, Donaldson entertained troops at
Camp Upton, where Irving Berlin was stationed and where
Berlin put on *Yip, Yip Yaphank*. Berlin and Donaldson became friends. After the war, Donaldson joined the recently-
founded firm of Irving Berlin, Inc., for which he wrote a long
succession of hits which made him one of Tin Pan Alley's
leaders in the 1920s. This skein began just before the new
decade opened with "How Ya Gonna Keep 'Em Down on the
Farm?", "You're a Million Miles From Nowhere," and "My
Mammy," all to lyrics by Sam M. Lewis and Joe Young.

When Al Jolson heard "My Mammy"—which Bill Frawley
was then singing on the Vaudeville circuit—he felt it was his
kind of a song, and he interpolated it into *Sinbad* where he
was then also singing Gershwin's "Swanee." Performed on one
bended knee, and with white-gloved hands outstretched, "My
Mammy" became at once one of Jolson's most memorable
specialties.

In 1922, Donaldson entered into a partnership with the
lyricist, Gus Kahn, that was initiated with a smash, "My
Buddy." This collaboration proceeded fruitfully with "Carolina
in the Morning," "Beside a Babbling Brook," and "Yes Sir,
That's My Baby." (However, Donaldson's big number for
1927, "My Blue Heaven," was to lyrics by George Whiting.)
The Donaldson and Kahn team was also responsible for the
complete score of *Whoopee,* starring Eddie Cantor, which
Ziegfeld produced in 1928, and which yielded "Making
Whoopee" (since become a Cantor trademark), "My Baby Just
Cares for Me," and "Love Me or Leave Me," the last successfully revived a quarter century later in the motion-picture
biography of Ruth Etting to which it gave the title.

In 1928, Donaldson left the firm of Irving Berlin to join
up with Mose Gumble, song plugger *par excellence,* to

establish the new firm of Donaldson, Douglas, and Gumble. This house issued the *Whoopee* song hits, and in the ensuing few years such others as "Just Like a Melody Out of the Sky," "Little White Lies," and "You're Driving Me Crazy," all to Donaldson's own lyrics.

George W. Meyer, born in Boston in 1884, first studied bookkeeping, then worked as an oculist in New York. When his song, "Lonesome," written with Kerry Mills to lyrics by Edgar Leslie, sold a million copies in 1909 he realized he was in the wrong business. After abandoning eyeglasses for songs, he wrote in 1914 "When You're a Long, Long Way From Home" (Sam M. Lewis), a staple in the repertory of such blues singers as Sophie Tucker and Grace La Rue, and in 1917 "For Me and My Gal" (Edgar Leslie and E. Ray Goetz), effectively revived a quarter of a century later by Judy Garland and Gene Kelly in a motion-picture musical that carried the same name. Three more aces were dealt by Meyer in the next three years: "Everything is Peaches Down in Georgia" (Grant Clarke), made famous by Al Jolson at the Winter Garden; "Now I Lay Me Down to Sleep" (Sidney Mitchell), later on a *tour de force* of Bert and Betty Wheeler in their Vaudeville act; and "Tuck Me to Sleep in My Old 'Tucky Home" (Sam M. Lewis and Joe Young).

Meyer wrote "Everything Is Peaches Down in Georgia" in collaboration with Milton Ager, a young man who was here tasting success for the first time. In his youth, Ager worked as a song plugger for the Chicago branch of Waterson, Berlin, and Snyder; also as an accompanist for Gene Green, a singer who toured the Orpheum Vaudeville circuit. He came to New York in 1914 to work as an arranger in the home office of Waterson, Berlin, and Snyder, when he started writing music of his own—initially piano pieces with Pete Wendling sold for $25.00 a number. After forming a permanent connection with William Jerome Music Company, Ager began writing songs to lyrics provided by his publisher, William Jerome.

Producing his first hit by collaborating with Meyer on "Everything Is Peaches," Ager hit his stride with two popular items written with Cliff Hess to lyrics by Howard Johnson: "Freckles," in 1919, and "I'm in Heaven When I'm in My Mother's Arms," in 1920. In the latter year Ager began a words-and-music partnership with Jack Yellen that proved uniquely fruitful, contributing such impressive Tin Pan Alley winners as "Who Cares?" (introduced by Al Jolson in *Bombo* in 1922), "I Wonder What's Become of Sally," "Crazy Words, Crazy Tune," and "Ain't She Sweet?"

Richard A. Whiting, born in Peoria, Illinois, in 1891, was an office manager for Remick's branch office in Detroit, when, in 1913, he published his first songs. These tentative efforts earned him virtually nothing. But within the next three years he wrote "It's Tulip Time in Holland" (Dave Redford), "Mammy's Little Coal Black Rose," and "They Called It Dixieland" (Raymond Egan) which brought him royalties in excess of $50,000. But this was just a preliminary to his triumph, "Till We Meet Again" (Egan), one of the unforgettable songs of World War I; by Armistice time it sold over five million copies. In the 1920s, his best sellers included "Japanese Sandman" (Egan), "Ain't We Got Fun?" (Whiting), and with Ange Lorenzo, "Sleepy Time Gal" (Alden and Egan).

The song-writing career of Harry Ruby—born in New York City in 1895—was prefaced by training in Tin Pan Alley. After finishing high school, he found a job as staff pianist in the publishing firm of Gus Edwards. Various other firms in the Alley employed him after that, mostly in the capacity of song plugger. He also toured the Vaudeville circuit as pianist for two acts.

While making the rounds of Vaudeville theaters, he met and befriended Bert Kalmar, a vaudevillian who was also owner of a New York music-publishing firm. Kalmar prevailed on Ruby to come to work with him as pianist and song plugger.

Some time later, when a knee injury incapacitated Kalmar for his Vaudeville act, and he decided to devote himself to writing lyrics, he asked Ruby to work with him as composer. Their first job was some songs for Belle Baker's Vaudeville act, one of which, "He Sits Around," became one of her favorites. "When Those Sweet Hawaiian Babies Roll Their Eyes," "So Long! Oo-Long," and "Who's Sorry Now?" (the last written with Ted Snyder) gave the team of Ruby and Kalmar added status in the Alley between 1917 and 1923. In the latter year, they wrote their first Broadway score, for *Helen of Troy, New York*, book by Marc Connelly and George S. Kaufman. This was the first of several Broadway musicals with which they were associated, among which was *Animal Crackers* with the Four Marx Brothers.

Con Conrad, born as Conrad K. Dober on New York's East Side in 1891, came to Tin Pan Alley by way of the Vaudeville stage, where he had been appearing since his sixteenth year. During this period he started writing songs, but failed to get a winner until he became a member of the house of Waterson, Berlin and Snyder. This happened in 1920 when with J. Russel Robinson he wrote "Margie" (Benny Davis). Between 1921 and 1924, Conrad followed this initial victory with others equally impressive, including "Ma—He's Making Eyes at Me" (Sidney Clare), "Barney Google" (Billy Rose), and with Larry Spier "Memory Lane" (B. G. DeSylva).

Sammy Fain, born in New York City in 1902, spent his boyhood in the Catskill Mountains, where, without any formal instruction, he learned to play the piano and put tunes down on paper. Bent on making headway in popular music, he returned to the city of his birth after finishing high school and found a job in Tin Pan Alley as song plugger and staff pianist. He set his sights on songwriting. But before publishing his first song—"Nobody Knows What a Red-Head Mama Can Do" (Irving Mills and Al Dubin), in 1925—he appeared on the Vaudeville circuit, and sang and played over the radio in Brooklyn and Newark.

In 1927, Fain became acquainted with Irving Kahal. For the next seventeen years—up to the time of Kahal's death— Kahal wrote the lyrics to Fain's music, though sometimes with some outside help from other lyricists. "Let a Smile Be Your Umbrella" and the score for *Manhattan Mary*, starring Ed Wynn, both in the first year of their collaboration, and "Wedding Bells are Breaking Up that Old Gang of Mine," in 1929, brought them a bid from Hollywood, where they were destined to do their best work. Besides their activity in motion pictures, Fain and Kahal were responsible for such leading hits as "Was That the Human Thing To Do?", "When I Take My Sugar to Tea," and "I Can Dream, Can't I?" and scores for about half a dozen Broadway musicals and revues.

VI

Before the end of the 1920s there came out of Tin Pan Alley a song destined to become one of its all-time classics. It was "Star Dust," not by one of the veterans of the Alley, but by a comparative novice named Hoagy Carmichael. Carmichael was born in Bloomington, Indiana, in 1899. Sixteen years later he came to Indianapolis, where he suddenly gave up high school to become a cement mixer on a twelve-hour shift. He completed his high school education after returning to his native city in 1919, then decided to study law. To earn his keep while pursuing these studies, Carmichael played the piano (at which he was self-taught) in various vacation resorts, and organized and booked bands for university dances. This immersion in musical activity led him, in 1924, to write "Riverboat Shuffle," which was published as an instrumental number a year later and was successfully recorded by The Wolverines. (A new edition, in 1939, had lyrics by Dick Voynow, Irving Mills, and Mitchell Parish.) His second song,

"Washboard Blues" (Fred Callahan and Mitchell Parish) was also published and recorded.

After receiving his law degree, Carmichael opened a law office in Miami. He did not stay there long. A recording of "Washboard Blues" by Red Nichols convinced him that music was his domain. He returned to Bloomington, where he made a new recording of "Washboard Blues" with Paul Whiteman's Orchestra, in which he sang the chorus in his now-familiar rasping voice; this recording helped to make the number popular. He now plunged into the maelstrom of musical activity by playing the piano with various outfits, and by demonstrating Tin Pan Alley songs for bands and singers. While all this was going on he managed to write a little masterpiece, "Star Dust."

In his autobiography, *Stardust Trail*, Carmichael tells how he came to write the song. One night, in 1929, he was sitting on the so-called "spooning wall" at the University of Indiana and musing about a girl he had once loved and lost when she deserted him for somebody promising greater security. As he was thinking, and looking up at the star-studded sky, a melody came to him. He rushed over to "The Book Nook," which had a piano, and convinced its proprietor to stay open another half hour so that he could write his song.

In its first version, "Star Dust" was a piano rag without words. In this form it was introduced by Don Redman, without attracting notice. Jimmy Dolan, an arranger, recognized its commercial possibilities if it were played in slower tempo. Victor Young made such an arrangement, and in the new format it was introduced by Isham Jones, and after that was recorded by the Emile Seidel Orchestra with Carmichael at the piano. Now a sweet, sentimental tune, "Star Dust" called for a lyric, which was forthwith provided by Mitchell Parish. Published by Irving Mills in 1929, "Star Dust" now began a slow and cautious ascent to recognition. In the middle 1930s it was played by many splendid musicians who believed in it, among them Artie Shaw (whose recording had such appeal that in five years' time it sold over two million records). Other performers also contributed to the mounting fame of the song, including the Mills Blue Rhythm Band, Eddy Duchin, and André Kostelanetz. By the end of the 1930s, "Star Dust" had firmly established itself as an all-time favorite. It was recorded over three hundred times, was made into forty-six different arrangements; the lyric was translated into forty languages. It is probably the only popular song ever recorded on both sides of a single disk, one side by Tommy Dorsey, the other by Benny Goodman.

While "Star Dust" was soaring to popularity, Carmichael settled in New York where he wrote "Rockin' Chair," to his own lyrics, and "Lazybones" with Johnny Mercer. For a recording of "Rockin' Chair," Carmichael made jazz history by assembling a band which numbered Bix Beiderbecke, Jimmy and Tommy Dorsey, Jack Teagarden, Gene Krupa, Benny Goodman, Bud Freeman, and Joe Venuti. Carmichael went on to extend his career by writing music for the movies, and after that by offering his distinctly personal style of singing and his Hoosier accent in featured roles in motion pictures and on radio and television.

VII

Up to the World War I period, most composers in Tin Pan Alley depended for their income on the royalties they received from the sale of sheet music. It sometimes happened that a composer's songs were played by numerous orchestras, and sung by numerous performers, without having the sheet music move in sizable quantities. Such a composer would, then, see his work grow popular without profiting from this development. It also happened that places of amusement exploited the popular music of the day to promote their businesses, thus deriving monetary advantage from the music while the composers themselves did not.

The inequity of this situation, as far as the popular-music composer was concerned, struck Victor Herbert one day. In 1913 he dined at the fashionable Shanley Restaurant, then situated on 43rd Street in New York where the Paramount Theatre can be found today. Shanley's employed an orchestra which, on the day Herbert was there, played excerpts from his operetta *Sweethearts*, as well as the music of other operetta and Tin Pan Alley composers. It suddenly occurred to Herbert how unjust it was for a restaurant to use the copyrighted work of composers in promoting its business without compensating the author. He consulted his attorney, Nathan Burkan, and they decided to make a test case out of the situation. The litigation dragged on for four years, through all the levels of American courts. In 1917, after two setbacks in the lower courts, the United States Supreme Court ruled in Herbert's favor. Justice Oliver Wendell Holmes said in part: "If music did not pay, it would be given up. If it pays, it pays out of the public's pocket. Whether it pays or not, the purpose of employing it is profit, and that is enough."

This battle convinced Herbert and several others of the crying need for an organization to protect and promote the financial interests of the American popular music. Even before he had received the blessing of the Supreme Court, Herbert had joined with Sousa, George M. Cohan, George W. Meyer and several others in creating a society protecting the performing rights of its members. The idea was hatched by thirty-five men in Lüchow's Restaurant near Union Square early in 1914. On February 13 of the same year these men launched an organization called The American Society of Composers, Authors, and Publishers (ASCAP, for short) at a meeting at the Hotel Claridge in which 150 composers and lyricists and about 20 publishers participated. George Maxwell was elected president and the other officers included Victor Herbert, Glen MacDonough, and John Golden. Soon the machinery was set up by which any outfit using music for public consumption could be licensed to use the work of ASCAP members for a stipulated royalty or fee.

For seven years there was no income to speak of. Many bitter court battles had to be fought to compel restaurants, cabarets, theaters, and so forth, to pay for music which up to now they had been using free. But slowly the opposition succumbed; six thousand restaurants, hotels, cabarets, motion picture theaters were compelled to pay a fee to ASCAP for the use of copyrighted music of its members through special licenses issued by that organization. In 1921, the members of ASCAP, numbering about 250, were beginning to draw modest royalties for the first time as the organization divided a melon of about $80,000. In 1922, the intake rose to $143,000, and in 1923 to almost $200,000.

Eventually, performance fees had to be paid to ASCAP by any organization that used music for profit: hotels, restaurants, cocktail bars, night clubs, radio and television stations, recording companies, motion picture theaters, and producers. Thus, with every possible source of public performance caught in its net, ASCAP became a powerful agency, protecting the financial interest of the American composer. By the middle 1950s it had branch offices in over thirty American cities and affiliations with similar groups in over twenty European countries. Over 4,000 members now divided the approximately $20,000,000 annual income from 30,000 licenses.

The income, after deduction for running expenses, was divided equally between the publishers on the one hand, and the composers and lyricists on the other. Originally, the amount received by any composer or lyricist depended upon an arbitrary rating assigned to him, a position varying with the writer's importance. Composers like Irving Berlin, George Gershwin, Jerome Kern, Cole Porter, or Richard Rodgers were given top rating, or "AA positions," and up to World War II their income from ASCAP amounted to about $25,000 a year. After 1950 a more equitable method of distributing royalties was evolved. The new method was dependent upon the number of performances received by a composer or lyricist through the various media. Thus in the middle 1950s, composers and lyricists most often performed—men like Richard Rodgers, Oscar Hammerstein II, Irving Berlin, Cole Porter, Otto Harbach, Ira Gershwin, and the estates of George Gershwin, Jerome Kern, and Lorenz Hart—could count on about $50,000 a year. (Since Berlin and Porter received ratings both as composers and as lyricists, each drew $100,000.) One step below—in the $30,000 to $40,000 a year bracket—came Harold Arlen, Arthur Schwartz, Jule Styne, Frank Loesser, Hoagy Carmichael, Jimmy McHugh, and the Sigmund Romberg estate, among others. In the $20,000 to $30,000 a year group appear Walter Donaldson, Jimmy van Heusen, the estate of Victor Herbert, besides many, many others. Thus under the new arrangement, a composer and lyricist who is no longer productive, or no longer alive, but whose work is still vital and widely heard, could still receive top fees, if his music or lyrics are performed as often as those of his still productive competitors. What this means to a writer was once described by Deems Taylor when he pointed out that Stephen Foster died with thirty-eight cents in his purse, but that if he were alive today he could count on anywhere from $20,000 to $40,000 a year from ASCAP, even if he stopped writing a note of music.

A rival to ASCAP came into existence in the fall of 1940 as a result of the bitter struggle erupting between that organization and the radio networks. In 1940, a five-year contract between ASCAP and radio expired. In negotiating a new contract, ASCAP demanded about $9,000,000 a year, or twice what it had been receiving. The radio executives refused to pay a fee they regarded as outrageous. In defiance, radio set up an organization of its own, Broadcast Music Incorporated (BMI) to produce music for radio broadcasting. In 1941, the music of all ASCAP members left the air, and only the works of young and comparatively unknown composers affiliated with the new BMI—or music in the public domain, like the songs of Stephen Foster—was heard. The fight continued right into the fall of 1941, when a compromise was reached. ASCAP accepted a new five-year contract renewed at its termination for an additional five years, in which it was offered a fee of about $3,000,000, about a third of the amount originally demanded.

This, to be sure, represented a defeat for the giant organization. A rival group had come into being which in a decade would draw about $6,000,000 a year and which within the first three years produced such substantial song hits as "The Breeze and I," adapted by Al Stillman from Ernesto Lecuona's *Andalucia;* "I Hear a Rhapsody" by George Fragos and Jack Baker; "I Don't Want to Set the World on Fire," by Eddie Seiler, Sol Marcus, Bennie Benjamin, and Eddie Durham; "Deep in the Heart of Texas," by June Hershey and Don Swander; and "Pistol Packin' Mama," by Al Dexter. Moreover, in the first year after the compromise, the net income of ASCAP was almost half of what it had previously been. But the defeat was only temporary. In 1944, ASCAP earned $6,000,000; between 1945 and 1947, $7,000,000 a year; in 1948, $8,000,000; and in the middle 1950s, $20,000,000 a year. If anything, ASCAP has since grown more gigantic and influential. Today it is a major force in American popular music—the most significant agency protecting the financial rights and privileges of its members.

VIII

Tin Pan Alley—both as a street and as the methods and esthetics with which the street is associated—passed out of existence in or about 1930. The giant development of the recording industry, radio, television, the juke box, and talking pictures opened for the song business fabulous new worlds of exploitation, which made obsolete the older techniques of writing and selling songs.

Each of the above media became, in varying degrees, significant influences in our popular music. The year 1919 was the first in which the record business was responsible for making a song a hit. In that year George Stoddard wrote "Mary" (not to be confused with the song of the same name by George M. Cohan) which he failed to get either performed or published. Somehow he managed to convince the Victor company to record it and, in about three months, it sold 300,000 disks and earned for him a royalty of $15,000.

The recording industry was now to become an instrument for popularizing unknown songs—particularly after the boom in records in the middle 1930s. In 1939, forty-five million popular records were sold; a decade later, this figure was tripled. Records now not only became a rich source of revenue for the song business—bringing in somewhere in the neighborhood of $10,000,000 a year—but they also became a means of bringing new songs to the American people, in recordings by the public's singing favorites. When Eddie Cantor signed the then unprecedented five-year contract with Brunswick, in 1920, at a guarantee of over $200,000, he became one of the first of many singing stars who, through the years could on a single disk bring overnight popularity to a hitherto unknown song— from Cantor and Jolson through Bing Crosby, Kate Smith, and Frank Sinatra to Perry Como, Eddie Fisher, Johnnie Ray, and (perhaps the greatest phenomenon produced by the record industry) Elvis Presley.

The radio, whose importance in our social scheme became evident in the 1920s, also helped produce song hits—and new singing stars. The voices of the Happiness Boys, Whispering Jack Smith, Morton Downey, Rudy Vallée, Bing Crosby, Kate Smith, among others, dominated the airwaves in the 1920s and 1930s. Each was able to make a song successful, sometimes with a single broadcast. In the early history of radio broadcasting Rudy Vallée became identified with "I'm Just a Vagabond Lover," which he wrote with Leon Zimmerman; Bing Crosby with "Where the Blue of the Night Meets the Gold of the Day," by himself, Roy Turk, and Fred E. Ahlert; Kate Smith with "When the Moon Comes over the Mountain," written by her collaboratively with Harry Woods and Howard Johnson; Morton Downey with "Carolina Moon," by Benny Davis and Joe Burke. These were the theme songs for the broadcasts of these outstanding radio personalities, serving to identify them to their audiences; but there were many other songs which each of these performers brought to nationwide success through the radio microphone.

As radio grew and developed, small stations began dotting the country, each catering to a limited geographical sphere. Unable to purchase live entertainment for its daily schedule, these stations resorted to the expediency of filling in some of their hours with phonograph music. The popularity of this kind of broadcasting by smaller stations became so widely prevalent that, finally, a major record company instituted legal suit to prevent the broadcast of recorded music. A decision handed down by the United States Circuit Court finally upheld the rights of any radio station to use records for its programs.

Recorded programs over the air led to the birth of the disk jockey, a term apparently coined by *Variety* in 1937 to designate radio announcers who played records with interpolated remarks about the various recordings, and who answered requests telephoned by listeners for special numbers. After World War II—with jockeys like Martin Block of the "Make Believe Ballroom" in New York and Al Jarvis in Hollywood—the disk jockey became a power in the music business. He was a potent force in creating hits and keeping them alive in public interest.

In 1935, radio provided a valuable and fairly accurate barometer of popular-song successes with "The Hit Parade," a weekly program presenting the ten "top" tunes of the week, based on record and sheet-music sales, frequency of juke box performance, and so forth. This program was inaugurated on April 20, 1935 with Kern's "Lovely to Look at" (Dorothy Fields and Jimmy McHugh) as the number 1 song, and with other numbers including Kern's "I Won't Dance," (Fields and McHugh), Warren's "Lullaby of Broadway" (Al Dubin), and George Gershwin's "Soon" (Ira Gershwin).

In the next quarter of a century, "The Hit Parade"—originally with Mark Warnow as the conductor, but after his death taken over by his brother, Raymond Scott—continued to point up first on the radio, then on television, the varying fluctuations in the fortunes of the week's top songs. Berlin's "White Christmas" appeared more often on this program than any other song: thirty-two times. The next four were: Richard Rodgers' "People Will Say We're in Love'" (Oscar Hammerstein II), thirty; "Harbor Lights" by Hugh Williams (Jimmy Kennedy), twenty-nine; and Sammy Fain's "I'll be Seeing You" (Irving Kahal) and Harry Warren's "You'll Never Know" (Mack Gordon), twenty-four each. "Too Young" by Sid Lippman (Sylvia Dee) had the greatest number of appearances in the Number 1 slot with twelve; "Because of You" by Dudley Wilkinson (Arthur Hammerstein) was second with eleven. Three songs assumed the Number 2 position most often with seven appearances each; two of them were by Richard Rodgers, "Bewitched" (Hart) and "No Other Love" (Oscar Hammerstein II).

Television became a force to reckon with in the song industry through avenues other than "The Hit Parade." A song like "Let Me Go, Lover," used as an integral part of a dramatic presentation by Studio One in 1954, could literally sweep into the best-seller class as sheet music and recording as a result of that one television presentation. The power of television to sell a song was again proved in the next two years with Jimmy van Heusen's "Love and Marriage" (Sammy Chan) heard in the

musical adaptation of Thornton Wilder's *Our Town,* and with
"When You're in Love" by Arthur Schwartz (Maxwell Anderson), from the musical adaptation of Maxwell Anderson's *High Tor,* starring Bing Crosby.

IX

Old techniques for issuing and publicizing songs thus made
way for new, as a single record, radio program, motion picture,
or television broadcast could bring a song to many millions,
often at a single performance. The old sources of revenue—the
sale of sheet music, and royalties from recordings and Broadway productions—seemed niggardly when compared to the rewards offered not only by these but also by other new media.

If the popular song had been big business in Union Square
and on 28th Street, it was now ready to become a mighty
trust. Smaller firms were swallowed by larger ones, and the
larger ones by still greater ones, as capital from Hollywood
and radio corporations was available for the purchase of these
houses. When sound came to the screen, and the talking picture
needed as many songs as it could put its hands on, the Warner
Brothers put through a giant deal of $10,000,000 to buy out
three leading Tin Pan Alley firms: Harms, Witmark, and Remick. Rival motion-picture studios followed the lead of the Warners in buying out other major publishing houses. Tin Pan Alley
was now receiving its death blow. Publishers not consumed by
Hollywood left 28th Street either for lavish offices in Radio City
or Hollywood or to concentrate in the Brill Building at 1619
Broadway. The song business was still operating in high gear,
but it was Tin Pan Alley no more. The old methods, the old traditions were gone.

The song plugger now became a "contact man" whose
sphere of activity was the record company, the radio and television studio, Hollywood, and "meetings" where leading performers heard the new songs. The job of selling songs for major
performances was now greatly complicated. Many bandleaders

and singing stars had partnerships in publishing houses; many radio networks were in the record business, and so were some songwriters; many publishing houses had their own artist bureaus; and some record companies had affiliated publishing interests. With each having his own ax to grind, the receptivity to songs by outside firms was greatly diminished.

Sheet music no longer was the lifeblood of the industry. Now it was the phonograph record, more than any other single element, that spelled success or failure for a song. As Abel Green wrote in *Variety:* "More than ever, an inanimate object—a vinylite platter running three minutes, regardless of the 33, 45 or 78 speed—is king of Tin Pan Alley. The pop-music business seems to revolve almost entirely around the revolving biscuit." With 22,000,000 phonographs in use, half a million juke boxes with an annual intake of $250,000,000, and 2,000 disk jockeys spinning records before a radio microphone, a song had to be on a record before it could hope to make the grade. Because a hit song was now heard so often, and in so many different places, the life of a hit was curtailed. Before 1925, a hit was expected to survive sixteen months and sell over a million copies of sheet music; a quarter century later its life span was only a few weeks, and a sale of 250,-000 copies of sheet music was considered excellent.

X

In the old Tin Pan Alley, popular composers were usually musically illiterate troubadours who dictated thirty-two bar choruses to an amanuensis. But in the new song industry, popular composers were generally sophisticated and knowledgeable musicians capable of employing the fullest resources of serious music in their popular writing. Nevertheless, one songwriting practice, prevalent on 28th Street, flourished even more richly in the publishing houses of the 1940s and 1950s: borrowing melodies from classical music and classical composers.

In the closing decades of the nineteenth century, Percy

Gaunt borrowed the tune of the Neapolitan folk song, *"Spagnola,"* for "The Bowery," and Joseph J. Sullivan used a fragment from Wagner's *Lohengrin* for "Where Did You Get That Hat?" In 1906, Vincent Bryan, himself a songwriter, told an interviewer for the New York *Herald:* "Filching is the only thing that counts in the songwriting business. All you need to compose a song that will sell is a good memory." And three years before that, a lyricist provided the following formula for writing hit songs:

> *As for the music, you'll manage that easily*
> *Get a few songs that were written before.*
> *Swipe 'em, and change 'em, and have 'em sung breezily,*
> *Get an arranger, you'll want nothing more.*

The practice of using other people's melodies for a popular song became big business in 1918 when Harry Carroll wrote "I'm Always Chasing Rainbows" (Joseph McCarthy). Carroll, a café-house pianist and after that a composer for Winter Garden productions, had produced a sizable quota of hit songs before he dipped into the classics for his ideas. By 1913 he had written "The Trail of the Lonesome Pine" (Ballard Mac-Donald) and, in 1914, "By the Beautiful Sea" (Harold R. Atteridge), each a million-copy success. Then in 1918, he lifted a principal melody from Chopin's Fantasie-Impromptu in C-sharp minor and with words by McCarthy introduced it in the Broadway musical, *Oh Look,* as "I'm Always Chasing Rainbows." It became a leader in Tin Pan Alley, and one of Carroll's greatest money-makers. And it proved to Tin Pan Alley tunesmiths that tune-lifting was a highly profitable trade.

In 1920, Vincent Rose, collaborating with Al Jolson, wrote "Avalon," which Jolson helped to skyrocket to popularity. The composer here helped himself to an aria from Puccini's opera, *Tosca,* changing the minor of the aria to a major key. Since all of Puccini's music was strictly protected by international copyright, his publishers brought suit against Rose. At the trial, on January 28, 1921, the plaintiffs had a trio play "Avalon" after a phonograph recording of the *Tosca* aria had been heard. The similarity was so striking that the publishers of Puccini's music were awarded damages of $25,000 and confiscation of all future "Avalon" royalties. A small recording company, which had gambled all its resources on the recording —and which, for a time, appeared to have won the jackpot— had to go out of business.

But as long as Tin Pan Alley composers confined their larceny to music in the public domain, their efforts were more rewarding. Franz Schubert earned only a little more than $500.00 from an entire lifetime of magnificent creation. But Sigmund Romberg, lifting only a single theme from the *Unfinished Symphony* earned over $100,000 in royalties from "Song of Love." This song appeared in his operetta, *Blossom Time*, made up of Schubert's melodies—a score that probably earned for Romberg through the years close to a million dollars.

In the early 1920s there was a minor epidemic of tune borrowing. Pieces like Rimsky-Korsakov's *Scheherazade, Song of India,* and *Hymn to the Sun;* Cui's *Orientale;* Ponchielli's "Dance of the Hours" from *La Gioconda;* Liszt's *Liebestraum;* MacDowell's *To a Wild Rose*—even, strange to say, works like the funeral march from Chopin's *Sonata in B minor* and the Negro spiritual, "Deep River"—were either presented in jazzed-up versions or used with lyrics for popular consumption. This practice led Ernest Newman, England's foremost music critic, to bellow: "Paws off!" In France, the French Society of Composers issued a formal protest. Even in this country there was some strong opposition. Several publications devoted to Negro interests attacked the practice of adapting Negro spirituals for Tin Pan Alley tunes. And the principal music critic of the New York *Times,* Richard Aldrich, wrote in 1924: "One of the most successful and lucrative methods of writing a song is to take the ideas of some musician who has written something that the world values, and change it just enough to make it seem something different—and, of course, cheaper and commoner."

But the opposition of serious musicians and critics did not keep tunesmiths from invading and trespassing on the private property of the masters. In our own day innumerable hits owe their origin to the serious musical repertory. Mozart was brought out of the eighteenth-century drawing room into the twentieth-century honky-tonk in Raymond Scott's "In an 18th-Century Drawing Room." The sedate Tchaikovsky *Concerto in B minor* was transformed by Erskine Butterfield into a "Boogie de Concerto." At one time, Tchaikovsky's music was heard more often on "The Hit Parade" than the songs of any other single composer, not excluding Gershwin, Berlin, Rodgers, Porter, or Kern. Tchaikovsky was reincarnated in "The Things I Love" (Harold Barlow and Lew Harris), "Our Love" (Larry Clinton, Buddy Bernier, and Bob Emmerich), "On the Isle of May" (Mack David and André Kostelanetz), "Tonight We Love" (Bobby Worth, Ray Austin, Freddy Martin), "Concerto for Two" (Jack Lawrence and Robert C. Haring), "Moon Love" (Mack David, Mack Davis, and André Kostelanetz). Chopin's *Polonaise in A-flat major* became "Till the End of Time" (Buddy Kaye and Ted Mossman)—and for nineteen consecutive weeks made "The Hit Parade." The same authors, Kaye and Mossman, went to Rachmaninoff's *Second Piano Concerto* for "Full Moon and Empty Arms." A theme from Wagner's *Tristan und Isolde* was used by Robert Henning and Heinz Provost for "Intermezzo." The Argentine tango, *"El Choclo"* became at the hands of Lester Allen and Robert Hill "Kiss of Fire," while Lecuona's *Andalucia* was transformed by Al Stillman into "The Breeze and I." Johnny Burke, under the assumed name of K. C. Rogan, rewrote a little piano piece for children by Robert Schumann into "Wild Horsemen." Even such comparatively esoteric composers as Debussy, Ravel, and Borodin were raided: Debussy's *Reverie* became "My Reverie" (Larry Clinton); Ravel's *Pavane pour une Infante défunte*, "The Lamp Is Low" (Mitchell Parish, Peter De Rose, and Bert Shefter); and Borodin's Polovtsian Dance from *Prince Igor*, "Stranger in Paradise" (Robert Wright and George Forrest).

XI

Whatever the faults of the old Tin Pan Alley of 28th Street, and they were many, it still had been capable of producing composers like Irving Berlin, Jerome Kern, George Gershwin, Ernest R. Ball, and others like them. It is an interesting—indeed, a significant—fact that since the death of the old Tin Pan Alley, there has not arisen a single new composer of first rank whose roots lie in the song business itself. Since the middle 1930s, the new men in popular music are those who received their recognition, stimulation, and assignments from the stage, screen, and radio.

The truth is that, unlike the old Tin Pan Alley, the song industry today is not receptive to unknown composers. It is difficult to conceive of a teen-ager penetrating the holy walls of our present-day song publishers the way Irving Berlin, Jerome Kern, and George Gershwin did many years ago, to get a hearing with the principal executives, and to find their embryo efforts published. The mountain of songs by unknown composers regularly issued by the Alley in years gone by has today been reduced to a mole hill. The large publisher today is indifferent to any new songs whose angles of exploitation are not assured by a distinguished performer or bandleader willing to introduce it; a large record company ready to put it on a disk; a Broadway show, motion picture, national radio hookup, radio or television program prepared to provide a springboard for its launching. Such a situation makes the emergence of new young composers extremely difficult.

When the death of old Tin Pan Alley became an established fact, *Downbeat*, the magazine of popular music, conducted a national contest to find a new name with which to christen our popular-song industry. The none-too-satisfactory name that was finally coined was "crew-cut music." Perhaps what the American popular music industry needs most today is not just another name to replace that of Tin Pan Alley. Perhaps what it needs most is another Tin Pan Alley, like the one that had existed and flourished in Union Square and on 28th Street.

chapter ten

JAZZ BECOMES
A SOPHISTICATED LADY

THE SOPHISTICATION of jazz—the effort to bring to it the discipline and richness of materials found in serious music—was a tendency prevalent in the best songs of George Gershwin, Jerome Kern, and other leaders in Tin Pan Alley in the 1920s. Though these songs had little blood relationship with the original product produced in New Orleans and Chicago, they came to be known as "jazz." The same tendency to enrich jazz also prevailed in the performances of the Paul Whiteman Orchestra, a pioneer in presenting popular music in symphonic dress; and it is found in the richly inventive symphonic arrangements that Ferde Grofé prepared for Whiteman. Finally, this tendency prevailed in the symphonic-jazz compositions of George Gershwin and Ferde Grofé, among others, in which elements of good jazz were successfully combined with the forms, techniques, and methods of the classical art.

It was a significant development in our popular music when the three most productive exponents of symphonic jazz in the early 1920s—Whiteman, Grofé, and Gershwin—decided to work collaboratively, each ploughing his respective field. Together, and within a short period, they were able to integrate the style of symphonic jazz and to bring it to universal acceptance.

Paul Whiteman and Ferde Grofé came to jazz by way of good music; George Gershwin, although he studied piano and harmony, through Tin Pan Alley. All three had a common goal. They were convinced that jazz—which in the 1920s meant not the hot music of New Orleans but more generally American popular music of all kinds—was a significant musical idiom, worthy of the attention of serious composers. Whiteman and Grofé served their apprenticeship in symphony orchestras. Both felt that their rightful place was in popular music. Before long each abandoned his respective job to organize a jazz orchestra. Their paths crossed in 1919, and it is at this point that jazz music in America arrived at a turning-point.

Paul Whiteman was the son of a well-known music educator in Denver, where he was born in 1890. After studying the violin, Paul became a member of the Denver Symphony Orchestra. During this time he sometimes gathered some of the men of the orchestra for impromptu rag sessions. After an additional period as violinist of the San Francisco Symphony Orchestra, he abandoned serious music for popular. It is believed that the final push sending him to jazz was a performance of hot music heard in a San Francisco dive. In any case, he found a job with a small jazz band, then lost it because he could not play in true rag style. For the next few months he tried assimilating ragtime idiom. In 1917 he organized a band of his own, but before it could give many performances, America was at war and Whiteman was mustered into the Navy. After the war, Whiteman reorganized his band and filled several engagements in California. A successful appearance at the Alexandria Hotel in Los Angeles marked the beginning of the Paul Whiteman Orchestra. Whiteman was so well liked there that he remained at the hotel for a full year.

At this decisive moment in his career, when he approached

the threshold of success for the first time, he met Ferde Grofé and engaged him as orchestrator. Grofé, like Whiteman, was the son of serious musicians, born in New York City in 1892. He spent his childhood in music study, then in 1909 joined the Los Angeles Symphony as violist. For a while he combined his activity with the symphony orchestra with engagements with ragtime bands. Then he left symphonic music and organized a jazz band of his own. He was conducting that band in a Los Angeles dance hall in 1919 when Whiteman heard him. The ingenuity of Grofé's orchestrations led Whiteman to engage Grofé for his own orchestra. From then on, through 1924, Grofé wrote all the orchestrations played by the Whiteman orchestra; and the Whiteman orchestra played them in carefully prepared performances. Grofé's imaginative musical settings, which revealed a sure understanding of orchestral sound and of the possibilities of each instrument, and Whiteman's suave and elegant performances, created a new era for popular music.

The Paul Whiteman Orchestra—which at various periods included such outstanding jazz artists as Bix Beiderbecke, Red Nichols, Jimmy and Tommy Dorsey, Joe Venuti, Bing Crosby, and Mildred Bailey—now went from one triumph to another: on phonograph records, which sold in the millions; on the Vaudeville stage, where it was a headliner; at the Palais Royal night club in New York; in such important Broadway musical productions as the *Ziegfeld Follies* and the *George White Scandals;* and, in the spring of 1923, in an extensive tour of Europe. Whiteman was now crowned by press and public "the king of jazz," the title of a motion picture in which he starred for Universal in 1930.

But symphonic jazz in the early 1920s was ruled not by a single king but by a triumvirate. There was not only Paul Whiteman, but also Ferde Grofé; and with them there was the composer, George Gershwin. The songs that Gershwin was writing for the various editions of the *Scandals* beginning with 1920—

and others interpolated in various other musical productions on Broadway—played no small part in making jazz a sophisticated art. Songs like "Do It Again" (B. G. DeSylva), which Irene Bordoni introduced in *The French Doll* in 1922, and "I'll Build a Stairway to Paradise" (B. G. DeSylva and Arthur Francis) and "Somebody Loves Me" (Ballard MacDonald), both in the *Scandals* between 1922 and 1924, were in their own class. Besides possessing a warm, fresh, and at times, a highly personal lyricism, they revealed an inventiveness of rhythmic technique, a dexterity in the use of changing meters and staggered accents, and at times an unorthodox harmonic approach that set them sharply apart from the popular songs of that day. No wonder, then, that so serious a musician as Beryl Rubinstein—a concert pianist, and later on director of the Cleveland Conservatory—could as early as 1922 speak of Gershwin as "a genius." Rubinstein told a newspaper interviewer: "With Gershwin's style and seriousness, he is not definitely of the popular music school, but is one of the really outstanding figures in this country's serious musical efforts. . . . This young man has great charm and a most magnetic personality, and I really believe that America will at no distant date honor him for his talent . . . and that when we speak of American composers, George Gershwin's name will be prominent on our list."

Recognition of the artistic importance of Gershwin's popular songs came from still another, and no less unexpected, corner. On November 1, 1923, Eva Gauthier, a celebrated concert singer, gave a recital in Aeolian Hall, New York, in which she performed works by such old masters as Byrd, Purcell, and Bellini, and such moderns as Schoenberg, Milhaud, and Hindemith. With remarkable courage and independence, she interpolated into her program one group devoted entirely to American jazz—the first time that any concert artist dared to make such a move. In this group she included Berlin's "Alexander's Ragtime Band," Jerome Kern's "The Siren's Song"

(P. G. Wodehouse), Walter Donaldson's "Carolina in the Morning," and three songs by George Gershwin, "I'll Build a Stairway to Paradise," "Innocent Ingenue Baby" (A. E. Thomas and Brian Hooker), and "Swanee." A fourth Gershwin song, "Do It Again," came as an encore, and was received so thunderously that it had to be repeated.

"It seemed to one listener," wrote Deems Taylor in his music column in the New York *World* the following morning, "that the jazz numbers stood up amazingly well, not only as entertainment but as music. . . . What they did possess was melodic interest and continuity, harmonic appropriateness, well-balanced and almost classically severe form, and subtle and fascinating rhythm—in short the qualities that any sincere and interesting music possesses."

For this popular-song group, Mme. Gauthier called upon George Gershwin to serve as her accompanist. Deems Taylor continues: "The singer reappeared, followed by a tall, black-haired young man who was far from possessing the icy aplomb of those to whom playing on the platform at Aeolian Hall is an old story. He bore under his arm a small bundle of sheet music with lurid black and yellow covers. The audience began to show signs of relaxation; this promised to be amusing. . . . Young Mr. Gershwin began to do mysterious and fascinating rhythmic and contrapuntal stunts with the accompaniment." When this same concert was repeated in Boston a month later, H. T. Parker said of Gershwin's accompaniments in the *Evening Transcript:* "He diversified them with cross-rhythms, wove them into a pliant and outspringing counterpoint; set in pauses and accents; sustained cadences; gave character to the measures where in the singer's voice was still. . . . He is the beginning of the age of sophisticated jazz."

Carl van Vechten was another to recognize the significance of an event that for the first time brought not only American popular music, but also George Gershwin into a serious concert auditorium. He wrote: "I consider this one of the very most

important events in American musical history. The Philharmonic will be doing it in two years."

II

It was, perhaps, inevitable that the three outstanding exponents of symphonic jazz—Whiteman, Grofé, and Gershwin
—should team up for a single effort. When they did, another
slice of popular-music history was carved.

Paul Whiteman had, of course, been playing Gershwin's
songs since 1920, and Grofé had orchestrated them. But Whiteman entered into a more direct collaboration with Gershwin
in 1922 when the Whiteman Orchestra played in the pit of the
Scandals. For the 1922 edition, George Gershwin wrote the
music for a one-act Negro jazz opera, *Blue Monday*, libretto
by B. G. DeSylva. Since Whiteman and his orchestra were in
the pit, the conductor had to work with Gershwin in preparing
the opera for performance. This took place at the Globe Theatre on August 29, 1922, with a cast that included Lester Allen,
Jack McGowan, and Coletta Ryan.

The setting for the little opera was a basement café on
Lenox Avenue, in New York's Harlem. There Joe and Tom are
rivals for Vi's love. When Joe decides to pay a secret visit to
his mother—and is ashamed to own up about such a sentimental
journey—Vi suspects he is about to have a rendezvous with
another woman. Tom stirs up Joe's girl to a point where, blind
with jealousy, she shoots and kills Joe. When he dies, Vi sees a
telegram that confirms that Joe had been telling the truth.

The somewhat silly libretto lacked credibility. If the opera
had any interest it was because of a few high moments in the
Gershwin score: the poignant "Blue Monday Blues"; the moving spiritual, "I'm Going to See My Mother"; the full-blooded
aria, "Has Anybody Seen My Joe?" In moments such as these a
perceptive listener can detect suggestions and anticipations of
creative powers which matured years later in *Porgy and Bess*.
But *Blue Monday* was, as a whole, an apprentice effort; it

lacked integration and dramatic truth; it suffered from a loss of musical continuity; its recitatives were naïvely put together.

Blue Monday disappeared from the *Scandals* after the opening night. George White felt that the somber mood of the opera chilled the audience to a point where it was incapable of enjoying the numbers that followed. Besides some of the New York reviewers had been destructive. Several years later, on December 29, 1925, Paul Whiteman revived the opera in a Carnegie Hall concert. Now renamed *135th Street*, it was given with a new cast headed by Blossom Seeley and Benny Fields. Whiteman again revived the opera a decade later at another Carnegie Hall concert; it was introduced over television on the "Omnibus" program on March 29, 1953; and a part of it was seen in the Gershwin screen biography, *Rhapsody in Blue*.

For the second Whiteman revival of *135th Street*, in 1936, the opera was given in a new orchestration by Ferde Grofé. But more than a decade earlier Grofé had joined forces with Whiteman and Gershwin to create what has since been accepted as a red-letter day in American music: the première of the *Rhapsody in Blue*.

The story of how the *Rhapsody in Blue* came to be written has often been told, and not always accurately. The basic facts are these. Late in 1923, Whiteman planned to bring his orchestra into a serious concert auditorium with a program devoted entirely to American popular music. His purpose was to prove that jazz was an idiom commanding respect. To give his concert added significance he asked Gershwin to write for him a new jazz work, for Whiteman had not forgotten the profound impression that *Blue Monday* had made upon him a year earlier, how it had revealed to him the new horizons which jazz could reach. Gershwin said he would write such a work for Whiteman, but being overwhelmed by his commitments for the theater he soon forgot his promise. One day, however, late in the winter of 1923 he read a brief notice in the New York *Herald Tribune* to the effect that he was writing a "jazz symphony" for Whiteman's forthcoming concert at Aeolian Hall on February 12, 1924. That announcement, and the imminence of the concert, galvanized him into action. Some ideas for a large orchestral work in the jazz idiom had already occurred to him and had been put down in a notebook. He now went to work in earnest, choosing the form of the rhapsody because its free and elastic form allowed him greater freedom in working out his ideas. He completed his music in a two-piano version on January 7, 1924. Ferde Grofé completed the orchestration for piano and jazz orchestra on February 4, and Ira Gershwin christened the new work *Rhapsody in Blue*.

Whiteman's historic concert took place at Aeolian Hall on Lincoln's Birthday of 1924. Though the house was over-crowded—and filled with celebrities not only from Tin Pan Alley and Broadway, but also from Carnegie Hall—it resulted in a deficit of $7,000 which Whiteman paid from his own pocket. For Whiteman had spared no expense in making the concert a gala affair, regarding it as he did an artistic event of major importance. Hugh C. Ernst explained to the audience in an introductory talk: "The experiment is to be purely educational. Mr. Whiteman intends to point out . . . the tremendous strides which have been made in popular music from the day of discordant Jazz, which sprang into existence about ten years ago from nowhere in particular, to the really melodious music of today."

This was Whiteman's complete program:

I. True Form of Jazz
   a. Ten years ago—"The Livery Stable Blues"
   b. With modern embellishment—
      "Mama Loves Papa" .... Baer

II. Comedy Selections
   a. Origin of "Yes, We Have No Bananas" .... Silver
   b. Instrumental Comedy—"So This Is Venice" .. Thomas
     (Adapted from *The Carnival of Venice*)

III. Contrast—Legitimate Scoring vs. Jazzing
    a. Selection in True Form—"Whispering" .. Schoenberger
    b. Same Selection with Jazz Treatment

IV. Recent Compositions with Modern Score
    a. "Limehouse Blues" .... Braham
    b. "I Love You" .... Archer
    c. "Raggedy Ann" .... Kern

V. Zez Confrey (Piano)
    a. Medley of Popular Airs
    b. "Kitten on the Keys" .... Confrey
    c. "Ice Cream and Art"
    d. "Nickel in the Slot" .... Confrey
      (Accompanied by the orchestra)

VI. Flavoring a Selection with Borrowed Themes
    "Russian Rose" .... Grofé
    (Based on the *Volga Boat Song*)

VII. Semi-Symphonic Arrangement of Popular Melodies
    a. "Alexander's Ragtime Band" .... Berlin
    b. "A Pretty Girl Is Like a Melody" .... Berlin
    c. "Orange Blossoms in California" .... Berlin

VIII. A Suite of Serenades .... Herbert
    a. Spanish
    b. Chinese
    c. Cuban
    d. Oriental

IX. Adaptation of Standard Selections to Dance Rhythm
    a. "Pale Moon" .... Logan
    b. "To a Wild Rose" .... MacDowell
    c. "Chansonette" .... Friml

X. George Gershwin (Piano)
    Rhapsody in Blue .... Gershwin
    (Accompanied by the orchestra)

XI. In the Field of the Classics
    Pomp and Circumstance .... Elgar

This program—in which the Victor Herbert *Suite,* like Gershwin's *Rhapsody,* was a world première—was a strange, almost indiscriminating, potpourri of the good and the bad in popular music; and none of it was *real* jazz. It was not a program able to sustain the interest of the discriminating listener; the similarity of style and orchestral coloring in the various numbers and the lack of any genuine sustaining musical interest made the concert, after a while, a bore. But for the Gershwin *Rhapsody in Blue,* the event might well have been a failure. Up to the moment the Gershwin *Rhapsody* appeared on the long program, the audience showed increasing signs of fatigue and restlessness. Then came the opening clarinet trill of the *Rhapsody in Blue,* and the audience was magnetized to attention. This was something definitely new—a refreshing, even exciting, change from the dull routines that had preceded it. The opening clarinet yawp plunged into the first theme—a brash, impudent, saucy subject that not only set the mood for the entire work but was the voice for the entire era of the frenetic and convention-shattering 1920s. Other ideas, no less infectious, followed, culminating in the broad rhapsodic slow section for strings which has since become one of the most celebrated melodies in serious American music, and Whiteman's signature music. The *Rhapsody* came to a close with a brief and dramatic coda.

The *Rhapsody in Blue* gave point and meaning to an otherwise dull and poorly organized program. It was the one work that pointed out the future of symphonic jazz and suggested its possibilities. Single-handed, the *Rhapsody* converted Whiteman's concert from an exotic novelty, to be forgotten a day later, into a musical event of historic importance.

The reaction of the music critics was varied. There were those whose enthusiasm knew no limits. Henry O. Osgood, assistant editor of *Musical Courier,* said that the première of the *Rhapsody in Blue* was a more important event than that of Stravinsky's *The Rite of Spring.* Henry T. Finck felt that Gershwin was "far superior to Schoenberg, Milhaud, and the rest of the futurist fellows." Gilbert W. Gabriel wrote about the composition that the "beginning and the ending of it were stunning. . . . Mr. Gershwin has an irrepressible pack of talents, and there is an element of inevitability about his piece." W. J. Henderson described the music as "highly ingenious" and Deems Taylor felt it displayed "a latent ability on the part of this young composer to say something of considerable interest in his chosen idiom."

At the opposite pole stood critics like Lawrence Gilman and Pitts Sanborn. "How trite and feeble and conventional the tunes are, how sentimental and vapid the harmonic treatment, under its disguise of fussy and futile counterpart," lamented Gilman. Sanborn complained that the music "runs off into empty passage work and meaningless repetition."

The critics may analyze and dissect, praise or blame. But in the last analysis it is the music public, and not the critics, who raise a musical work to the status of a classic. The music public of the entire world has elevated the *Rhapsody in Blue* to a position of first significance among the outstanding works of the twentieth century. It is doubtful if there is any other serious musical work written since 1900 that has been played so often as Gershwin's, that is loved so universally, that is so well known in so many different places. It has been arranged for solo piano, two pianos, eight pianos; for piano and symphony orchestra, and violin and symphony orchestra; for an orchestra of harmonicas, and an orchestra of mandolins. It has been interpreted as a Grecian ballet, a modernistic ballet, and a tap dance. In 1930, the Roxy Theatre in New York paid Gershwin $10,000 a week to appear on its stage and play the work; while in the same year Fox paid the biggest figure ($50,000) offered up to then for a musical composition to be included in a motion picture. In 1946, the *Rhapsody* gave its name as a title for the Gershwin screen biography. The royalties from the sale of sheet music, records, and performance rights have reached beyond $250,000 in a quarter of a century. The *Rhapsody in Blue* made Gershwin wealthy; and it carried him to world recognition as a serious composer.

More important even than its immense financial success and its world-wide popularity is its influence on the music of our generation. The *Rhapsody in Blue* was the liberation of jazz from Tin Pan Alley; it brought jazz into the free open world of serious music where from this time on it would occupy a place of honor. What Walter Damrosch later said of Gershwin's subsequent *Concerto in F,* applies as well to the *Rhapsody.* "Various composers have been walking around jazz like a cat around a plate of hot soup, waiting for it to cool off so that they could enjoy it without burning their tongues, hitherto accustomed only to the more tepid liquid distilled by cooks of the classical school. Lady Jazz, adorned with her intriguing rhythms, has danced her way around the world. . . . But for all her travels and her sweeping popularity she has encountered no knight who could lift her to a level that would enable her to be received as a respectable member in musical circles. George Gershwin seems to have accomplished this miracle. He has done it boldly by dressing this extremely independent and up-to-date young lady in the . . . classic garb."

The *Rhapsody in Blue* was by no means the first piece of serious music to use popular American idioms. Before the *Rhapsody* there were works like Debussy's *Golliwog's Cakewalk,* Satie's *Parade,* Stravinsky's *Ragtime,* and Milhaud's ballet *La Création du monde*—each of which incorporated within larger classical forms the techniques and styles of American popular music. But none of these works, either individually or collectively, had the impact on the music world that the *Rhapsody in Blue* had. The *Rhapsody* succeeded where all other similar works had failed. It brought complete acceptance to American popular music among most serious musicians everywhere. Henceforth, many of America's and Europe's most celebrated composers were to exploit jazz techniques and styles for serious efforts. Jazz, regarded by so many composers as an ugly stepchild before 1924, suddenly assumed dignity and a handsome appearance.

III

Gershwin himself pointed the way with other works, each increasingly ambitious either in structure or in deployment of jazz materials. Soon after the première of the *Rhapsody*, Gershwin was commissioned by Walter Damrosch, conductor of the New York Symphony Society, to write a new jazz orchestral work for his organization. Gershwin chose to write a piano concerto. He completed his *Concerto in F* on November 10, 1935, this time doing his own orchestration, a practice he followed for all subsequent serious works. The following December 3, the *Concerto* was introduced in Carnegie Hall at a concert of the New York Symphony Society, Walter Damrosch conducting, with the composer as soloist.

Jazz was no less prominent in the *Concerto* than it had been in the earlier *Rhapsody*. The new work opens with an abandoned Charleston theme in the kettledrums and woodwinds. The work abounds with other racy jazz ideas, including a poignant poetic subject for muted trumpet that opens the second movement, and a wonderful melody for the strings in the same movement that is the heart of the entire work; both these subjects, for all their aristocratic beauty, were obviously born on the other side of the musical tracks.

The *Concerto* showed a definite advance in Gershwin's symphonic-jazz writing. There is greater variety and richness of thematic ideas than in the *Rhapsody*, and these ideas are worked out with greater elasticity and technical assurance. The progress in musical know-how and the artistic growth are perceptible in all subsequent serious works by Gershwin. In 1926 he wrote three jazz Preludes for the piano, which he himself introduced at a concert at the Hotel Roosevelt in New York, in which he was assisting artist to the operatic contralto, Marguerite D'Alvarez. The first Prelude, in B-flat major, is a skillful blend of the tango and the Charleston. The second, in C-sharp minor, is a blues melody, and is the most famous of the set, familiar not only in its original version but also in numerous transcriptions. By contrast, the third Prelude, in E-flat major, effervesces with leaping jazz rhythms.

Less than two years after that, during a European vacation, Gershwin completed a new orchestral work, a tone poem, *An American in Paris,* introduced by the New York Philharmonic-Symphony under Damrosch on December 13, 1928. Describing the feelings of an American tourist as he strolls along a Parisian boulevard, *An American in Paris* was the most successful effort by Gershwin to combine jazz and symphonic writing. Jazz appears in the brisk popular melody for the trombones early in the score; in the wailing blues melody for muted trumpet which is the core of the composition; and in a piquant Charleston tune for two trumpets. Modern symphonic writing is found in the saucy walking theme, in the harmonic writing often coated with modernistic acid, and in the brilliant orchestration which included two actual Parisian taxicab horns.

The *Second Rhapsody,* in 1931, grew out of a brief orchestral sequence that Gershwin wrote for his first motion-picture assignment, *Delicious.* Here he gives a tonal portrait of the sights and sounds of a large city. This *Rhapsody* opens with an incisive rhythmic subject descriptive of riveting, and has for its principal melodic subject a spacious blues first heard in the strings and then in the brass. The *Second Rhapsody* was introduced by the Boston Symphony under Serge Koussevitzky —the composer at the piano—in Boston on January 29, 1932.

The *Cuban Overture* in 1932 (originally entitled *Rhumba*) and the *Variations on I Got Rhythm,* in 1934, show remarkable forward strides by the composer in the use of counterpoint in the first work, and in the art of thematic development in the second. The *Cuban Overture* came after Gershwin had spent a brief holiday in Havana where he was fascinated by its native rhythms and percussion instruments. In his *Overture,* he incorporated both elements: the rhythms of the rhumba and the habanera; and such Cuban instruments as the Cuban sticks, the gourd, and the maracas. The *Cuban Overture* was first heard at a concert at the Lewisohn Stadium in New York, on August 16, 1932, Albert Coates conducting.

Gershwin wrote the *Variations on I Got Rhythm* for a concert tour he was making with an orchestra in 1934, in a program made up of his works. The *Variations* were introduced in the first of these appearances, in Boston on January 14, 1934. "I Got Rhythm" is, of course, one of Gershwin's best-known and most dynamic songs; it comes from the musical comedy *Girl Crazy.* In an extended work for piano and orchestra, Gershwin subjects this vigorous theme to many subtle changes of mood, atmosphere, and feeling; from a melancholy dirge to a brilliant eruption of pyrotechnics; from a dolorous blues lament to an athletic melody full of spirit and the joy of life.

Gershwin's last serious work was his greatest—the folk opera, *Porgy and Bess,* first performed by the Theatre Guild in Boston and New York in the fall of 1935, and making world history from 1952 to 1956 in a tour that embraced Europe, the Near East, the Soviet Union, countries behind the Iron Curtain, Scandinavia, Mexico, and South America.

Though the opera employs both jazz and popular elements, this is no jazz opera, and consequently cannot come in for detailed discussion in a book on popular music. *Porgy and Bess* is a profound and moving folk drama in the *genre* of Musorgski's *Boris Godunov,* deeply grounded in the soil of Negro life, backgrounds, experiences, and music. As this author wrote in his biography of Gershwin:* "*Porgy and Bess* was Gershwin's inevitable achievement . . . for it represents, at

---

* A *Journey to Greatness:* The Life and Music of George Gershwin, by David Ewen. New York: Henry Holt & Co., 1956.

last, the meeting-point for the two divergent paths he had
all his life been pursuing—those of serious and popular music.
The serious musician is found at his best in the musically
distinguished tone speech, in the powerful antiphonal choruses,
in the expressive dissonances and chromaticisms, in the brilliant
orchestration, in the effective atmospheric writing, in the skillful
use of counterpoint in the duets and particularly in the last-
scene trio. The popular composer emerges in the jazz background of several choruses . . . in the two songs of Sportin'
Life, 'It Ain't Necessarily So,' and 'There's a Boat That's Leavin'
Soon for New York,' and in Crown's sacrilegious blues ditty, "A
Red-Headed Woman Makes Choochoo Train Jump Its Track.'
Yet there is no feeling of contradiction, no sense of incongruity,
in this mingling of the serious and the popular, for the popular
is as basic to Gershwin's design as the serious, with its own specific function."

IV

Gershwin pointed a direction which many composers followed. There were others in Tin Pan Alley who, encouraged
by Gershwin's example and success, attempted creative en-
deavors more ambitious than the thirty-two bar popular song.
The most significant of these was Ferde Grofé. In the year of
the *Rhapsody in Blue*—1924—Grofé wrote for Paul Whiteman the *Mississippi Suite* in which jazz techniques are adroitly
used: in the second section, for example, where Huckleberry
Finn is described. More celebrated—indeed, possibly the best
known jazz-symphonic work since the *Rhapsody in Blue*—is
the *Grand Canyon Suite*, in 1931. The *Suite* is a five-move-
ment picture of one of America's natural wonders. The names
of the respective movements give the clue to their program-
matic content: Sunrise; The Painted Desert; On the Trail
(the best known section of the set, and utilized by a famous
cigarette company as its musical signature on radio and tele-

vision); Sunset; and Cloudburst. In this work the use of jazz is more discreet than in the *Mississippi Suite;* but the melodic and rhythmic content is unmistakably of jazz origin.

Like Grofé, Robert Russell Bennett earned his living as an orchestrator of other people's music. He was, and still is, the ace orchestrator for the Broadway musical stage. In between his more profitable chores on Broadway, he has found the time to write many serious musical works. Some are filled with those popular elements he had assimilated on the musical stage, and these include: *Charleston Rhapsody* (1926); *March,* for two pianos and orchestra (1930); *Concerto Grosso,* for jazz band and orchestra (1932); and *Variations on a Theme by Jerome Kern* (1933).

Jerome Kern was encouraged by André Kostelanetz, the famous conductor, to write two works in forms more spacious than the song to which he had hitherto confined himself. *Scenario,* in 1941, was an extended symphonic work made up of the principal themes and songs from *Show Boat,* a skillful integration of the basic melodic materials from that production. About a year later, Kern wrote a second large orchestral work, this time with original thematic ideas: *Mark Twain: A Portrait for Orchestra.* This was a work in four sections touching on episodes in Twain's career. Both works are filled with that gentle and personal lyricism that Kern brought to his best songs, and they are the sum of ingratiating lyric parts.

Duke Ellington's best work for symphony orchestra is *Black, Brown and Beige,* introduced by his orchestra in Carnegie Hall in 1943. Ellington prefers calling this "Negro music," but it is really jazz, filled as it is with blues, ragtime, and jazz colorations. The work was intended by the composer as a "tonal parallel to the history of the Negro in America." Other and later large orchestral works by Ellington, in which the popular element is pronounced, are: *Liberia Suite,* written in 1947 on a commission from the Liberian government to commemorate the 100th anniversary of the founding of that African republic; *Harlem,* a suite introduced at an Ellington concert at the Metropolitan Opera House in 1951; and *Night Creature,* first heard in Carnegie Hall in 1955.

Less ambitious in purpose and design than the symphonic works of Gershwin, Grofé, Bennett, and Ellington are the semi-classical numbers of men like David Rose and Leroy Anderson, who utilize popular elements in their orchestral writing with charm, humor, and pleasing effect. David Rose, born in London in 1910, came to this country in his fourth year. A comprehensive musical education was completed at the Chicago Musical College, after which Rose worked for several years for various radio stations as pianist and arranger. He first attracted attention during World War II with what is still one of his most delightful instrumental pieces, "Holiday for Strings," published in 1943. One year later he wrote the music for, and conducted, the Army Air Force production written by Moss Hart, *Winged Victory.* Other pleasing numbers in the style of "Holiday for Strings" are "The Dance of the Spanish Onion," "Big Ben," and "Escapade."

The light classics of Leroy Anderson are even better known; few composers have used the idioms and approaches of popular music in light instrumental works with greater freshness, variety, wit, and originality than Anderson. He was born in Cambridge, Massachusetts in 1908, and received his academic education on a scholarship at Harvard, where he received the Phi Beta Kappa key and the degrees of Bachelor and Master of Arts. His musical training began in boyhood at the New England Conservatory and continued with private teachers in Boston. For one year he led the Harvard University Band; for two years he taught music at Radcliffe; and for several years after that, he worked as choirmaster, organist, and as arranger and guest-conductor of the Boston Pops Orchestra. It was for the Boston Pops Orchestra that he wrote his first semi-classical piece, "Jazz Pizzicato," and it was a hit. The

Boston Pops Orchestra, under Arthur Fiedler, continued to introduce his pieces, all of which were enthusiastically received by audiences. His best-known and most frequently heard compositions are "Jazz Legato," "Fiddle Faddle," "The Syncopated Clock," "The Waltzing Cat," "Sleigh Ride," "The Typewriter," and "Blue Tango." The last is scored for fifty violins, and despite the fact that it has no lyrics, became the top juke box favorite in 1952, and sold over two million records.

Serious composers have discovered from Gershwin that jazz techniques and styles could be effective within the patterns and formats of the most serious classical works. Aaron Copland, at the dawn of his career that eventually brought him to leadership among American composers, discovered jazz and wrote two major works in that style: *Music for the Theatre* (1925), an orchestral suite in which a dance movement is unadulterated jazz; and the *Piano Concerto* (1926), where the second movement makes extensive use of jazz materials. John Alden Carpenter wrote the first important ballet in jazz style in *Skyscrapers*, introduced at the Metropolitan Opera House in 1926. Jazz appears in the music of other important serious American composers: in *Daniel Jazz* (1923), and the *Jazz Suite* (1925) by Louis Gruenberg; *Jazz Symphony* (1927), and the opera *Transatlantic* (1930) by George Antheil; *New Year's Eve in New York* (1929) by Werner Janssen; *Chorale and Fugue in Jazz* (1931), *Swing Sinfonietta* (1936) and the *Boogie-Woogie Etude*, by Morton Gould; in the ballet, *Fancy Free* (1944), by Leonard Bernstein.

In Europe, too, serious composers took a cue from Gershwin. Maurice Ravel, probably the most significant French composer of the twentieth century, freely admitted his debt to Gershwin when he wrote the *Sonata for Violin and Piano* (1927), the last movement of which is a blues, and the *Concerto for Left Hand and Orchestra* (1931), the last part entirely in jazz style. The influence of Gershwin may have been less immediate on other European composers—and less openly acknowledged—but it is there anyway. On the crest of the wave of the fabulous success of the *Rhapsody in Blue* came jazz operas by Ernst Krenek (*Jonny spielt auf*), Paul Hindemith (*Neues vom Tage*), and Kurt Weill (*Mahagonny* and *Die Dreigroschenoper*). Jazz also appeared in such varied symphonic works as Arthur Honegger's *Concertino for Piano and Orchestra*, Constant Lambert's *Rio Grande*, William Walton's *Façade*, Kurt Weill's cantata *Lindbergh's Flight*, and Rolf Liebermann's *Concerto for Jazz Band and Orchestra*.

V

Jazz—the sophisticated lady of New York, not the primitive from New Orleans and Chicago—became a dominating voice in our popular music of the 1920s. Jazz concerts in serious concert halls became a practice as Vincent Lopez brought his orchestra into the Metropolitan Opera House, Paul Whiteman and Benny Goodman and Duke Ellington to Carnegie Hall. Jazz orchestras, specializing in the symphonic treatment of popular music, multiplied and flourished—heard throughout the country in hotels, night clubs, Vaudeville, musical-comedy and motion-picture theaters led by such acclaimed jazz musicians as Vincent Lopez, Ben Bernie, Paul Whiteman, Abe Lyman, Duke Ellington, Leo Reisman, Guy Lombardo, and many others.

The importance of jazz, or its demoralizing influence, became a hotly-fought issue. One educator said that "its influence is as harmful and degrading to civilized races as it always has been among the savages from whom we borrowed it. If we permit our boys and girls to be exposed indefinitely to this pernicious influence, the harm that will result may tear to pieces our whole social fabric." One physician discovered that jazz was capable of inducing inebriation. "Reason and reflection are lost," he wrote, "and the actions of the person are directed by the stronger animal passions. In other words, jazz affects the brain through the sense of hearing, giving the same results as whiskey or any other alcoholic drinks taken into the system by the way of the stomach."

The President of the Christian and Missionary Alliance Conference charged that "American girls of tender age are approaching jungle standards. . . . Little American girls are maturing too quickly under the hectic influence of jazz." John Roach Straton denounced jazz from his pulpit in New York as "music of the savage, intellectual and spiritual debauchery, utter degradation." A city ordinance banned jazz in Zion City, Illinois, together with other sinful practices. The celebrated American composer and educator, Daniel Gregory Mason, said of jazz: "It is not a new flavor, but a kind of curry or catsup strong enough to make the stale old dishes palatable to unfastidious appetites. . . . It is a meaningless stirabout, a commotion without purpose, an epilepsy simulating muscular action. It is the musical counterpart of the sterile cleverness we find in so much of our contemporary conversation, as well as in our theatre and books."

Others spoke up for jazz with equal fervor and conviction. Within the august halls of Harvard University there took place a symposium on jazz conducted by Prof. Edward Burlingame Hill. The League of Composers in New York—guardian of the most serious principles of modern music—held a jazz conference. Such outstanding musical artists as Fritz Kreisler, Leopold Stokowski, and Marguerite d'Alvarez came vigorously to its defense. Mrs. Charles S. Guggenheimer said in an interview that a chair of jazz should be established at the American Academy in Rome. Actually a course in jazz music was instituted at the New School for Social Research in New York. "I like to think," said a noted journalist, Hiram K. Motherwell, "that it is the perfect expression of the American city, with its restless bustle and motion, its multitude of unrelated details, and its underlying rhythmic progress towards a vague Somewhere. Its technical resourcefulness continually surprises me, and its melodies, at their best, delight me."

One of the most touching tributes to jazz came from Marguerite d'Alvarez. In reply to John Roach Straton's scathing denunciation of jazz, she said simply: "I want nothing better than that Gershwin's *Piano Concerto* be played over my grave."

chapter eleven

THE HEYDAY OF
THE MUSICAL COMEDY

In 1914, Jerome Kern succeeded George M. Cohan as a major composer for the American musical comedy as distinguished from the American operetta. In that year, Kern had his first outstanding Broadway stage success in *The Girl from Utah,* and his first resounding song hit in "They Didn't Believe Me" (Herbert Reynolds), with a two-million copy sheet-music sale. But there were two lesser gems in the same score: "You're Here and I'm Here" and "I'd Like to Wander with Alice in Wonderland," lyrics by Reynolds.

Kern had arrived. Only one year later he helped to revolutionize the American musical comedy with the verbal help of a new partner. Guy Reginald Bolton, of English birth, had started out as an architect in New York, where he designed the Soldiers and Sailors Memorial on Riverside Drive. He turned to the theater in 1911 by helping to write a play, *The Drone,* produced that year. That was the sum total of his stage experience when he teamed up with Kern in 1915.

Kern and Bolton decided to create a new kind of musical production—a radical departure from the extravaganzas and revues then in vogue—by emphasizing small casts, economical sets, intimacy of tone, and informality of manner. Their first venture, *Nobody Home,* in 1915, was only a mild success. But in the same year, *Very Good, Eddie,* clicked big. Everything about that production was compact and economical, and the acting and singing were pitched in a low key. *Very Good, Eddie* helped to create a new *genre* in the American musical theater that soon came to be known as the "Princess Theater Shows" after the theater in which they were produced.

A third side was soon added to the Bolton and Kern partnership, an addition that helped create one of the most successful writing triangles on musical Broadway in the 1910s. This was P. G. Wodehouse, already famous for such novels as *Psmith in the City* and *Psmith, Journalist.* It will be recalled that some years earlier Kern and Wodehouse had collaborated on several songs while working in Frohman's office in London. Wodehouse came to the United States in 1909, where he soon made his mark both as a novelist and as a drama critic. In the latter capacity he attended the opening-night performance of *Very Good, Eddie.* Kern and Bolton then suggested to Wodehouse that he join them in writing for the musical stage. Their first combined effort was *Have a Heart,* Bolton writing the book, Kern the music, and Wodehouse the lyrics.

This trio introduced a new sophistication and vivacity into the musical theater of that day. Their greatest success was *Oh Boy!,* in 1917, which had a Broadway run of 475 performances, besides four companies on the road. Pointing out the qualities that set *Oh Boy!* sharply apart from the other musicals of the period, Guy Bolton wrote in *The Dramatic Mirror* of that period: "It was straight, consistent comedy with the addition of music. Every song and lyric contributed to the action. The humor was based on the situation, not interjected by comedians." Then Bolton added that "realism and Americanism" were other distinguishing traits of this musical. Even if *Oh Boy!* did not achieve everything Bolton believed it should, it was an important step forward in integrating the various elements of the musical theater into a single creation.

The songs Kern had thus far written already gave evidence of a strong creative talent: an instinctive feeling for an original turn of the melodic phrase; a partiality toward intriguing rhythms. These songs included "They Didn't Believe Me" and "You're Here and I'm Here" from *The Girl from Utah;* "You Know and I Know" (Schuyler Greene) from *Nobody Home;* "Babes in the Wood" and "Nodding Roses" (Greene) from *Very Good, Eddie;* "Magic Melody" and "Till the Clouds Roll By" (Wodehouse and Bolton)—the latter a title subsequently used for the Jerome screen biography—from *Oh Boy!;* and "The Siren's Song" (Wodehouse) from *Leave It to Jane.*

The years following World War I were bountiful with Kern successes both in songs and stage productions. Marilyn Miller starred in two of these Kern musicals. In *Sally,* in 1920, she brought an indescribable radiance to one of Kern's most beautiful songs, "Look for the Silver Lining" (B. G. DeSylva). But this number, despite general belief, did not originate in *Sally.* Kern had included it a few months earlier in *Good Morning, Dearie,* and liked it so well that he decided to use it for his star in *Sally. Sunny* followed five years later. The luster of the star, still undimmed—and a melodious score that included "Who" (Harbach and Oscar Hammerstein II)—would have insured the future of any production, and they spelled success for *Sunny.*

Up to 1925, since working with the "Princess Theater Shows," Kern functioned more or less within traditional molds. But these molds were stifling him. He felt the need to step beyond the barriers and restrictions set for him by the musical theater of that day. He wanted to write music for a play that had distinction and plausibility of plot, validity of characterization, authenticity of atmosphere. He was certain that good entertainment need not be sacrificed for good art.

It was with these ideas in mind that Kern (against the studied judgment of the bigwigs of Broadway, and the sincere advice of his closest friends) went to work on *Show Boat*. But that is another, and later, story.

II

Irving Berlin also dominated the traditional musical theater of the 1910s and 1920s, remaining one of its most productive composers from then on.

Berlin's first appearance as a composer for the stage took place soon after he wrote "Alexander's Ragtime Band." On June 16, 1911 he contributed four songs to *Jardin de Paris*, a musical revue produced by Florenz Ziegfeld atop the Amsterdam Theatre. Three years later Charles B. Dillingham, planning a ragtime musical comedy starring Vernon and Irene Castle, asked Berlin, the recognized king of ragtime, to write the score. *Watch Your Step*, produced in 1914, had thirteen numbers, among them ragtime melodies like "The Syncopated Walk," and nostalgic and sentimental pieces like "Play a Simple Melody."

After *Jardin de Paris*, Berlin wrote the music for about twenty Broadway productions, all of them successes in varying degrees. After World War I, he contributed twelve songs to the *Ziegfeld Follies of 1919*. One was "Mandy," a carry-over from his all-soldier show *Yip, Yip, Yaphank*, which Marilyn Miller helped make a success of the first magnitude in the *Follies;* another was "A Pretty Girl Is Like a Melody," one of his best, and one to which he has always been particularly partial. A third Berlin song was the slightly suggestive, "You'd be Surprised," then as later an Eddie Cantor favorite.

In 1921, Berlin joined with Sam H. Harris in building a new Broadway theater, the Music Box on 45th Street. Within this house they planned to produce musical shows combining smartness with spectacular beauty, sophistication with wit. The four editions of the *Music Box Revue*, between 1921 and 1924, were a bountiful source of Berlin songs, beginning with "Everybody Step" and "Say It With Music," in 1921, and in later editions continuing with "Lady of the Evening," "Crinoline Days," "What'll I Do?", and "Pack Up Your Sins."

After writing the score to the *Ziegfeld Follies of 1927* Berlin lapsed into a period of silence as far as the stage was concerned, a period that lasted about five years and in which he wrote some of his most beautiful ballads. Many of these were inspired, as we have explained earlier, by his romance with and marriage to Ellin Mackay.

A year or so after his marriage, Berlin wrote the ballad, "The Song Is Ended." It was almost as if he had had a prophetic glimpse at what was lying in store for him. For after writing this song, Berlin was mysteriously paralyzed into creative inactivity. He destroyed most of what he wrote; whatever he tried writing suddenly seemed to him trite or repetitious. Never before had he known such a period of frustration. To make matters worse, during this same period he saw his vast fortune crumble in the economic debacle following the stock market crash in 1929. He needed new song hits not only to satisfy his creative urges and to bolster his self-confidence, but also to make a living.

The road back to success began in 1931 with his score to *Face the Music*, produced in 1932, with a book by Moss Hart, who had recently won Broadway with his satire on Hollywood, *Once in a Lifetime*, written with George S. Kaufman. The Berlin score—which contained "Let's Have Another Cup o' Coffee," "Soft Lights and Sweet Music," and "I Say It's Spinach"—was slick and professional; it was still not Berlin at his best.

A stroke of luck came Berlin's way in 1932 when two old ballads—"Say It Isn't So" and "How Deep is the Ocean?"—were revived and became hits. This fresh taste of success may have proved the invigorating tonic he needed. In 1933 he seemed to find new strength in his music for a topical revue, *As Thousands Cheer*, book once again by Moss Hart. Its best song was adapted from a number Berlin had written in 1917 and which, as "Smile and Show Your Dimple," had been a failure. In its new version, renamed "Easter Parade," the song was made into a production number for the first act finale and was introduced by Clifton Webb and Marilyn Miller. Other songs in the revue were by no means of inferior vintage—all of them new. One was "Heat Wave," with Ethel Waters adding several degrees to the temperature with her torrid rendition; another, "Not for All the Rice in China."

As *Thousands Cheer* ran up the respectable total of 400 performances. The next time Berlin appeared on the Broadway stage as composer, seven years later, it was with a triumph of equal magnitude, *Louisiana Purchase,* with William Gaxton and Victor Moore. Several distinguished Berlin numbers included the title song, "It's a Lovely Day Tomorrow," and "You're Lonely and I'm Lonely."

During World War II, Berlin was primarily occupied with the production and world-wide performances of his second all-soldier show, *This Is the Army.* He returned to Broadway in 1946 with what has proved to be the greatest stage success of his entire career: *Annie Get Your Gun,* which ran 1,147 performances in New York. Ethel Merman was starred as Annie Oakley, a girl handier with a gun than with a man, in one of her most strident, brash, and irresistible characterizations. Never before had Berlin come up with such an opulent score. At one time, three of these songs appeared simultaneously on the "Hit Parade," the only time that any show was thus represented on this radio program. Never before had he produced so many numbers that fit so neatly into the over-all design of the play. A love song like "They Say It's Wonderful" might sound a bit corny off-stage (especially the lyrics), but it was just the kind of love song for Annie, a backwoods girl. A homespun waltz like "The Girl that I Marry" is on the sentimental side—but not when sung by Fred Butler who, with his size and brusqueness, mellows sentiment with charm. "Doin' What Comes Naturally" and "You Can't Get a Man with a

Gun" acquire an even sharper edge of humor, and the risqué lines have a keener point, when heard as part of the play, particularly in the earthy rendition of Ethel Merman. Nor do these songs exhaust the melodic richness of the score, which also includes "There's No Business Like Show Business," "Anything You Can Do," "I Got the Sun in the Morning," and "I'm an Indian, Too," the last used for an eye-filling production number.

Miss Liberty, in 1949, had a book by one of America's most distinguished playwrights, Robert Sherwood, three-time recipient of the Pulitzer Prize for drama, now making his bow in the musical theater. Berlin's best songs had an ingratiating charm: "Let's Take an Old-Fashioned Walk," "Paris Wakes Up and Smiles," and an effective setting of the Emma Lazarus poem inscribed on the base of the Statue of Liberty, "Give Me Your Tired." But the consistent brilliance and the wide gamut of Berlin's musical writing in *Annie Get Your Gun* were not to be found here, nor were they found in *Call Me Madam*, in 1950. Yet the Berlin score for the latter play had one or two delights: "It's a Lovely Day Today," "You're Just in Love," and "I Like Ike," the last starting a movement that ultimately culminated in the White House.

III

All the while that George Gershwin was justifying the high hopes the concert world had for him, he did not abandon the musical theater.

In 1924, he wrote the music for *Lady Be Good*, starring Fred and Adele Astaire, in which he revealed new creative powers in popular-song writing. A number like "Fascinating Rhythm" used changing meters with virtuoso skill, while the title song had repeated triplets in cut time that produced an intriguing effect. But the best song in that score was deleted from the production during its out-of-town tryouts, because the general consensus was that it arrested the action of the play and lacked popular appeal. It was "The Man I Love," Gershwin's own favorite among his songs—unforgettable for its contrapuntal background of a descending chromatic scale to a melody made up of a six-note blues progression. It first became popular in London, largely through the enthusiasm and influence of Lady Louis Mountbatten. Not until about half a dozen years after it was written did it achieve acceptance in this country; since then it has become an all-time Gershwin favorite.

Lady Be Good was a milestone in Gershwin's stage career because it was the first Gershwin musical comedy for which his brother, Ira, wrote all the lyrics. From this time on, the Gershwins were one of the most successful words-and-music partnerships on Broadway. Ira consistently provided George with smart, deft, neatly turned verses capable of stimulating a composer's imagination. After *Lady Be Good,* and up to 1930, the Gershwins were represented on Broadway by half a dozen or so musicals of which only three had more than passing interest: *Tip-Toes,* in 1925, which had "That Certain Feeling," "Sweet and Low Down," and "Looking for a Boy"; *Oh Kay,* in 1926, with Gertrude Lawrence making her first appearance in an American-written musical, and with such song gems as "Someone to Watch Over Me," "Clap Yo' Hands," "Maybe," and "Do, Do, Do"; and *Funny Face,* in 1927, whose melodic treasures numbered " 'S Wonderful," "Let's Kiss and Make Up," and "The Babbit and the Bromide," the last one of Ira Gershwin's most brilliant lyrics.

The year of 1930 was a banner one for George Gershwin. It brought *Girl Crazy,* a major box-office success, and *Strike Up the Band,* an artistic one. *Girl Crazy* was a veritable cornucopia of Gershwin riches. It had one of his most poignant love songs, "Embraceable You," and one of his most mellow ballads, "But Not For Me." It had a charming take-off on hillbilly tunes in "Bidin' My Time," a satire on the Frankie-and-Johnny type of ballad in "Sam and Delilah," and a high-voltage tune in Gershwin's best rhythmic vein, "I Got Rhythm." Not the least of the salient attractions of *Girl Crazy* was the volcanic performance of Ethel Merman, here making her bow in the musical-comedy theater. When she appeared on the stage and threw her large brassy tones across the footlights in "Sam and Delilah" and "I Got Rhythm," the impact of singer on audience was cataclysmic. Merman obscured all the other luminaries in a star-studded stage, even the glamourous Ginger Rogers, also making her Broadway bow, and one of the great buffoons of the Broadway stage, Willie Howard.

Strike Up the Band was financially less rewarding than *Girl Crazy*, but its influence on our musical theater was more lasting. Here was one of the few musical productions of that period to reveal a political conscience. *Strike Up the Band* was a keen political travesty highlighting a war between the United States and Switzerland over the issue of chocolate. This theme provided the authors, George S. Kaufman and Morrie Ryskind, with the opportunity to regard war with mockery, to chuckle at the foibles of international diplomacy, to sneer at the frequent absurdities to which international relations descend, and even to rib big business. And there was a generous dose of mockery and malice in Gershwin's music. Rarely before in our popular music has martial pomp been so completely deflated as in the march, "Strike Up the Band"; American chauvinism was reduced to proper size in "A Typical Self-Made American"; military grandeur was ridiculed in "The Entrance of the Swiss Army." Several other numbers were in Gershwin's most aristocratic lyrical manner, particularly the languorous ballad, "Soon," and "I've Got a Crush On You."

With *Strike Up the Band* the authors veered toward a new direction in the theater. Good as it was, *Strike Up the Band* was but a hint of better things to come. One year later, the same authors of text and music created a second musical

satire in *Of Thee I Sing*, a devastating musical commentary
on the political scene at home. The core of the play is a
Presidential campaign in which Wintergreen and Throttle-
bottom—respectively played by William Gaxton and Victor
Moore—run on a "love ticket" and are elected President and
Vice-President of the United States. The story digresses frequently to point a sharp finger of ridicule at the comedy-of-
errors of the Washington political scene, at political rallies, at
the Senate and Supreme Court, and at the forgotten men of
American politics, the Vice-President. Ira Gershwin's breezy
lyrics neatly caught the spirit of the text in some of his deftest
and most needle-pointed verses; so did George Gershwin's
music. At every point, the music helps to stress and underline
every satiric suggestion and implication of the play. "Wintergreen for President" lampoons political campaigns. The title
song is a blow at patriotic songs and Tin Pan Alley in a single
stroke, beginning like a solemn hymn and suddenly descending into Tin Pan Alley sentiment—"of thee I sing, *baby*." In
several other instances two birds are again killed with one
stone: Viennese waltzes and American motherhood in "I'm
About to Become a Mother"; grand opera pretensions and the
dignity of the Senate in the Senate scene. But the score was
remarkable not only in details. Some of the songs themselves
could stand apart from the over-all texture and command
attention: "Of Thee I Sing," "Who Cares?" and "Love Is
Sweeping the Country" have become deservedly popular.

Of Thee I Sing, then, was mature entertainment with bite,
sting, and malice. It was that *rara avis*, a musical with an
adult mentality. And it made theater history. Beside being
the only Gershwin musical to have two touring companies
simultaneously, it was the first American musical comedy by
anybody whose text was published in book form, and the first
American musical comedy to win the Pulitzer Prize for drama.

Discounting *Porgy and Bess*, which is an opera, Gershwin
had two more musicals on Broadway, both in 1933, both

failures. *Let 'Em Eat Cake* was an unashamed attempt to imitate *Of Thee I Sing*. The text had some memorable satirical moments, and the score included "Mine." But this musical was, as Brooks Atkinson reported, "strained, dull, and dreary." *Pardon My English* was an all-around unhappy adventure, with a feeble play, and a cast that included a strange and bewildering conglomeration of foreign accents. It closed in about a month. The music was for the most part second-rate Gershwin, with only "The Lorelei," and "Isn't it a Pity?" to commend it.

After *Porgy and Bess*, in 1935, Gershwin deserted Broadway for Hollywood, and up to the time of his untimely death in 1937 he concentrated on writing for the screen.

IV

When George Gershwin withdrew as a composer of the *Scandals*, in 1924, he was replaced by the songwriting team of De Sylva, Brown, and Henderson. Buddy De Sylva and Lew Brown collaborated in writing lyrics; Ray Henderson was the composer. For the next half-dozen years or so, the three men worked so intimately and harmoniously that it was not always clear where the work of one ended and that of the other two began. There were times when the composer Ray Henderson helped to write lyrics, and when the two lyricists provided ideas to the composer. And, as if to complicate matters further, there were also times when Buddy De Sylva collaborated with somebody else in writing the musical-comedy book. Consequently, in discussing the musicals of De Sylva, Brown, and Henderson—and their songs—it is necessary to speak of them as a single creative entity.

We concern ourselves with this trio of writers immediately after Gershwin, not only because this happened to be the order of succession in the *Scandals*, but for another significant reason. Like the Gershwin of *Strike Up the Band* and *Of Thee I Sing* De Sylva, Brown, and Henderson were interested in the immediate world around them. Their best musicals departed basically from a long prevailing tendency in musicals to emphasize the boy-meets-girl theme in a romantic and picturesque setting by presenting different facets of contemporary American life.

The dynamo of this trio was Bud De Sylva, born in New York City in 1895. In his freshman year at the University of Southern California, he produced a college show, played the ukulele in a Hawaiian band, and started writing song lyrics. Al Jolson took a fancy to some of these lyrics and after setting them to his own music introduced them at the Winter Garden. When De Sylva recovered from the shock of receiving his first royalty check as lyricist—the figure read $16,000—he came to the conclusion that there was a more promising future for him in the New York theater than in college. He came to New York in 1919 and immediately went to work on contract for Remick. With Arthur Jackson he wrote the lyrics for George Gershwin's first complete musical, *La, La Lucille*. Important assignments now came his way profusely. During the next few years his lyrics were heard in Kern's *Sally*, in the *Ziegfeld Follies of 1921*, the *Greenwich Village Follies of 1921*, Victor Herbert's *Orange Blossoms*, and the *Scandals* when George Gershwin was its composer. On the one hand he could produce the words for such formidable song hits as "April Showers," music by Louis Silvers, which Jolson interpolated into *Bombo* and by which he will always be remembered. On the other hand, De Sylva collaborated in writing songs that started out as hits and ended up as classics: Kern's "Look for the Silver Lining," Victor Herbert's "A Kiss in the Dark," and Gershwin's "Somebody Loves Me."

De Sylva was associated with the two Georges—White and Gershwin—until 1925, when Gershwin withdrew from the *Scandals* to be replaced by Ray Henderson and Lew Brown. By 1925, Lew Brown had also achieved an impressive background as lyricist, with one of the most popular ballads of

World War I, "I May Be Gone For a Long, Long Time," made famous by Grace La Rue in *Hitchy-koo of 1917,* and "Oh By Jingo" and "I Used to Love You," all to music by Albert von Tilzer. Then in 1922 he teamed up with Bud De Sylva to write the lyric for "Georgette." The music was by Ray Henderson. The fruitful partnership of De Sylva, Brown, and Henderson had begun.

Ray Henderson, born in Buffalo in 1896, had been trained as a serious musician at the Chicago Conservatory. While there he earned a regular income playing pop tunes on the piano at parties and by filling engagements as pianist with a Vaudeville act that included an Irish tenor and a Jewish comedian. Once out of the Conservatory, he left serious music to take on a job as song plugger for Leo Feist. After holding various other minor jobs in Tin Pan Alley he impressed Louis Bernstein, of the firm of Shapiro, Bernstein & Co., who henceforth did what he could to advance the composer's career. One of the things Bernstein did for Henderson was to introduce him to the lyricist, Lew Brown. The first two songs by Brown and Henderson— published by Shapiro, Bernstein—became popular: "Humming" and "Georgette."

At times with Lew Brown, and at times with other lyricists, Henderson wrote several more songs that proved to be publishing bonanzas. Among them were "Alabamy Bound" (De Sylva and Bud Green) and "Five Feet Two, Eyes of Blue" (Sam M. Lewis and Joe Young). He now became George White's first choice to succeed Gershwin as composer for the *Scandals.* De Sylva, Brown, and Henderson wrote all the songs and lyrics for the editions of 1925, 1926, 1928, and 1931. Among their triumphs were "Black Bottom," "The Birth of the Blues," "My Song," 'Life Is Just a Bowl of Cherries," and "That's Why Darkies Were Born."

With an assist from Laurence Schwab, who helped De Sylva with the book, the songwriting team completed in 1927 their first musical comedy, *Good News.* Its setting was Tait College, where the emphasis was on football and fraternities rather than on the curriculum. The college spirit was introduced into the production without preliminaries: three rousing "rah-rahs" were shouted by the men of the orchestra just before the opening bars of the overture. Throughout the evening the college spirit was intensified by such rousing tunes as "Varsity Drag," "On the Campus," "Good News," and "Girls of Pi Beta Phi." Two other excellent songs had less animal exuberance and more sentiment: "Lucky in Love," and the hit song, "The Best Things in Life Are Free," which later became the title of a screen biography of this songwriting trio.

Hold Everything, in 1928, once again lampooned the contemporary scene, this time the prize fight game being the specific target, with Bert Lahr cast as a badly mawled pugilist, and Victor Moore as his hapless and much victimized manager. One of the foremost song hits by De Sylva, Brown, and Henderson appears in this musical: "You're the Cream in My Coffee." *Follow Through*, in 1929, had Jack Haley cavorting in a swanky golf club in a pungent commentary on country life and the golfing set. Text and music were in the happiest De Sylva, Brown, and Henderson vein, the score including "Button Up Your Overcoat" (its rhythms neatly tapped out by the quicksilver toes of Eleanor Powell), "My Lucky Star," "I Want to Be Bad," and "You Wouldn't Fool Me." The last of the De Sylva, Brown, and Henderson musicals—*Flying High*, in 1930—was also a smash hit. It concerned airmail pilots and their ambition to crash through the obscurity of their humdrum lives by establishing flying records. An excellent score included "Thank Your Father," "Good For You, Bad For Me," and "Wasn't It Beautiful While It Lasted?"

Hollywood and the motion pictures broke up this winning combination, but only after it had produced some of the early song successes in the history of the talking pictures. De Sylva became a motion-picture producer, occasionally returning to Broadway to put on stage musicals for which he did no writing.

When he died in Hollywood in 1950 he was still a top man in show business—and on both coasts.

While De Sylva was in Hollywood, Brown and Henderson collaborated on two musicals, neither of which had the freshness or exhilaration that had made the De Sylva, Brown, and Henderson products so appealing. For a while after that, Brown and Henderson parted company. Brown went out to the coast as a producer in Hollywood, while Henderson completed some musical chores for Broadway, including scores for the *Scandals of 1935* and the *Ziegfeld Follies of 1943*, besides contributing music to the screen. Eventually, Brown and Henderson reestablished their partnership by opening a new publishing firm of their own in New York.

In 1944, an old De Sylva, Brown, and Henderson song, "Together,"—written sixteen years earlier—was revived, and acclaimed as one of the ten best of that year. In 1947, there came a new brilliant screen adaptation of *Good News*, and in 1956 *The Best Things in Life Are Free*, the screen biography of the songwriting trio. These were belated reminders of the glory that once was De Sylva, Brown, and Henderson in its heyday in the 1920s.

V

Gershwin's *Strike Up the Band* and *Of Thee I Sing* were two of several attempts by the musical theater of the 1920s and 1930s to establish a closer relationship between word and melody in songs, and in the musical play among songs, dances, and the spoken text.

One pair of writers proceeded toward this goal conscious of what it was trying to do, and endowed with the talent and imagination to achieve its aim: Rodgers and Hart. This was— together with the Gershwins—the most successful words-and-music team in the theater of that period. Rodgers and Hart wrote twenty-seven musical shows (only four of which were box-office failures) and about a thousand songs (over fifty of which belong with the best in our popular music)—and in a little over two decades.

Lorenz Hart was the lyricist, Richard Rodgers the composer. They were opposites in every possible way: temperament, outlook, glandular makeup, living and working habits. Yet it is doubtful whether any pair in the musical theater ever worked together with such singleness of thought and such harmony of purpose as they did—that is, unless that pair be Rodgers and Hammerstein of a later era.

It was the lyrics of Hart whose impact was first felt most strongly. When Hart started writing, the lyric was, generally speaking, a sadly neglected and illiterate stepchild in Tin Pan Alley. It combined shopworn clichés, bromides, and naïve sentiments with bad prosody, grammar, and halting meters and rhymes. The best lyrics of Irving Berlin, Ira Gershwin, and Cole Porter frequently had a cultivated air in those days; but it must be remembered that these men did their best work after they had been affected by the one-man revolution in lyric writing instigated by Hart.

He had a virtuoso's technique in using not only the more formal poetic procedures but also tripping exterior and interior rhymes, glib male and female rhymes, and other slick devices found in good light poetry. He had a way with a phrase that was highly personal; a feeling for figures of speech that avoided the trite and the obvious. His wit and sophistication were not afraid to dart in unexpected directions. And when he was sentimental, as every commercial lyricist had to be, it was usually with restraint and good taste. Frequently his lines leaped with the agility of Nijinsky floating through space in *The Afternoon of a Faun;* and then, just like Nijinsky, they would come to rest easily and gracefully.

His freedom and dexterity of movement and thought would certainly have been arrested, if not completely smothered, had he not been lucky enough to find an ideal musical collaborator. Richard Rodgers was a composer with an elastic range of idea and feeling, the resiliency to turn to many different styles, the skill to arrive at a fresh thought with simplicity and directness, the independence to think for himself instead of echoing the ideas of other men. He refused to function within those routined patterns and styles that served composers for the theater under many different circumstances and in many different contexts. As he kept on working with his collaborator, and developing and growing with him, he began to conceive of the musical-comedy score as a whole rather than a collection of individual numbers, each part having a subtle affinity with every other part, a family resemblance so to speak. Rodgers felt strongly, and Hart with him, that a song which did not derive its immediate stimulation from the play for which it was intended could not be integral to the play; and a song that was not integral to the play was a superfluity.

He was also able to think in dimensions larger than the song form. Through marches, ballets, dream sequences and extended recitatives he endowed his scores with a breadth and amplitude not usually encountered on the musical stage of the late 1920s and early 1930s. Beyond all this, he had an instinct for good theater and a taste for good writing that made it possible for him to understand and sympathize with the subtlest demands of his collaborator. (In later musicals, Rodgers would take a hand in the production, and sometimes even in the writing of the book.) Lorenz Hart, for his part, had a sound critical sense for music, and an intuitive feeling for good melody. These two co-workers, then, not only plowed their own fields, but often provided one another with a welcome helping hand.

They were both novices when they met for the first time in 1918. Hart was twenty-three, Rodgers only sixteen. Both had been born in New York and raised in a comfortable middle-class background. Rodgers first visited Hart at the latter's home on West 119th Street and spent the afternoon with him. He was deeply impressed by Hart's sophistication, knowledge of poetry, and ideas about lyric writing. Rodgers, in turn, played for Hart some of the tunes he had written. Before the day was over each knew that he would henceforth work with the other.

They began working together soon after their first meeting, and it was not long before they found at least one receptive ear. This was Lew Fields, one-time partner in the celebrated dialect-team of Weber and Fields, and more recently a Broadway producer. One day Rodgers played for Fields some of the songs he had written with Hart. "Any Old Place With You" appealed to the veteran showman who decided to interpolate it into his musical, *A Lonely Romeo,* then already running. This was in 1919. Lew Fields, then, had the historic role of leading Rodgers and Hart into the Broadway theater—possibly the first occasion that the music of a seventeen-year-old composer was heard on the professional stage in New York.

In the fall of the same year, Rodgers entered Columbia College where he wrote the music for the Varsity show, *Fly With Me*—the first time a freshman was thus honored. The show was seen at the Hotel Astor Ballroom in the spring of 1920. Lew Fields liked it so much that he bought the songs for a musical he was planning for Broadway, *The Poor Little Ritz Girl.* The show opened on July 28, 1920, the rest of its musical score by the veteran, Sigmund Romberg. What attracted favorable attention, however, was not the music but Larry Hart's lyrics. Heywood Broun wrote in *The World:* "The neglected lyric gets more of its due than usual, for the song entitled 'Mary, Queen of Scots' seems to us the most rollicking ballad we have heard in a twelvemonth."

Rodgers and Hart collaborated on a second Columbia Varsity show, and on other songs that were not published or performed. Somewhat discouraged, Rodgers decided to study music. He enrolled in the Institute of Musical Art in 1921, a student in harmony, ear training, and musical history. A temporary break in these studies allowed him to conduct a tabloid version of a

Lew Fields musical which the Shuberts were then sending on the road. As for Hart, he returned to a job held before he collaborated actively with Rodgers—that of translating and adapting Viennese operettas for the Shuberts. He saved his money and used it to produce two Broadway shows without music, both failures.

In 1923, after Rodgers left the Institute of Musical Art, the collaboration of Rodgers and Hart was resumed. They wrote several musicals for which Herbert Fields contributed the book, but none found interested producers. While waiting for recognition, Rodgers and Hart wrote about thirty amateur shows for churches, synagogues, schools, and clubs, getting only a pittance for such efforts. They also wrote a three-act comedy, *The Melody Man,* under the thinly-disguised pseudonym of "Herbert Lorenz," produced by Lew Fields in the spring of 1924, and a failure. Once again discouraged, and in debt, Rodgers— now twenty-two—decided to quit the theater for good.

He was about to take a job as a salesman for a babies' underwear firm for fifty dollars a week when a friend called to tell him that the Junior Group of the Theatre Guild was about to present an intimate, satirical revue to raise money for tapestries for the recently constructed Guild Theatre. The friend further informed Rodgers he had the necessary connections to get the group to use Rodgers and Hart songs. There would be no remuneration; but the importance of being associated with the Theatre Guild could not be overestimated. Rodgers and Hart agreed to co-operate.

The Garrick Gaieties, as the revue was called, was scheduled for only two performances, on the afternoon and evening of May 17, 1925. But it aroused such interest, and gathered such critical accolades, that four more performances were scheduled. Then a regular run was started on June 8, and continued for about twenty-five weeks. Of the twenty-three numbers in the sprightly show, Rodgers and Hart contributed six songs, the best being "Manhattan" and "Romantic You and Senti-

mental Me." The Rodgers and Hart songs, like the entire production, had vivacity, freshness, and at times the impertinence
of youth. *Variety* reported that the Rodgers and Hart numbers
clicked "like a colonel's heels at attention." The success of the
Gaieties led to a second edition the following season. This had
four songs by Rodgers and Hart, among them the still familiar
"Mountain Greenery."

The *Garrick Gaieties* proved to be the making of Rodgers
and Hart. The formerly elusive producers now sought them out.
One of the shows they had written before the *Garrick Gaieties*
was now produced—*Dearest Enemy,* which started a nine-
month run on September 18, 1925. "Here In My Arms," was
its hit song, and it is still frequently heard. In 1926, Rodgers
and Hart had four new productions on Broadway, and a fifth
in London. The year of 1927 brought *A Connecticut Yankee,*
a musical-comedy adaptation and modernization of the Mark
Twain story. Hart was never more agile in his versification or
crisper in his wit. "Something like your knob is used as a door
knob, that's why I feel at home with you"—so runs a passage
in the tongue-in-the-cheek love song called "I Feel At Home
With You." The pseudo-Arthurian phraseology mixed with
American jargon in "Thou Swell"—the "thous" and "wouldsts"
co-existing with terms like "lalla paloosa"—is equally amusing.
And "On a Desert Island With Thee" boasted some of the finest
lines found in any song lyric of the 1920s.

Since the *Gaieties,* Rodgers' music had been growing in
suaveness and assurance. It achieved a new high with "My
Heart Stood Still," to this day one of his best songs. The lyric
came to Hart after a characteristically perilous taxi ride in
Paris, when his girl friend exclaimed: "Oh, my heart stood still."
"My Heart Stood Still" was completed in London and appeared
in a London revue, *One Dam Thing After Another,* produced
by Charles B. Cochran in the spring of 1927. It quickly became such a pronounced hit in England that a false rumor
gained circulation that Florenz Ziegfeld offered to buy it.

Rodgers and Hart, however, knew its value and bought the song back from Cochran, intending it for one of their own American productions. Since their next American effort was *A Connecticut Yankee,* the song was fitted in there.

It was about a decade after *A Connecticut Yankee* before Rodgers and Hart were associated with a musical comedy both as good or as successful as that one. Meanwhile there was a long succession of minor plays, more entertaining than original. If these plays are remembered today it is for their best songs: "You Took Advantage of Me" (said to be the favorite of the then King of England when he wooed and won Wallis Simpson) in *Present Arms;* "With a Song in My Heart" (later Jane Froman's theme song and the title of her screen biography) in *Spring Is Here;* "A Ship Without a Sail" in *Heads Up;* "Ten Cents a Dance," made famous by Ruth Etting in *Simple Simon.*

After *America's Sweetheart,* in 1931, a satire on the movies and Hollywood, there was a five-year hiatus in which Rodgers and Hart worked in the screen capital. By the time they returned to Broadway, in 1936, they were beginning to think along new lines as far as the musical theater was concerned. They were now talking about "musical plays" as distinguished from musical comedies; plays in which, as Hart explained, "the songs are a definite part of the show and not extraneous interludes without rhyme or reason." They wanted song and dance and humor to spring naturally from the situation, each number to become a "plot number." They wanted the music to carry the action onward, not to hinder it. They were also thinking of paying greater attention to ballet and less to formal routines.

Their first effort in this new direction was *On Your Toes,* in 1936 (the first time Rodgers and Hart had a share in writing the book) in which they collaborated with George Abbott. This musical invaded boldly the world of ballet, concentrating on the backstage life of a ballet troupe—then a highly original subject for musical-comedy treatment. More significant still was the integral way that ballet was used in the story pattern. There were actually two principal ballets, both with choreography by George Balanchine and starring Ray Bolger, making his first major appearance on the musical stage. One was a hilarious satire on the more formal traditions; the other, "Slaughter on Tenth Avenue," was a ballet in the American style and tempo.

A great deal in *On Your Toes* betrayed the lines and wrinkles of premature age when it was revived in 1954—but not "Slaughter on Tenth Avenue," probably Rodgers' best music in a larger mold. As Richard Watts Jr. wrote: "A sizable number of jazz ballets have passed this way since its first appearance, but it is still something of a classic in its field." Songs in *On Your Toes* might prove more popular—say, "There's a Small Hotel" and "It's Got to Be Love." But the ballet score was more significant by indicating that the more ambitious forms of serious music were not beyond Rodgers' reach.

Babes in Arms in 1937—the first musical in which Rodgers and Hart received no outside help in the writing of the book—was no less courageous and independent in combining play, song, and dance into a single dramatic purpose. It also had an exciting ballet, "Peter's Journey," once again with Balanchine choreography and spacious music. It had three provocative songs: "Where or When," "Johnny One Note," and "The Lady Is a Tramp." And it had an all-time favorite, "My Funny Valentine." As Robert Coleman remarked in his review: "Rodgers and Hart thrust aside the conventional musical-comedy formula in favor of novelty, surprise, and freshness."

In *I'd Rather Be Right*, in 1937, Rodgers and Hart joined George S. Kaufman and Moss Hart in a topical political satire in the vein of Gershwin's *Of Thee I Sing*. The Gershwin musical had used a Presidential campaign with fictitious characters. *I'd Rather Be Right* had an American President who looked, talked, and acted like Franklin Delano Roosevelt, penetratingly portrayed by George M. Cohan in one of the outstanding characterizations of his long stage career. In using actual names in the news, and commenting sardonically on current events, this musical was a source of none too innocent merriment. No single song stands out prominently. The score was better as a whole than in individual parts. In numbers like "A Homogeneous Cabinet," "A Little Bit of Constitutional Fun," "We're Going to Balance the Budget," and "Off the Record" composer and lyricist made a conscious attempt to interrelate music and play more intimately and indivisibly than they had heretofore done.

After coming to grips with the realities of Washington politics, Rodgers and Hart returned to ballet and fantasy for which they had previously shown such a deft touch. They themselves adapted a Hungarian play by John Vaszary into a musical which became one of their happiest efforts at musical-play writing. *I Married an Angel,* starring Vera Zorina, an alumna of the Ballet Russe, provided her with an ample opportunity to exhibit her terpsichorean art—particularly in the "Honeymoon Ballet." But, though emphasized, ballet was beautifully integrated into the half-real world in which Count Willy Palaffi marries an angel. An ideal balance between fantasy and broad humor was another salient feature of the play, while the title song and "Spring Is Here" added appreciably to the over-all charm.

Some of the musicals engaging Rodgers and Hart after *I Married an Angel* pointed up a growing audacity on their part in selecting books—a healthy attempt to provide the musical theater with new horizons through the exploitation of unusual subjects. *The Boys from Syracuse,* in 1938, went for its plot to Shakespeare (a decade before Cole Porter's *Kiss Me Kate*), and introduced two of Rodgers' most beguiling and original melodies in "This Can't Be Love" and the waltz, "Falling in Love With Love." *By Jupiter,* in 1942, went to classical antiquity by adapting Julian F. Thompson's comedy about Greek Amazon women and their war against the Greeks. The score had two song hits in "Nobody's Heart Belongs to Me" and "Careless Rhapsody" and some skillful extended vocal writing in the final-etto to Act 2.

It took courage and independence for musical-comedy writers to go to Shakespeare or Greece for their themes. But perhaps even greater fortitude was required for them to write a show like *Pal Joey* in 1940. *Pal Joey* originated as a series of sketches in letter form by John O'Hara in *The New Yorker*. Built around a highly disagreeable person, these pieces uncovered some of the less palatable facets of life on Chicago's South Side, including blackmail, illicit love, crass opportunism, downright skullduggery. It was not the kind of material to lend itself to escapist musical theater, certainly not the kind of material musical-comedy writers reach for. Rodgers and Hart recognized these facts. Yet they felt that O'Hara's stories might bring a new virility to the musical stage through a closer identification with everyday life. "If it is possible to make an entertaining musical comedy out of an odious story, *Pal Joey* is it," reported Brooks Atkinson. "Although *Pal Joey* is expertly done, can you draw sweet water from a foul well?" But theatergoers seemed to find sustenance in foul water. The tempo was irresistible; the impact, a kind of animal energy. The Rodgers and Hart songs were in their most appealing sophisticated vein, frequently as hard-boiled and earthy as the characters who sang them.

During the original run of the play, its hit song was "I Could Write a Book." Vera's song, "Bewitched, Bothered and Bewildered" passed by without too much notice. But, in 1950, this song was revived on the radio suddenly and inexplicably to climb to the top rung of the Hit Parade ladder. This popularity of a nine-year-old song tempted the farsighted executive of Columbia Records, Goddard Lieberson, to record the complete score of the show; and this, in turn, stimulated a Broadway revival in 1952 that proved so successful that it ran more than 500 performances, breaking all records for a revival.

By Jupiter, in 1942, was the last musical by Rodgers and Hart. Its run of over a year was the longest of any Rodgers and Hart show. It would have lasted even longer if its star, Ray Bolger, had not embarked on a USO tour to entertain American troops in the Pacific. Thus, the partnership of Rodgers and Hart ended on a note of triumph.

But the partnership was over. Always somewhat shiftless, irresponsible, oversensitive, and disorderly in his habits, Lorenz Hart grew increasingly undisciplined with the growth of his fame and prosperity. Working with him, ever a trial to test the patience of a saint, had become torment for Rodgers. Besides, Hart was mentally and physically ill, an alcoholic. During the writing of *By Jupiter* he had had to be hospitalized; work on the musical went by fits and starts, often inside the hospital itself. After the *By Jupiter* opening, Hart went off to Mexico for a few months in a futile attempt to run away from himself. He returned more weary than ever, more depressed, more effete, more inclined to escape through drinking. He had lost all interest in success or the theater. Therefore, when in 1942, the Theatre Guild asked Rodgers and Hart to adapt Lynn Riggs' dramatic folk play, *Green Grow the Lilacs* into the musical *Oklahoma!* Hart bowed out gently but definitely. After all those years, Rodgers had to seek out a new collaborator.

Having lost the will to work, Hart soon lost the will to live. On March 31, 1943, *Oklahoma!* opened at the St. James Theatre to inaugurate not only the new musical-comedy team of Rodgers and Hammerstein but also a new era in the musical theater. A few months later, on November 17, *A Connecticut Yankee* was revived in a slightly modernized form, with six new songs for which Hart had painfully managed to provide the lyrics. On opening night, Hart disappeared from the theater while the performance was still going on. No one knows where he went. Forty-eight hours later he was found unconscious in his hotel room. He died a few days later, on November 22, of double pneumonia. He was only forty-eight.

VI

As our social historians have written, the 1920s were a period of license and iconoclasm, cynicism and sex emancipation, fads and rackets, uninhibited humor and freedom of behavior.

Cole Porter is the spirit of the 1920s in song and lyrics. We find in him the callous response of an age to romance and love, remote from the cloying sentimentality and antiseptic cleanliness of so many Tin Pan Alley songs of the period. He is the arch cynic whose love is often for sale; who can be true to you only in his fashion; to whom that seemingly crushing love affair is just one of those things.

If his attitude toward love reflected the spirit of the 1920s, so did his partiality for dilettantism and catchpenny philosophies. He sprinkles through his lyrics, with a firecracker succession of scintillating rhymes, all kinds of cultural, literary, and geographical allusions. His lyrics sprawl across the worlds of esoterica, exotica, and erotica. And his suave and well-groomed melodies, like his lyrics, fastidiously avoid the tender and the sentimental. They prefer sensuality to sentiment, throbbing excitement to deep feeling.

His personal and artistic credo was "anything goes"—even as it was the banner under which the 1920s marched to catastrophe. Like a character out of an F. Scott Fitzgerald novel, Porter was the sophisticate searching ceaselessly for the fullest riches life can yield; he was the high priest of life's pleasures. Fortunately he was also something of a genius, with a genius' compulsion to create.

He was born to wealth, on a seven-hundred acre fruit farm in Peru, Indiana, in 1892. At Yale, he led the glee club, helped to write and produce college shows, and wrote football songs; two of the latter, "Bulldog" and "Bingo" became famous. After a brief span at Harvard Law School he transferred to the School of Music.

His first Broadway show, *America First,* in 1916, was a fiasco. Porter remarked wryly that this failure was responsible for sending the author of the book, Lawranson Riggs, to the priesthood ("possibly in penance") and himself to the Foreign Legion ("as escape"). This Foreign Legion business was no gag. Porter joined the French desert troops in North Africa and ultimately received the *Croix de Guerre* from the French government for helping to sustain the morale of his fellow soldiers. When America became involved in World War I, Porter was shifted to France, where he was assigned to teach American soldiers the technique of French gunnery. At this time he acquired a luxurious Paris apartment and became one of Europe's playboys and most gracious hosts—the war notwithstanding. His military duties apparently were not too onerous since they allowed him to entertain in the grand manner and to write songs. His festivities—and the crisp, smart, and frequently sexy little songs he performed for his guests—attracted the élite of Paris. One was the beautiful American socialite, Linda Lee Thomas, divorced wife of the publisher of the *Morning Telegraph.* Linda and Cole fell in love and planned to marry as soon as the war ended.

Immediately after the Armistice, Porter returned to the United States for a brief visit to his family. On the boat he met Raymond Hitchock, the Broadway producer who since 1917 had been putting on an annual revue, called *Hitchy-Koo,* in which he himself starred. Delighted by some of Porter's songs, Hitchock engaged him to write the score for the next edition of his show, in 1919. Porter complied with about a dozen numbers. One was his first commercial success, "An Old Fashioned Garden," which actually had been written some years earlier while he was still in uniform.

Once back in Paris, Porter married Linda and set up a fashionable establishment where the parties were brilliant and prolonged. Guests came for the evening, and sometimes stayed on for a week. At one time, the Porters engaged the Monte Carlo

Ballet for one of their parties. On another occasion, at the whim of a moment, all guests were transported by motorcade to the Riviera.

In 1923, the Porters brought their gay life to Venice, to the Rezzonico Palace where Browning had died. They had a floating night club constructed which could accommodate over a hundred guests. They had Elsa Maxwell plan elaborate games for them, such as a treasure hunt through the canals, and arrange sumptuous balls. The 1920s were here, and the Porters were doing their best to set the tone for the era.

How music did not get lost in all these feverish celebrations and frenetic diversions remains something of a minor miracle. Actually, in Paris, Porter found both the time and the inclination to do some serious studying at the Schola Cantorum with Vincent d'Indy, one of the most renowned musicians of the day. He also kept on writing songs—sometimes risqué, always sophisticated—songs like "Settembrini," in which there appears the pithy comment that "these Lido boys are mere decoys." His friends—who included the Prince of Wales, Noel Coward, the Princess de Polignac, Cecil Beaton, and Elsa Maxwell—admitted he had creative talent, but also insisted that it was not the kind that could be put up for sale. "The reason is as plain as the nose on my face," Elsa Maxwell once told him. "You are too good. Your standards are too high. The wit and poetry of your lyrics are far beyond them. But one day you will haul the public up to your own level, and then the world will be yours."

Elsa Maxwell was, of course, right. The score Porter wrote in 1919 for *Hitchy-Koo*, and the five songs he contributed in 1924 to the *Greenwich Village Follies* proved that he was not at ease when he tried to meet the public on its own level. He was at his best in the intimacy of a living-room, surrounded by admiring friends, where he could sing as he felt, without inhibitions or fear of censorship.

At the Lido in Venice, E. Ray Goetz, the Broadway producer, moved into the Porter orbit. Goetz was then planning a musical, *Paris*, starring his wife, Irene Bordoni, which needed the kind of slick and suave songs that Porter was writing. He assigned Porter to do the score. The five numbers that Porter produced, in 1928, had three in the subtly suggestive vein that was to make him famous: "Let's Misbehave," "Let's Do It," and "Babes in the Wood."

A year later, Porter wrote the songs for two more Broadway plays. *Fifty Million Frenchmen* had "Find Me a Primitive Man" and "You Do Something to Me." *Wake Up and Dream* was the showcase for Porter's masterpiece, "What Is This Thing Called Love?" In 1930, a chic revue, *The New Yorkers*, was made memorable by still another Porter gem, "Love for Sale."

Porter's identity as a songwriter was now established. With a wry and frequently sardonic air, and always with an elegant manner, his lyrics passed, as Fred Lounsberry remarked, "from the esoteric to the lowbrow, the idealistic to the iconoclastic, the sophisticated to the sentimental." His individuality as a composer was also evident: the long sweeping lyric line, almost Semitic in character, and in a minor-mode languor, often refusing to stop to breathe after the sixteenth bar; the nervous throbbing of an irresistible rhythm in the background; the deep purple moods and the sensually exciting climaxes.

Once he had settled down to the business of being a professional songwriter there was nothing of the dilettante about him. He became a careful and methodical workman, capable of intense preoccupation with the job at hand, fastidious about meeting deadlines. By 1930, the playboy of the social world had become a composer who had won the respect of his colleagues and the admiration of a large public. His songs were among the smartest and most original, both in subject matter and in treatment, heard in or out of the Broadway theater of that period. He had succeeded in doing what Elsa Maxwell had prophesied he would: lift the public to his own level. But he had only begun. After 1930, he participated in more successful musical productions, and was responsible for a longer succession of song hits than any other man, with the exception of Irving Berlin or Richard Rodgers.

The reign of Cole Porter on Broadway began officially in 1932 with *Gay Divorce* (the movies later added an extra "e" to the last word), a frothy bedroom farce with Fred Astaire. It brought gaiety to the Broadway scene for almost 250 performances. But it is remembered today only because it gave birth to one of the most distinguished songs by an American, "Night and Day," a title subsequently taken over by Hollywood for Cole Porter's screen biography.

Two years later came *Anything Goes*, for many years described by commentators on the Broadway scene as "the highest point in Cole Porter's career . . . a climax he has never surpassed." Howard Lindsay and Russell Crouse wrote the book, whose setting was a luxury liner carrying a curious assortment of passengers, including Public Enemy No. 13 disguised as a Reverend (Victor Moore), and an indomitable lady who posed as a night-club hostess (Ethel Merman). Some of the choicest treasures in this remarkable production were found in Cole Porter's songs. The sardonic attitudes, ecstatic moods, and sexy overtones with which he was already identified were found in "All Through the Night," "I Get a Kick Out of You," and "Anything Goes." There were other kinds of songs, too: songs with light-handed wit and gaiety, as in "There'll Always Be a Lady Fair," a gentle take-off on sailor chanteys; patter songs with the neatness and dispatch of Gilbert and Sullivan, as in "You're the Top"; songs with bold brass and vigor, and obviously written with Merman in mind, as in "Blow, Gabriel, Blow."

It took Porter four years to be involved in another musical as satisfying and as successful as *Anything Goes*. In 1938 Bella and Samuel Spewack adapted their stage success, *Clear All Wires*, into a musical-comedy book. With Porter's music, and starring William Gaxton, Sophie Tucker, and Victor Moore, *Leave It to Me* became a delightful newspaper yarn that trailed all the way to the Soviet Union, entwining a sadly be-fuddled American Ambassador (Victor Moore) who could only dream of the time he would go home again and enjoy double banana splits.

William Gaxton, Sophie Tucker, and Victor Moore repre-sented the cream of show business. Yet when the curtain de-scended on the opening-night performance, it was none of these who stole the limelight, but a little girl from Weather-ford, Texas. Shedding her ermines in a simulated strip-tease at the wayside of a Siberian railroad, this unknown named Mary Martin sang in a quavering and childlike voice: "While tearing off a game of golf, I may make a play for the caddy; but when I do, I don't follow through, 'cause my heart belongs to daddy." A minor role had suddenly assumed major propor-tions through Mary Martin's incomparable way with "My Heart Belongs to Daddy." An obscure performer had suddenly become one of the all-time greats of the musical-comedy stage.

Leave It to Me inaugurated for Porter a new cycle of suc-cesses that included *Du Barry Was a Lady,* with Bert Lahr, in 1939; *Panama Hattie* with Ethel Merman, in 1940; *Let's Face It,* with Danny Kaye in 1941; and *Something for the Boys,* once again with Ethel Merman, in 1943.

Three successive failures came after that. Then, apparently having rid his system of some third-rate music and lyrics, Porter engaged upon the most consistently brilliant score of his career, that for *Kiss Me Kate,* in 1948. The springboard for the Bella and Samuel Spewack book was Shakespeare's *The Taming of the Shrew.* The adaptation shifted nimbly from present-day Baltimore, and the love entanglements of troupers performing Shakespeare, to Shakespeare's Padua and the tribu-lations of Petruchio and Kate. Elizabethan dialogue became a companion to Cole Porter sophistication.

Many distinguished elements made up the phenomenal success of *Kiss Me Kate*, which ran over 1,000 performances: a scintillating book; the performances of Alfred Drake, Lisa Kirk, Harold Lang, and Patricia Morison; the dances of Hanya Holm. But the most significant element was unquestionably the songs of Cole Porter. Veins tapped successfully in earlier shows stood out more prominently than ever. Rarely were his moods more darkly indigo than in "Were Thine That Special Face" and "So In Love"; rarely had his flair for parody and satire been so prominent as in "Wunderbar" and "Always True to You"; rarely did he leap from gaiety to broad humor with such agility as in "Brush Up Your Shakespeare" and "I Hate Men"; and rarely did he touch a discreet pornography with such deftness and inoffensiveness as in "Too Darn Hot" and "Where Is the Life that Late I Led?"

The critics raved over *Kiss Me Kate*, and with good cause. They found much less to exult over in *Can-Can*, in 1953. Nevertheless, audiences found so much entertainment in this nostalgic excursion into Bohemian Paris of 1893 that the musical had a long and profitable run. What Porter's songs lacked in brilliance they made up for in providing the proper feeling of nostalgia and sentiment, particularly in "I Love Paris" and "C'est Magnifique."

The critics on the whole were more partial to *Silk Stockings*, in 1954, a highly successful transfer to the musical-comedy stage of a motion-picture satire about the Soviet Union in which Greta Garbo had starred—*Ninotchka*. Porter's skillful parodies of Russian choral music, on the one hand, and his winning and nostalgic songs "All Of You" and "Without Love" were not the least of the production's strong suits.

VII

Vincent Youmans belongs with the giant figures of the American musical theater of the 1920s. He wrote the score for two of the great stage successes of that decade, *No, No, Nanette* and *Hit the Deck*. Some of his songs have long ago been assured a permanent place in the American repertory: "Tea for Two," "Sometimes I'm Happy," "Through the Years," "Without a Song," "Hallelujah," "I Want to Be Happy," "Flying Down to Rio," "More Than You Know," "Rise 'n' Shine," "Carioca" . . . and so on. His creative imagination, gift for a neatly turned melody, dramatic instinct, economy and preciseness, instinct for always finding the proper music for each episode and mood—all this gave many critics of the 1920s good cause to acclaim him one of our foremost popular composers.

This assurance comes to us from his successes. But, strangely enough, it comes to us even more strongly from his failures. Musical plays like *Rainbow* (which ran only 29 performances in 1928) and *Through the Years* (20 performances in 1932) suggested a new concept of the musical theater. That concept had to be realized by others, but Youmans must be considered a pioneer in this virgin territory.

He was born in New York City in 1898. He started taking piano lessons when he was four, but his father, a successful businessman, led him first to engineering, then to finance. During World War I, Youmans enlisted in the Navy where he produced musical shows for which he occasionally wrote songs. John Philip Sousa, then conductor of Navy as well as Army bands, liked one of his numbers and played it; other Navy bands followed suit until it became known to sailors everywhere. Ten years later, this same song became even more popular in *Hit the Deck:* "Hallelujah."

After the war, Youmans found a job as staff pianist for Harms. His first stage score was for *Two Little Girls in Blue* which had a profitable run in 1921. Youmans' sprightly songs, to Ira Gershwin's lyrics, were in the spirit of the whole gay production; one of these clicked big, "Oh Me, Oh My, Oh You." *Wildflower,* in 1923, was even more successful. Here he joined Herbert Stothart in writing a score that included two salient items, the title song and "Bambalina," both to lyrics by Otto Harbach and Oscar Hammerstein II. Then came a triumph—*No, No, Nanette*. After a brief try-out in Chicago, it opened in London in 1925 to achieve what was for that city the unprecedented record of 665 performances. In the fall of 1925 it came to Broadway for another marathon run. After that it encircled the globe, brought by seventeen different companies to Europe, South America, China, New Zealand, and the Philippines. It yielded for its producer a profit of over $2,000,000 and for the composer more than $500,000.

No, No, Nanette was at times, a good, at times an hilarious show—that is, within the limits set and prescribed by the existing stage conventions. Comedy was one of its strong points. Vincent Youmans' songs, his best up to then (lyrics by Irving Caesar) provided another. A disarming simplicity concealed the skill with which each was constructed: the ease with which the melodic line moved, the natural way in which the accents fell, the subtlety of the rhythmic pulse and syncopation. The economy of Youmans' writing was most apparent in the two hit songs of the production, "Tea for Two" and "I Want to Be Happy."

Youmans' next major Broadway musical came less than two years later. Herbert Fields made a musical adaptation of the Broadway comedy *Shore Leave* and called it *Hit the Deck*. With Youmans doubling as composer and co-producer, *Hit the Deck* exceeded the Broadway run of *No, No, Nanette* by twenty-four performances. The songs (this time with lyrics by Leo Robin and Clifford Grey) included two all-time Youmans' favorites: "Hallelujah," which the composer had written when he was in uniform, and "Sometimes I'm Happy," the latter once again a seemingly effortless creation that seems to have been written all in one piece and at one sitting.

Between 1927 and 1932 Youmans appeared on Broadway with a series of box-office disasters. But he did not have to be ashamed of two of these failures since each, in its own way, represented a courageous effort to bring a new spaciousness and artistic validity to the musical stage. *Rainbow*, in 1928, was a romantic play by Laurence Stallings and Oscar Hammerstein II set in California during the Gold Rush days of 1849. If any single musical deserves recognition as the forerunner of *Oklahoma!* for adjustment of music to play, this is it. *Through the Years,* in 1942, was another attempt to write a musical play instead of a musical comedy. This was Brian Hooker's adaptation of *Smilin' Through,* Jane Cowl's sentimental play long popular on stage and screen, now acquiring a new glow and radiance through Youmans' music. Two of its songs are deservedly famous, the title song (the composer's own favorite) and "Drums In My Heart."

Individual songs rather than the productions in which they are found bring significance to other Youmans musicals of this period. A few of these show the composer's growing technical mastery, his increasing assurance in arriving at exactness of musical expression and compactness of form, his developing articulateness. *Great Day* in 1929 had "More Than You Know" and "Without a Song" (William Rose and Edward Eliscu). *Smiles,* in 1930, might have had one of Youmans' classics, "Time On My Hands" (Harold Adamson and Mack Gordon) if the star, Marilyn Miller, had not objected to it so vigorously; consequently, the composer left it out of his show and issued it as a separate number. *Take a Chance,* in 1932, boasted another Youmans' gem, "Rise 'n' Shine" (Bud De Sylva), in the style of a revivalist hymn. *Take a Chance* was Youmans' last appearance on Broadway as composer. In 1933 he went to Hollywood to write music for *Flying Down to Rio.*

Youmans was laid low in 1933. The passion and intensity with which he always worked contributed to undermining his delicate health. A victim of tuberculosis, he had to quit all work and withdraw into a Colorado sanatorium. Not until about a decade later was he well enough to consider going back to the theater. He now planned a new kind of musical production called the *Vincent Youmans Ballet Revue,* embracing the classic and modern dance, good music (classic as well as popular), beautiful costuming and scenery, and even interludes for puppets. The show opened in Baltimore early in 1944 and met a frigid reception. It expired out of town without ever reaching New York—collapsing under the weight of its own pretentious aims.

This was Youmans' swan song. His health once again broke down, and he had to enter a New York hospital early in 1945. One year later, he returned to a Colorado sanatorium, from which he was never destined to emerge alive, and where he died in April 1946.

chapter twelve

THE REVUE BECOMES
SOPHISTICATED

IN THE 1920s and early 1930s the revue, like the musical comedy, outgrew the rompers of childhood to assume a mature dress.

For many years after 1894—when the first *Passing Show* had introduced to the stage a new kind of musical entertainment consisting of Variety in an elaborate format—the revue had been following familiar patterns. It was a festival for the eye, an opiate for the senses. It glorified the female figure, emphasized costuming, scenery, and stage techniques. Over-all effect was given precedence over detail. For years, the revue provided entertainment through splendor and glamour; stimulation and provocative originality belonged to other branches of the theater.

More than any other single person, Florenz Ziegfeld had been responsible for the personality assumed by the Broadway revue in the 1910s and 1920s. Father of the *Follies,* which for two decades was the yardstick by which all other revues were measured, he was the producer in the grand manner, the Sergei Diaghilev of the American musical theater. His was the courage to think and plan in grandiose designs; his the recklessness to

[264]

ignore budgets while mounting his incomparably lavish productions. He once paid an actress $650 a week, and had her wear a $1,200 gown, just to walk across the stage in a single scene. He ordered a gold set at the cost of $25,000, only to discard it unhesitatingly because it proved too garish. He bought for his shows the finest talent available without looking at the price tag, and he paid salaries unheard-of at the time, not only for stars but also for the girls of the chorus. He was never one to compromise with his ideals. As the years passed, his revues grew ever more ambitious, more opulent, more extravagant with talent.

He presented his first *Follies* on the roof of the New York Theater on July 8, 1907. The stars—Emma Carus, Grace La Rue, and the burlesque team of Bickel and Watson—were supplemented by The Anna Held Girls, publicized as fifty of the most beautiful women ever presented on a single stage, some of them imported from Paris. "Mr. Ziegfeld," wrote one critic, "has given New York the best mélange of mirth, music, and pretty young girls that has been seen here in many summers."

Out of the later editions of the *Follies* stepped some of the all-time greats of the American theater, many of them unrecognized before Ziegfeld glorified them. Ziegfeld used to say that, since he demanded only the best, he was not interested in making stars but only in buying them. But the truth is that few producers did more than Ziegfeld to lift unknowns to the heights. Fannie Brice was a performer in a shabby burlesque house when Ziegfeld gave her the spotlight in 1910 for "Lovey Joe," a ragtime number by Joe Jordan and Will Marion Cook that first made her a star. W. C. Fields was an obscure comic in *Watch Your Step* before becoming famous with his pool-table act in the *Follies of 1915.* Ziegfeld engaged a comparative nobody from Vaudeville, put him in the *Follies of 1916,* and had him sing Albert von Tilzer's "Oh! How She Could Yacki, Hacki, Wicki, Wacki, Woo" (Stanley Murphy and Charles McCarron). The song launched one of the theater's fabulous careers, that of Eddie Cantor. From out of the ranks of the chorus line stepped such later stars as Mae Murray, Nita Naldi, Olive Thomas, Ann Pennington, Marion Davies, Lilyan Tashman, Harriet Hoctor, and many others.

Most of the music for the *Follies*, during its twenty-four year reign on Broadway, was written by such reputable Tin Pan Alley craftsmen as Raymond Hubbell, Louis A. Hirsch, Dave Stamper, and Harry Tierney—each of whom could be counted upon to produce with despatch and skill the kind of functional music required by the varied production numbers and by the respective stars. At intermittent periods Irving Berlin, Jerome Kern, Victor Herbert, Rudolf Friml, and Gus Edwards also wrote for Ziegfeld.

Songs, like stars, were made in the *Follies*. In 1908 Nora Bayes introduced one that henceforth was to be her musical trademark: "Shine On, Harvest Moon," which she wrote with her husband, Jack Norworth; and in the *Follies of 1930*, this same number was revived with striking effect by Ruth Etting. Irving Berlin's "A Pretty Girl Is Like a Melody" and "You'd Be Surprised," were written, as we have earlier remarked, for the 1919 edition. Other hit songs to come out of the *Follies* included: "Row, Row, Row" by Jimmy V. Monaco (William Jerome); "Oh! Gee, Oh! Gosh, Oh! Golly, I'm in Love," introduced by Olsen and Johnson, who also wrote the lyrics to Ernest Breuer's music; "Mister Gallagher and Mister Shean," which Gallagher and Shean both wrote and introduced; "Hello Frisco!" by Louis A. Hirsch (Gene Buck) and "Some Sweet Day" by Dave Stamper and Hirsch (Buck). Fannie Brice's sentimental *tour de force*, "My Man," adapted for the American public from a French song by Channing Pollock, Berlin's "Mandy," and Victor Herbert's "A Kiss in the Dark" (De Sylva), while first becoming popular in the *Follies*, actually originated in earlier and different stage productions.

Sex and spectacle were apotheosized not only by Ziegfeld but by the many who imitated him. Taking their cue from the master, many producers became famous and wealthy putting on annual revues of their own, many frankly imitative of the *Follies*. The Shuberts had the *Passing Show* and *Artists and Models,* whose principal musical contributors were Louis A. Hirsch, Jean Schwartz, Sigmund Romberg, and J. Fred Coots. "Smiles" by Lee S. Roberts (J. Will Callahan), first became famous in one of the *Passing Shows,* and so did Walter Donaldson's "Carolina in the Morning" (Kahn). George White had the *Scandals* in which George Gershwin and De Sylva, Brown and Henderson served their valuable apprenticeships. Irving Berlin helped produce, and wrote book and songs for the *Music Box Revue*. Raymond Hitchcock had *Hitchy-Koo,* for which Cole Porter wrote the music in 1919 and Jerome Kern in 1920, and where were introduced Harry Tierney's "M-I-S-S-I-S-S-I-P-P-I" (Bert Hanlon and Benny Ryan) and Albert von Tilzer's "I May Be Gone For a Long, Long Time" (Lew Brown). Earl Carroll produced the *Vanities* and John Murray Anderson the *Almanac,* neither of which made any particularly lasting additions to our popular-song literature.

Somewhat off the beaten track was the all-Negro revue. One of the earliest was *Shuffle Along,* starring Florence Mills and Noble Sissle, which first became successful in Harlem before stepping downtown for a short stay. One of the most triumphant of the all-Negro revues to follow was the *Blackbirds of 1928,* book and lyrics by Dorothy Fields, the cast headed by Adelaide Hall and Bill Robinson. This revue first brought to prominence a new name in popular music, that of Jimmy Mc-Hugh. Born in Boston in 1894, McHugh for a while ploughed the classical fields, following his music study, as a rehearsal pianist at the Boston Opera House. Then deciding to change to popular music, he found a job as staff pianist and song plugger in Irving Berlin's publishing firm. McHugh's first published song "Emaline" (George A. Little) came in 1921. His first hits appeared three years after that: "When My Sugar Walks Down the Street" (Irving Mills and Gene Austin) and "What

Has Become of Hinky Dinky Parley Voo?" (Al Dubin and Irving Fields). For several years, McHugh wrote the music for revues staged at the Cotton Club in New York's Harlem. Then, in 1928, he was engaged to write the music for the *Blackbirds*. This was his first Broadway score, and his first major success. Two of the principal numbers were "Diga Diga Doo" and "I Can't Give You Anything But Love," the latter reputedly inspired by a casual remark overheard by Dorothy Fields and McHugh outside of Tiffany's on Fifth Avenue.

After the *Blackbirds*, McHugh continued to bring winning numbers to various revues. "On the Sunny Side of the Street" (Fields), one of his best numbers, was a principal attraction of Lew Leslie's *International Revue* in 1930. In the same year, the *Vanderbilt Revue* introduced "Blue Again" (Fields). In 1939, *The Streets of Paris* brought the "South American Way" (Al Dubin), which helped to make Carmen Miranda a Broadway sensation. In the nine-year period between the *Vanderbilt Revue* and *The Streets of Paris*, McHugh worked in Hollywood where he became one of the screen's foremost composers.

The original *Blackbirds* was filled with the verve, excitement, passion, humor, and rhythm, for which Negro performers are famous. It ran almost two years and was the precursor of several other *Blackbird* revues between 1930 and 1939, none of which was able to match the original product in quality, spontaneity, and box-office appeal. But another all-Negro revue was more fortunate: *Hot Chocolates*, in 1929, for which Fats Waller wrote "Ain't Misbehavin'" (Andy Razaf).

II

Then, in the 1920s, a healthy reaction set in against the orgy of colors in set and costuming, the extravagance in stage effects, and the exaggerated importance placed on female nudity. There was dissatisfaction in some quarters with the tendency of the revue to slight so many other important elements of the musical theater, notably satire. A new trend developed toward simplicity, freshness of approach, subdued tones, and a relaxed, leisurely pace. The revue was now striving to appeal to intelligence as well as to eye and ear.

This revolution first took place not on Broadway but further downtown, on the East Side—in a little theater on Grand Street, the Neighborhood Playhouse. A group of little known writers and performers collaborated in 1922 in what they described as a "lowbrow show for highgrade morons," a satirical revue called *The Grand Street Follies*. Partly out of economic necessity, partly by intention, these *Follies* scrupulously avoided lavish sights and sounds, and large masses of performers. The emphasis was on laughter: satire, parody, mimicry, caricature. The show had so much sparkle and originality that the flow of theatrical trade soon moved downstream from Broadway to Grand Street. The *Grand Street Follies* stayed downtown through 1926; from 1927 to 1929 it was seen uptown on Broadway.

Each season this revue brought the penetrating impersonations of prominent stage stars by two superb mimics, Albert Carroll and Dorothy Sands; hilarious parodies of current ballets and plays; irreverent satires on the classic theater and opera. And with these came little melodies and bright-faced lyrics, often accompanied by economical and ingeniously contrived dances and production numbers. Everything was in a modest design—everything except the imagination, enthusiasm, and the talent of the performers and writers.

Broadway soon felt the impact of the *Grand Street Follies*. While the more elaborate revues continued to flourish, a new kind of production sought out and found a discriminating audience. Undoubtedly it was from the Neighborhood Playhouse in Grand Street that the Junior Group of the Theater Guild got the happy stimulation to put on their own *Garrick Gaieties* in 1925.

But the smart, frugal, and intimate revue thus far appealed only to a comparatively limited audience of sophisticated the-ater-goers. None of the editions of the *Grand Street Follies* had over 150 performances, while the longest run of the *Garrick Gaieties* was 174 performances. *Americana*, in 1926, succeeded in passing the 200 performance mark—still a modest success at best—even though it helped to carve out revue history. For it was in this production that Charles Butterworth, the comedian, made his stage debut, and for the first time Helen Morgan sat atop an upright piano to moan one of her plangent blues songs.

In 1929 a new intimate revue proved not only a substantial *succès d'estime* but also box-office magic. The first *Little Show* stayed on Broadway for about a year. With it, the informal, intimate, sophisticated revue became an integral part of show business. Since nothing on Broadway breeds imitation like success, everybody now seemed to get into the act of putting on intimate revues. The provocative columnist of the New York *World*—Heywood Broun—was the master-of-ceremonies of *Shoot the Works*, in 1931. In 1934, Leonard Sillman presented the first of his revues designed to provide opportunities for unknown performers and writers, aptly called *New Faces;* incidentally, those new faces included Imogene Coca and Henry Fonda, in 1934, and a year after that, Van Johnson. One smart revue, *Lend an Ear*, started out on the so-called straw circuit in 1941, and ended up on Broadway seven years later. Another such revue called itself the *Straw Hat Revue*, in 1941, and it brought to the Broadway stage (by way of an adult camp in Pennsylvania) Max Liebman and Danny Kaye. The most prosperous of these revue-importations was *Meet the People*, which originated in Hollywood in 1939 on a modest outlay of $3,600; coming to Broadway a year later with its incisive social viewpoints, sardonic commentaries on the political scene, and gay take-offs on torch songs and popular tunes lifted from the classics, it played to packed houses for almost a year.

III

Many composers, bringing their talent to these intimate revues, wrote smart and sophisticated songs in keeping with the general nature of these productions. None of these songwriters was more consistently productive and more consistently brilliant in this special branch of the theater than Arthur Schwartz. His apprenticeship had taken place—appropriately! —in the *Grand Street Follies* where a single song, "Baltimore, Md., You're the Only Doctor For Me" (Eli Dawson) was heard in 1925. One year later he contributed several more numbers to the *Grand Street Follies*. In 1929, the apprentice turned into master with the score for the first *Little Show*. From that time on, he associated himself with some of the brightest revues on broadway.

The first *Little Show* was a milestone and a turning point. Up to then Schwartz had been a more or less successful lawyer, to whom the writing of songs was only a pleasant avocation. After the first *Little Show* he was a professional, to whom the theater was bread and butter.

He was born in Brooklyn, New York, in 1900. He attended the city public schools, then New York University from which he was graduated with a Bachelor of Arts degree, and Columbia University, where in 1921 he received a degree of Master of Arts. For a while he contemplated a literary career, having done some writing for the college paper, but he finally bowed to the wishes of his father by taking up law at Columbia. While studying law, he supported himself by teaching English in a New York high school.

Wearing a Phi Beta Kappa key, Schwartz was admitted to the bar in 1924. He practiced law for four years and did quite well. But in 1928 he suddenly decided to exchange the law court for the stage. What had decided him in this drastic change of life had been a few minor successes as a songwriter. In 1923 he had a song in *Poppy*, starring W. C. Fields—"Alibi Baby," the first of his songs to be published. A year later "All Lanes Must Reach a Turning" appeared in *Dear Sir,* a musical whose score was by Jerome Kern. Then came the already-mentioned "Baltimore, Md." in the *Grand Street Follies*. For some time after that, Schwartz ghosted some songs for an ill-fated production that never reached Broadway, and doctored the songs for still another show that opened and closed out of town.

Before 1928 he had received heartening encouragement from a friend: Howard Dietz, an advertising man whose extracurricular activities included the writing of lyrics. Dietz's first published lyric had been to Schwartz's "Alibi Baby." He then wrote all the lyrics for *Dear Sir,* and three years after that worked with Morrie Ryskind in writing book and lyrics for the intimate revue, *Merry Go Round*.

The first important collaboration of Schwartz and Dietz was also their first triumph, the *Little Show*. Dietz wrote most of the lyrics and book; Schwartz contributed the main musical numbers. Here Libby Holman established herself as a striking new personality of the musical theater with her sultry renditions of "Moanin' Low" and "Can't We Be Friends?" (As it turned out, neither of these two songs was by Schwartz. The first was by the pianist in the orchestra pit, Ralph Rainger, with lyrics by Dietz; the other was by Kay Swift, to words provided by her husband, James Warburg.) Fred Allen, one-time juggler and ventriloquist, stopped the show each evening with his dead pan and his rasping voice as he delivered wry monologues and commentaries from a drawn curtain. The veteran of the company was Clifton Webb. His debonair manner when he sang Schwartz's "I Guess I'll Have to Change My Plan," and his suave dancing routines brought a touch of elegance, and a welcome change of pace, to the exciting proceedings. (The song, "I Guess I'll Have to Change My Plan" so neatly fits Webb's style and personality that it may come as a distinct shock to discover that Schwartz had written it two years earlier for an amateur production at a boys' summer camp.)

There were two other *Little Shows,* both of them with book and lyrics by Howard Dietz, and only one with a score by Schwartz. Neither had the informal and ingratiating personality and charm of its parent. The *Second Little Show,* in 1930, had Al Trahan and Jay C. Flippen. Schwartz's music here was of modest attainments, and the hit number came from somebody else—"Sing Something Simple," words and music by Herman Hupfeld. The *Third Little Show,* in 1931, was dominated by the personality of Beatrice Lillie, who introduced to the American theater Noel Coward's "Mad Dogs and Englishmen." The rest of the numbers were written by various composers, one of the most amusing being Herman Hupfeld's "When Yuba Plays the Rumba on the Tuba."

Much more in the manner, design, and tempo of the first *Little Show* was *Three's a Crowd,* in 1930. Once again Fred Allen, Libby Holman, and Clifton Webb were the stars, and once again Schwartz and Dietz provided the production with materials that had all the spice and savor of the original recipe. Allen's drawling monologues and Webb's sleek *savoir-faire* in song and dance lost none of their subtle timing. Libby Holman's now celebrated low moanin' was heard in Schwartz's "Something to Remember You By" and in "Body and Soul," the latter by Johnny Green (Edward Heyman, Robert Sour, and Frank Eyton).

An even higher standard was realized by Dietz and Schwartz in *The Bandwagon,* in 1931. Here Dietz had the support of George S. Kaufman in writing a book whose sketches, characterizations, and quips had the sting of acid; whose humor was more often derived from a sustained situation or a pointed characterization than from a surprise blackout line. It was in this show that Adele Astaire bowed out both from the theater and her long stage partnership with her brother, Fred; and it was here that Fred Astaire revealed a new adeptness at comedy. Schwartz's score included one of the best songs he has written, "Dancing in the Dark." Others included

"I Love Louisa" and "New Sun in the Sky," the latter inspiring an unforgettable dance conception.

Flying Colors, in 1932, was more ambitious in scope and format than either the first *Little Show* or *Three's a Crowd.* But it still had some of the ingredients that had made the two earlier revues so exciting, most notable of which was Clifton Webb. The newer performers included Charles Butterworth, a worthy replacement for Fred Allen, Imogene Coca, and Larry Adler and his harmonica. Of Schwartz's songs, three made a favorable impression: "Alone Together," "Louisiana Hayride," and "A Shine On Your Shoes."

Both *At Home Abroad* in 1934 and *Inside U.S.A.* in 1938 were primarily the frames for the buffoonery of Beatrice Lillie. In the former, Schwartz's best song was "Love Is a Dancing Thing," while in the latter the most prominent musical numbers were "Haunted Heart," "Blue Grass," and "Rhode Island Is Famous For You."

Vernon Duke was another popular-song composer incubated by the intimate revue. Three of his songs in the 1930 edition of the *Garrick Gaieties* represented his first musical efforts for the New York stage: "I'm Only Human After All" (Ira Gershwin and Yip Harburg), and "Shavian Shivers" and "Too, Too Divine," both with lyrics by Harburg.

Duke was born in Russia in 1903 as Vladimir Dukelsky, a name which he long used for his more serious symphonic and choral works. As a student at the Kiev Conservatory he received a thorough musical training. In 1918, the Revolution drove him from his native land. After taking a circuitous route by way of Constantinople he arrived in America in 1921 with the hope of making his way here as a popular composer—an ambition first aroused in Constantinople when he came upon the sheet music of Gershwin's "Swanee." In New York he contacted Gershwin, who gave him criticism and a helping hand, and who was also the one to make him assume the name of Vernon Duke for his more popular efforts. Duke did not make any headway in

popular music for some years; in that time he wrote ballet
scores, symphonies, and concertos that were performed by
many major musical organizations in Europe and America, and
mostly by the Boston Symphony under Koussevitzky. But in
1930 he broke the ice in popular music by selling three songs
to the third edition of the *Garrick Gaieties* which in turn
brought him a contract from Harms. Other songs were then
heard in later revues: "Let Me Match My Private Life With
Yours" (Harburg) in *Americana.* "Muchacha" (Harburg and
Jay Gorney) in *Shoot the Works,* and "Talkative Toes" in
Three's a Crowd. Success came in 1932 with his first full score
for a Broadway musical, *Walk a Little Faster,* a revue starring
Beatrice Lillie, lyrics by Yip Harburg. Since this score included "April in Paris"—to this day the song with which Duke
is most often associated—he was also the proud author of quite
a substantial hit. The idea for this song came to Duke while the
show was in preparation. He was dining at a place on 52nd
Street with Dorothy Parker, Robert Benchley, Monty Woolley
and several others—worrying over a new romantic number that
would suit the gifts of one of the stars of his show—when he
heard Dorothy Parker say: "Oh, to be in Paris now that
April's there!" Though Duke knew only too well that April
happens to be one of the most disagreeable months for Paris,
he seized upon the idea and immediately relayed it to his
lyricist, Harburg. The song went over well when the show tried
out in Boston, and while in New York nobody seemed to notice
it at first, it slowly caught on, particularly after Marian Chase
began singing it in night clubs and made a recording that sold
well.

IV

The mounting social and political tensions gripping the tur-
bulent 1930s could not be ignored by the musical theater. The
revue boldly entered the political arena on November 27, 1937,
when a new production faced the problems of the labor class

and the international scene with song, dance, and sketches, and at times with sentiment and laughter. That revue, *Pins and Needles*, did not actually belong to the professional theater. It was conceived and created by and for the International Ladies Garment Workers Union, with a cast recruited exclusively from the ranks of union members. As a product with a union label, *Pins and Needles* identified itself unequivocally with a progressive, and at times, leftist viewpoint. "Sing me a song with social significance, all other songs are taboo," was the refrain which served as a kind of *Leitmotif* for the entire production.

Beginning as a week-end adventure, and as an escapade for members of the Union and their friends, *Pins and Needles* turned out to be one of the greatest box-office triumphs of our musical theater. It remained on the boards for three years, achieving the staggering figure of 1,108 performances.

Pins and Needles made the social-political conscious revue popular. It did something else, too. It introduced a new and henceforth major songwriter to the Broadway theater—Harold J. Rome. Rome wrote all the songs for *Pins and Needles*, words as well as music. For some time after 1937, his songs were filled with social and political implications and were heard in several other well received leftist Broadway productions.

Born in Hartford, Connecticut in 1908, Rome was a child of the Great Depression. He studied law at Yale, but law bored him and after a year he went to the School of Architecture, from which he was graduated with a degree of Bachelor of Fine Arts in 1934. All the while he had been engaged in musical activities, earning his way through college and post-graduate school playing the piano in jazz bands. At Yale he took some courses in music and joined the college orchestra when it toured Europe.

In 1934 he tried earning his living in New York as an architect. In order to gain experience he had to take on a job without pay. To earn some money, he tried writing popular songs, sometimes the lyrics, at other times melodies, occasionally both. Gypsy Rose Lee helped him get one of his lyrics published, and one of his songs was used by the Ritz Brothers in a movie. Encouraged, he suddenly decided to give up architecture and devote himself completely to writing songs.

In the summer of 1935 he found a job at Green Mansions, an adult summer camp in the Adirondack Mountains of New York. In its theater an original musical was put on weekly, written by staff men, and performed by a resident company. Rome was hired to write some of the material and help with the production. He worked at Green Mansions for three summers, in which time he wrote lyrics and music for about ninety songs.

One of his collaborators there was Charles Friedman. Friedman had been invited by the International Ladies Garment Workers Union to put on an amateur musical show with union personnel. He needed songs, and he asked Rome to write them. That amateur show was *Pins and Needles,* which carried Rome both to Broadway and fame.

Now identified with songs of a left-wing slant, Rome was commissioned by Max Gordon to write music and lyrics for a new political revue, *Sing Out the News,* book by Charles Friedman. The political consciousness of *Pins and Needles* prevailed in the new revue, though not with the bite and sting of the original. It had one of Rome's best political songs, "Franklin D. Roosevelt Jones," a moving tribute of the common man to the President.

Let Freedom Ring, in 1942, came next, but since it was more propaganda than entertainment, it was rejected by audiences and departed unlamented after only eight performances. The highlight of this revue survived long after the revue closed: "The House I Live In," an effective production number pleading for racial and religious tolerance, popularized some years later by Frank Sinatra.

Rome entered the Army in 1942, where he wrote Army shows and orientation songs. He also toured the Pacific combat zone. His only commercial chore while in uniform was a song for the *Ziegfeld Follies of 1943.*

Once out of the Army, he returned to Broadway with his greatest success since *Pins and Needles*—a brilliant topical revue that started a two-year run in 1946, *Call Me Mister.* As its title suggests, *Call Me Mister* was inspired by the-then recent shift of millions of Americans from Army to civilian status. Much of the revue was concerned with either a sentimental or satiric treatment of Army life; much to similar approaches to the readjustment problems of the veteran. There were also social and political overtones in other sketches and numbers that had little to do with Army life. But what stole the show had neither military nor political interest. It was a hilarious travesty on the American craze for South American music, "South America Take It Away," in which Betty Garrett became a star.

The changing political climate after the end of World War II chilled the theater-goer to political revues. It is, then, no occasion for surprise that with his next revue, *Bless You all,* in 1950, Rome should be involved with a production seeking out non-provocative subjects for humor, such as movie stars from the South, miracle drugs, and the Parent-Teachers Associations. The two main songs were also completely devoid of political awareness: "When" and "You'll Never Know What Hit You."

When Rome next appeared on Broadway it was with *Wish You Were Here,* in 1952, his first musical comedy. And here his divorce from political realities becomes complete.

chapter thirteen

HOLLYWOOD

THE MOVIES as a source for new popular songs and a medium to circularize them did not assume significance until they had acquired a voice.

The solitary piano, or the orchestra, which provided background music for the silent movies generally went for material to Tin Pan Alley, the stage, or the existing repertory of semi-classics. Such music—used to heighten suspense or intensify emotions, to point up atmosphere and background—was stereotyped. Set pieces were used for set situations: say, Sinding's "Rustle of Spring" for bucolic scenes; Tobani's "Hearts and Flowers" for tragedy; *brio* passages from Rossini or Suppé for climaxes and suspense.

Digression from the practice of using familiar music was rare. One took place as early as 1916 when Victor Herbert was commissioned to write original music for *The Fall of a Nation*, presented at the Liberty Theatre in New York. This was the first occasion when an original musical score was written for a motion picture.

But not until the screen became vocal did it become a most potent agency for the creation and distribution of new popular songs.

II

Experiments with sound films had been going on for some time. On April 15, 1923, Dr. Lee de Forest presented a program of Phonofilm at the Rivoli Theatre in New York that included Eddie Cantor and Weber and Fields. By 1926, the practicability of applying sound to films was firmly accepted by Warner Brothers, who then formed the Vitaphone Corporation to present sound pictures, entering into an agreement for this purpose with the Western Electric Company. The first Warner public presentation of sound pictures took place at the Warner Brothers Theatre in New York on August 6 of the same year. The first half of the evening was devoted to a program of good music by leading concert artists and the New York Philharmonic Orchestra under Henry Hadley. The second part consisted of a silent picture—*Don Juan* starring John Barrymore. What gave this picture significance and added interest was the fact that it had a synchronized musical score, written expressly for this purpose by Major Edward Bowes, David Mendoza, and Dr. William Axt.

Many now predicted that the future of the movies lay with sound. But there were also many who remained skeptics. The latter remembered that before sound films could be distributed, theater owners everywhere would have to go to the formidable expense of wiring their theaters; that expensive Hollywood equipment would overnight become obsolete; that many glamorous stars of the silent screen—valuable properties to their studios—would lose their magic when they opened their mouths to speak. William Fox insisted that "there will never be the much-dreamed-of talking pictures on a large scale. To have conversation would strain the eyesight and the sense of hearing at once, taking away the restfulness one gets from viewing pictures alone."

But the Warner Brothers insisted that sound was here to stay, and were willing to gamble on their judgment. They not only set up a program to produce such films, but even went to the expense of wiring several theaters where their pictures could be presented. Grudgingly, and in response to public demand, other producers followed the Warner lead in experimenting with sound. Fox presented the first sound Movietone News and a series of Movietone short subjects in 1927. Studios now began recording and synchronizing musical backgrounds for all major film productions, often with new music. And theater owners were compelled to install sound equipment or else lose their clientele.

The theme song became a fad. For the first time popular songs written directly for the movies rivaled in popularity those meant for the stage. In 1926 there was "Charmaine" by Erno Rapee (Lew Pollack) in *What Price Glory;* in 1927, "Diane," once again by Rapee and Pollack, in *Seventh Heaven,* and "Ramona," by Mabel Wayne (L. Wolfe Gilbert) in the picture of the same name; in 1928, "Jeannine, I Dream of Lilac Time" by Nathaniel Shilkret (L. Wolfe Gilbert) in *Lilac Time,* and "Angela Mia" by Rapee and Pollack in *Street Angel.* Recognizing that the popularity of theme songs provided a powerful means for publicizing titles of motion pictures, Hollywood moguls soon insisted that some of these songs bear the same name as the picture. *Varsity Girl* had "Varsity Girl, I'll Cling to You"; *Woman Disputed,* "Woman Disputed, I Love You"; *Wild Party,* "My Wild Party Girl"; *Madonna of Avenue A,* "My Madonna"; *The Pagan,* "Pagan Love Song." It took Dorothy Parker to reduce this practice to absurdity. Engaged to write lyrics for a film called *Dynamite Man,* she submitted a song called "Dynamite Man, I Love You."

The screen, which had just burst into melody, was now ready to erupt into speech and song.

On October 6, 1927, Warner Brothers presented in New York *The Jazz Singer,* based on the Broadway play of the same name by Samson Raphaelson. Al Jolson was starred in the role created on the stage by George Jessel, that of a cantor's son who rejects the synagogue to become a jazz singer, only to substitute for his ailing father on the Day of Atonement services. This was meant to be a silent film with background music. But an experiment was tried to inject novelty: midway in the picture, in a café scene, Jolson sang "Dirty Hands, Dirty Face," by Edgar Leslie, Grant Clarke, Jimmy Monaco, and Jolson himself. The sudden break of silence, and introduction of Jolson's magnetic singing style, immediately made the silent picture obsolete, launched the age of the talking picture, and established Warner Brothers as an empire in the celluloid industry. When this song was first filmed on the Warner Brothers set, Jolson spontaneously abandoned the script to shout out to the "extras" in the café set one of his pet stage cries: "Wait a minute, you ain't heard nothin' yet!" The spoken line proved so effective that the director decided to leave it in the picture. Other songs by Jolson, and a scene of dialogue between him and his screen mother, were also interpolated. Jolson sang some of his old favorites including "Toot, Toot, Tootsie," by Gus Kahn, Ernie Erdman, and Dan Russo; Donaldson's "My Mammy"; and Irving Berlin's "Blue Skies." In the final scene he also gave a poignant rendition of the old Hebrew prayer, "Kol Nidrei." (Joseph Rosenblatt, the world-famous cantor, had been engaged to dub in the singing of the "Kol Nidrei" for Jolson. But Jolson's own way of singing the traditional hymn was so moving that he was asked to do it for himself. Rosenblatt, instead, was used for a special concert-hall sequence in which he gave some traditional Jewish and Hebrew songs.)

The triumph of *The Jazz Singer* was uncontested. It was acclaimed wherever it played and it grossed what for that time was the unprecedented figure of $3,000,000.

When the first all-talking picture—*Lights of New York*, in 1928, produced by the Warner Brothers—gathered a profit of almost $2,000,000, Hollywood had to admit that sound was here to stay. The once-skeptical Fox now brought out an all-talkie of his own in 1929. MGM produced the first motion-

picture revue in *The Broadway Melody,* which added a chapter
to the early history of talking pictures by being the first musical
to win the Motion Picture Academy Award, instituted one year
earlier, as the best picture of the year. Its score, by Nacio Herb
Brown (Arthur Freed) yielded two substantial hits: "Broadway Melody" and "The Wedding of the Painted Doll."

The Broadway Melody, a box-office smash, set the pattern
for numerous similar films. In 1929 Fox brought out the *Fox
Movietone Follies,* and in 1930 *The King of Jazz,* starring Paul
Whiteman. Warner Brothers produced *The Gold Diggers of
Broadway,* whose music by Joe Burke (Al Dubin) included
"Painting the Clouds with Sunshine" and "Tip Toe Through
the Tulips." Other Warner Brothers musicals included *The Show
of Shows,* while Paramount presented *Paramount on Parade*
and MGM *Hollywood Revue.*

Musical comedies and plays with interpolated songs also entered the market. In 1929, Paramount introduced Maurice
Chevalier to the American public in *Innocents of Paris.* Here,
among other songs by Richard Whiting (Leo Robin), Chevalier
sang one with which he was henceforth to be associated,
"Louise." Firmly entrenched as a new movie idol, Chevalier
appeared in the same year with Jeanette MacDonald in Para-
mount's *The Love Parade,* winning still more female hearts with
songs like "My Love Parade" and "Paris Stay the Same" by
Victor Schertzinger (Clifford Grey). Paramount also presented
The Cocoanuts, the first Four Marx Brothers' picture, for which
Irving Berlin wrote a haunting ballad, "When My Dreams
Come True." Warner Brothers starred Fannie Brice in "My
Man," where she sang not only that ballad but also many of
the comic songs she had helped make famous in the *Ziegfeld
Follies* and other Broadway musicals.

The songwriting team of De Sylva, Brown, and Henderson
had a hand in the music for two of the best liked musicals in the
early history of talking pictures: *The Singing Fool* with Al
Jolson, and *Sunny Side Up* with Janet Gaynor and Charles

Farrell, both released in 1929. *The Singing Fool* was the first motion picture to play the New York Winter Garden, scene of so many Jolson stage successes; the first motion picture to charge the top admission price of $3.00; the first motion picture to gross over $4,000,000. Jolson sang three numbers, each of which clicked: "I'm Sittin' On Top of the World," "It All Depends On You," and what is probably one of the most succussful motion-picture theme songs ever written, "Sonny Boy." A fourth song, "There's a Rainbow Round My Shoulder," was by Billy Rose, Dave Breyer, and Jolson.

The songs of De Sylva, Brown and Henderson also helped make *Sunny Side Up* the gentle and lovable musical it was, particularly "Keep Your Sunny Side Up," "If I had a Talking Picture Of You," and "I'm a Dreamer."

The large market for screen revues and musicals put a heavy premium on popular music, creating in Hollywood a new and seemingly insatiable demand for popular songs. To supply that need, the motion-picture producers made some significant moves. They bought out the motion-picture rights to all the Broadway musicals and operettas they could put their hands on. In the first few years of talking pictures many Broadway successes came to the screen. Among these were *Rio Rita, Sally, Show Boat, Animal Crackers, Follow Through, Good News, Hit the Deck, New Moon, No, No, Nanette, Sunny, Whoopee, The Vagabond King, The Desert Song,* and many, many others.

A second move to insure a steady supply of songs for the screen was the purchase of some of New York's most significant song-publishing firms, thus providing Hollywood with a large and handy reservoir of music to draw from. Still a third maneuver was the offer of fabulous fees to the foremost popular-song composers and lyrists of Broadway and Tin Pan Alley to work for motion pictures.

De Sylva, Brown, and Henderson came to the Coast in 1929, and immediately became engaged in the writing of two major films, mentioned earlier. They also wrote the numbers for *Say*

It With Songs, starring Al Jolson, and *Just Imagine*, in 1929 and 1930 respectively. Irving Berlin became associated with motion pictures in 1929 by writing the theme song for *The Cocoanuts* and three songs for *Hallelujah*, an MGM picture directed by King Vidor. Still in 1929, Walter Donaldson wrote his first complete motion-picture score, for *Hot for Paris*. In 1930, both Jerome Kern and Sigmund Romberg worked for the films for the first time, the former writing music for *The Three Sisters*, the latter for *Viennese Nights*. In 1931, George Gershwin appeared at the Fox Studios to produce a score for *Delicious*, while Rodgers and Hart came to First National to work on *The Hot Heiress*. In 1933 Vincent Youmans came to Hollywood to write original music for *Flying Down to Rio*, a Fred Astaire-Ginger Rogers musical that had "Carioca" and "Orchids in the Moonlight."

III

Most of the composers, previously dominating the musical scene on Broadway and in Tin Pan Alley, were now in Hollywood. In the first few years of talking pictures, three of its most prolific composers were men who had already made their mark in the East. They were Richard Whiting, Jimmy McHugh, and Harry Ruby.

In the two-year period of 1929 and 1930, Whiting wrote the scores for over half-a-dozen screen musicals. Two of them starred Maurice Chevalier (*Innocents of Paris* and *The Playboy of Paris*), one, Jeanette MacDonald (*Monte Carlo*). In the dozen or more screen musicals for which Whiting wrote the music after that, many outstanding songs were introduced; the best were "One Hour With You" (Leo Robin), soon to become Eddie Cantor's theme song on the radio; "When Did You Leave Heaven?" (Walter Bullock); and "Too Marvelous for Words" (Johnny Mercer).

Jimmy McHugh came to Hollywood in 1930 to write for *Love in the Rough*. From then on, his was one of Hollywood's busiest

pens. The wide range of his creative gift and the equally ample
span of his success as composer for the screen are pointed up by
songs like these: "The Cuban Love Song," "I'm in the Mood for
Love," "Don't Blame Me," and "I Can't Give You Anything But
Love," all to lyrics by Dorothy Fields; and "A Lovely Way to
Spend an Evening," and "It's a Most Unusual Day," lyrics by
Harold Adamson.

Harry Ruby hit a winner in Hollywood with his very first
screen effort: "Three Little Words" (Bert Kalmar), introduced
in 1930 in the Amos 'n Andy picture, *Check and Doublecheck.*
His songs continued to appear prominently in important motion
pictures, the finest of these being "I Love You So Much"
(Kalmar) and "Do You Love Me?" to his own lyrics.

The leaders of the Broadway musical stage were also richly
represented on the Hollywood set. After *Viennese Nights,* Sigmund Romberg wrote music for a second movie with a Viennese
background, *Children of Dreams.* Both pictures are forgotten.
So would be the one for which he wrote the score in 1934, *The
Night Is Young,* but for the fact that it was the point of origin
for one of Romberg's greatest ballads, "When I Grow Too Old
to Dream" (Oscar Hammerstein II). Romberg's last complete
score for Hollywood was *The Girl of the Golden West* in 1938.

Rodgers and Hart had their first major Hollywood success
in 1932 with *Love Me Tonight,* with Maurice Chevalier and
Jeanette MacDonald. This picture had the saucy, spicy Gallic
flavor for which Chevalier had already become famous. Not the
least of its condiments were the four Rodgers and Hart numbers, among the best they were to write for the screen: "Mimi,"
"He's Nothing But a Tailor," "Isn't it Romantic?" and "Love
Me Tonight." Actually, Rodgers and Hart wrote a fifth song
which was deleted when the picture went into production—
strange, for this was "Lover," one of their greatest. "Blue Moon"
—another Rodgers and Hart masterpiece—was also intended
for the movies but was inexplicably dropped from two different

pictures. Other Hollywood assignments included a dull Jolson movie, *Hallelujah, I'm a Bum*—whose sole interest lies in the fact that Rodgers and Hart experimented with the use of rhythmic dialogue—and an early Bing Crosby film, *Mississippi*.

Kern's best screen musicals appeared in the decade between 1935 and 1945, beginning with *I Dream Too Much*, starring Lily Pons. The screen, like the stage, inspired in Kern many high flights of melody: "The Way You Look Tonight" (Dorothy Fields) which appeared in the Fred Astaire-Ginger Rogers musical, *Swingtime*, and won the Academy Award in 1936; "Our Song" (Fields) in *When You're in Love*, with Grace Moore; "Dearly Beloved" (Johnny Mercer) in *You Were Never Lovelier* and "Long Ago and Far Away" (Ira Gershwin) in *Cover Girl*, both starring Rita Hayworth; "More and More" (Yip Harburg) in *Can't Help Singing*, with Deanna Durbin; and "All Through the Night" (Oscar Hammerstein II), in *Centennial Summer*, Kern's last motion picture.

One of Kern's most celebrated songs for the screen, however, did not actually emanate from one of his scores, but was interpolated into the Gershwin screen musical, *Lady, Be Good*. This was the only song that Kern ever wrote independently— that is, without a specific musical comedy or screen play in mind. One day, in 1940, his lyricist, Oscar Hammerstein II, telephoned him from New York to read him a lyric he had just written—a poem inspired by the recent tragic fall of Paris to the Nazis. Hammerstein wanted Kern to write music for it, even though Kern's melodies always came before the lyric, and though Kern never wrote music independent of some production. Apparently the fall of the city he loved was enough stimulation for Kern. The melody came to him instantly as Hammerstein read and reread the lyric over transcontinental phone; and the way Kern played it to Hammerstein, still over the phone, was the way it was finally published and sung. The song was "The Last Time I Saw Paris," popularized in night clubs by

Hildegarde and Sophie Tucker before being fitted into *Lady, Be Good*. There, as the only Kern song in an otherwise Gershwin score, it won the Academy Award for 1941.

Some of the most delightful musicals produced during the first decade of the talking pictures had old and new music by Irving Berlin. In 1935 there was *Top Hat*, the first of three Fred Astaire-Ginger Rogers song-and-dance films. One of its songs, "Cheek to Cheek," brought Berlin a royalty in excess of $250,000. The other two Astaire-Rogers films were *Follow the Fleet* in 1936 and *Carefree* in 1938. Between the two there appeared, in 1937, *On the Avenue* with Dick Powell and Alice Faye.

In 1938, Berlin contributed not only the songs but also the original story of *Alexander's Ragtime Band*. This picture was originally intended to be Berlin's screen biography, but in the writing it developed into a loosely-knit and somewhat formalized yarn about a jazz-band leader who is swept to success on the crest of the title song. Tyrone Power was the jazz-band leader in *Alexander,* and he was also the star in *Second Fiddle,* in 1939.

These sundry assignments in Hollywood resulted in the following new Berlin songs: "I'm Putting All My Eggs in One Basket," in *Follow the Fleet;* "The Night is Filled With Music," in *Carefree;* "I've Got My Love to Keep Me Warm," in *On the Avenue;* and "I Poured My Heart Into a Song," in *Second Fiddle*.

After a three-year absence, Berlin returned to Hollywood in 1942 to write the score for *Holiday Inn*—the Bing Crosby-Fred Astaire picture in which his classic, "White Christmas" was born. A year later he adapted *This Is the Army* for the screen.

Immediately after World War II, Berlin helped create two ambitious musical films, each bringing him a fantastic fee, and each directing attention to his rich creative history by presenting a cavalcade of some of his most famous songs. In 1946 there was *Blue Skies* with Bing Crosby and Fred Astaire, in which were heard the pearls of Berlin's minstrelsy from such early efforts as "Everybody Step" and "I've Got My Captain Working For Me Now" to such later gems as "A Couple of Song and Dance Men" and "You Keep Coming Back Like a Song." Two years later a second picture used a Berlin song as a title—and as a pivot on which the story revolved: *Easter Parade,* with Fred Astaire and Judy Garland, and with another armful of Berlin songs, old and new. The practice of using a famous Berlin song as the starting-point for the story, and as the title for the picture, continued in 1954 with *White Christmas* and *There's No Business Like Show Business.* The former had a new Berlin hit song in "Count Your Blessings."

After his single assignment in 1931—*Delicious*—George Gershwin stayed away from Hollywood for five years. When he returned with his brother Ira, they planted their roots permanently in the movie capital.

His first new score was for a gay Fred Astaire-Ginger Rogers musical, *Shall We Dance?* which had two delightful songs, "Let's Call the Whole Thing Off" and "They Can't Take That Away From Me." In 1937, Gershwin wrote the music for a second Fred Astaire picture, *Damsel in Distress,* in which "Foggy Day" and "Nice Work If You Can Get It" were heard. Samuel Goldwyn then engaged him and Ira Gershwin to write the songs for a bountiful screen revue, *The Goldwyn Follies.* George was able to write only five of these numbers, two of them—"Love Walked In" and "Love Is Here to Stay"—among his greatest. He collapsed while working on this assignment. On July 11, 1937 he died in the hospital after a fatal operation for a brain tumor.

The Goldwyn Follies was the last screen production for which George Gershwin wrote the music. But it was not the last production with Gershwin music. In 1945 his screen biography, *Rhapsody in Blue,* was produced; about this, more later. In 1947, *The Shocking Miss Pilgrim* introduced several Gershwin songs never before published or performed, but prepared for this production by Ira Gershwin with the assistance of Kay Swift; one of these—"For You, For Me, For Evermore"—was a veritable find. Two years later, the Gershwin storehouse was once again raided, this time for a Technicolor production inspired by Gershwin's tone poem, *An American in Paris,* and named after it. The tone poem was used as the musical background for an imaginative fifteen-minute ballet danced by Gene Kelly and Leslie Caron, with which the picture comes to its climax; and a handful of famous Gershwin songs helped along the romance of an American painter in Paris and a little French girl he pursues. So successfully were song and dance, sentiment and comedy fused in *An American in Paris* that it was chosen in 1951 the Academy Award winner as the best picture of the year. This was the fourth time that a musical received such an honor.

Cole Porter's first important screen score was for *Born to Dance,* in 1936, in which were introduced "I've Got You Under My Skin" and "Easy to Love." In *Rosalie,* in 1937, were found "In the Still of the Night," while "You'd Be So Nice to Come Home To" originated in *Something to Shout About,* in 1943, and "True Love" in *High Society* in 1956.

The screen, then, yielded a sizable quota of Cole Porter favorites. But one of these had been written much earlier, and was discarded by the composer, before the screen found it and made it popular. "Don't Fence Me In" was a cowboy ballad Porter had written in 1934. It cropped up in *Hollywood Canteen,* a decade later, sung by Roy Rogers, to become one of Porter's song triumphs, measured by sales of sheet music and records and by appearances on the Hit Parade.

IV

In 1934, the Motion Picture Academy recognized the importance of popular music for the screen by instituting a special award for the best song introduced in a motion picture. Some of these awards have since then been conferred on composers whose careers more rightfully belong to Tin Pan Alley or Broadway than to Hollywood. The very first award, for example, went to Con Conrad for "The Continental" (Herb Magidson) in the Fred Astaire-Ginger Rogers picture, *Gay Divorcée*. After that Jerome Kern won the honor twice for "The Way You Look Tonight" and "The Last Time I Saw Paris"; Irving Berlin and Richard Rodgers once each for "White Christmas" and "It Might As Well Be Spring," respectively; Hoagy Carmichael received it for "In the Cool, Cool, Cool of the Evening" from *Here Comes the Groom* in 1951; Sammy Fain twice, for "Secret Love" in *Calamity Jane* in 1953 and "Love Is a Many Splendored Thing" from the picture of the same name in 1955, both to lyrics by Paul Francis Webster.

But most of the Academy awards for popular songs were rightfully carried away by composers whose careers either began or were developed in Hollywood. For from the beginning of talking pictures, the motion-picture industry was able to produce its own share of successful songwriters.

Nacio Herb Brown was one of the first major popular composers to emerge to prominence in talking pictures. He preceded his musical career by fruitful business ventures in Los Angeles: first with a merchant-tailoring establishment catering to movie stars; then in real estate in Beverly Hills. Since he had been musical from childhood on, and had always played the piano (on one occasion he had worked as accompanist to a vaudevillian on the Orpheum Circuit) he had always dabbled in composition. His first song, "Coral Sea," written with King Zany, was published in 1920 and soon after this was introduced by the Paul Whiteman Orchestra at the Alexandria Hotel in Los Angeles. An instrumental number, "Doll Dance," was the high spot of a revue produced in Hollywood in the mid-1920s.

Since his business deals and investments made him wealthy, he had no intention of devoting himself seriously to songwriting. But, one day in 1928, Irving Thalberg of MGM induced him to write music for the movies; as a first assignment Thalberg offered him *The Broadway Melody,* then being planned by the studio as the first all-talking, singing revue. With Arthur Freed as his lyricist, Brown wrote "The Broadway Melody" and "The Wedding of the Painted Doll," among other numbers, and thus projected himself at once as the first successful composer made-in-Hollywood. Thalberg now prevailed on him to turn the management of his business activities to assistants so that more time might be available for music. In time, Brown achieved such a formidable success in music that he sold out all other ventures and concentrated on composition. For in the half-dozen or so years after *The Broadway Melody* he wrote a few of the most successful songs to come from the then still young talking screen, lyrics always by Freed: "You Were Meant For Me" and "Singin' in the Rain" in *The Hollywood Revue;* "The Pagan Love Song" in *The Pagan;* "Paradise" in *A Woman Commands;* "Temptation" in *Going Hollywood;* and "You Are My Lucky Star" in *The Broadway Melody of 1936.*

Nacio Herb Brown was the only one among the new Hollywood composers who was a home-grown product, whose songwriting experience had been developed exclusively in California. The other composers had served their apprenticeships in the East, and most of them had had a first taste of success in Tin Pan Alley or on Broadway. Nevertheless, their careers belong substantially to Hollywood because it was there that they did their best work and it was there that they realized their most impressive victories.

Harry Warren, for example, had written a number of creditable song hits before coming out to Hollywood in 1930. As a song plugger in Tin Pan Alley he made an initial bid for recognition with "Rose of Rio Grande" (Edgar Leslie) in 1922. This song brought him a staff job as composer for Shapiro, Bernstein & Co. In his next few years in Tin Pan Alley, Warren wrote "Where Do You Work-a, John?" (Mort Weinberg and

Charles Marks), "Nagasaki" (Mort Dixon) and "Where the Shy Little Violets Grow" (Gus Kahn). As a composer for Broadway revues, Warren earned additional laurels for "Cheerful Little Earful" (Ira Gershwin and Billy Rose) and "Would You Like to Take a Walk?" (Mort Dixon and Billy Rose) in *Sweet and Low*, in 1930, and with "You're My Everything" (Mort Dixon and Joe Young) in *The Laugh Parade* and "I Found a Million Dollar Baby" (Dixon and Billy Rose) in *Crazy Quilt*, both in 1931.

All this, however, was but a first step for Warren. After 1931, his career as a significant composer for the screen unfolded. He had actually been something of a pioneer in the motion-picture business. In his youth he had worked as an extra, assistant director, and pianist providing off-stage mood music, at the old Vitagraph lot in New York. He was, then, returning to an old love when he went to work for Hollywood in 1931, launching a new career as songwriter with "Crying for the Carolinas" and "Have a Little Faith in Me" (Sam Lewis and Joe Young) for *Spring Is Here*. How high he rose in his field can best be proved by pointing out that he won the Motion Picture Academy Award three times, the only composer to accomplish this thus far: for "Lullaby of Broadway" (Al Dubin) in *The Gold Diggers of 1935;* "You'll Never Know" (Mack Gordon) in *Hello, Frisco, Hello*, in 1943; and "On the Atchison, Topeka, and the Santa Fe" (Johnny Mercer) in *The Harvey Girls*, in 1946.

Other prominent Warren songs for the screen—all of them to lyrics by Al Dubin, with whom he worked most often and most fruitfully—included: "Shadow Waltz" in *The Gold Diggers of 1933;* "I'll String Along With You" in *Twenty Million Sweethearts;* "I Only Have Eyes for You" in *Dames;* "Forty-Second Street" and "Shuffle Along" in *Forty-Second Street;* and "Remember Me?" in *Mr. Dodd Takes the Air*. To lyrics by Johnny Mercer, Warren also wrote: "You Must Have Been a Beautiful Baby" in *Hard to Get;* "Jeepers Creepers" in *Going Places;* and "It's a Great Big World" in *The Harvey Girls*.

For Mack Gordon's lyrics, Warren wrote: "Chattanooga Choo-Choo" in *The Sun Valley Serenade* and "The More I see Of You" in *The Diamond Horseshoe.*

In 1939, Harold Arlen received the Academy Award for what is still one of his best known and most beautiful songs, "Over the Rainbow" (Yip Harburg). But he had been one of Hollywood's significant composers for about half-a-dozen years before that. Born in Buffalo, New York, in 1905, Arlen began participating in popular-music performances as early as his fifteenth year when he played the piano in night clubs and on lake steamers in or near Buffalo. He next led a trio which soon grew into a full-sized jazz band, for which he made all the arrangements, besides playing the piano and singing the vocal choruses. His arrangements were so good that a New York booking agent brought him to New York in 1927 to work for a night club. In New York, Arlen found a job as rehearsal pianist for Youmans' musical *Great Day.* While filling this post he branched out for the first time into songwriting, his first song actually being the result of an accident. While accompanying a Negro choral group in one of Youmans' numbers, Arlen improvised an accompaniment that made such an impression on the choral director that he encouraged Arlen to put it down on paper. With lyrics by Ted Koehler, it was published as "Get Happy" and introduced in the *9:15 Revue.* The show was a failure and soon forgotten; but Arlen's song became popular. When George Gershwin heard a try-out performance of the revue in New Haven he went backstage to tell the unknown Arlen that "Get Happy" was one of the best production numbers he had heard in years.

On the strength of that song, Arlen was engaged by Remick as staff composer. For about three years, up to 1933, he supplied songs for night club shows produced at the Cotton Club in Harlem, where Duke Ellington was appearing. With Koehler, Arlen wrote such sultry numbers as "Between the Devil and the Deep Blue Sea," "Minnie the Moocher's Wedding Day,"

and, most important of all, "Stormy Weather." These songs
deserve a special niche in American popular music, being the
first successful numbers written directly for and introduced in
a night club.

In 1933—the year in which "Stormy Weather" received its
sensational première by the Duke Ellington orchestra and the
remarkable blues singer, Ivy Anderson—Harold Arlen left for
Hollywood. He wasted neither time nor motion in putting his
best foot forward. "It's Only a Paper Moon" (Yip Harburg and
Billy Rose) was heard in the first picture with which he was
associated, *Take a Chance*. One of his most tender numbers,
"Let's Fall In Love" (Koehler), came a year later in his second
motion picture, of the same name. And, in 1939, Arlen won his
Academy Award with "Over the Rainbow," one of several songs
he wrote with Harburg for the Judy Garland extravaganza,
The Wizard of Oz. There is so much of Judy Garland's personality and history in this song that it is difficult to think of one
without the other. Over a decade later, when Judy began her
dramatic comeback with historic performances at the London
Palladium and the Palace Theatre in New York, she always
brought down the house with her tearful rendition of "Over
the Rainbow": sitting on the floor of the stage as she sang, her
feet dangling in the orchestra pit, a single light pointing to her
drawn, pale face and her tear-filled eyes.

Succeeding films continued to bring Arlen treasures: "Blues
in the Night" (Mercer) in the picture of the same name;
"That Old Black Magic" (Mercer) in *Star-Spangled Rhythm;*
"Happiness is a Thing Called Joe" (Harburg) in *Cabin in the
Sky;* "One for My Baby" (Mercer) in *The Sky's the Limit;*
"Accentuate the Positive" (Mercer) in *Here Come the Waves*.

Surely it is poetic justice that the man who wrote Judy Garland's theme song should also write the songs with which she
made such a triumphant return to the screen after a four-year
absence. Judy's rebirth as a screen star came with Harold
Arlen's music and Ira Gershwin's lyrics, in *A Star is Born*—a

1954 musical version of a 1937 screen success. Arlen's songs here were distinguished not only for their rhythmic appeal and lyricism but also because they served to heighten and intensify the tragic story. The songs always kept one eye on the story and the other on the star. Their elastic range gave Judy Garland's performance scope and dimension: for burlesque in "Love That Long Face"; for light-foot rhythm in "Gotta Have Me Go With You"; and for pathos in one of Arlen's best torch songs, "The Man That Got Away."

The team of Arlen and Gershwin produced several songs for a motion-picture starring another performer of the first magnitude, Bing Crosby. In *The Country Girl* the songs once again served the drama rather than punctuated it, once again helped the flow of the plot rather than impeded it.

Frank Loesser, who received the Academy Award for "Baby It's Cold Outside" in *Neptune's Daughter* in 1949, first became famous in Hollywood as a lyricist, and only much later did he start writing the music as well as the words. Born in New York in 1910 to a musical family, Frank never received formal musical instruction. He learned to play the piano by ear and to sing in an ingratiating and personal style. After a single year at the College of the City of New York, his schooling ended. He then held one job after another in rapid succession. All the while he tried writing lyrics. A ballad called "Armful of You" was sold to a vaudevillian for $15.00.

He was not yet twenty when he received a one-year contract from Leo Feist to write lyrics for that publishing house. None were considered good enough for publication, and at the end of the year Feist decided to dispense with his services. Only when he was no longer officially connected with that firm did it issue one of his lyrics, "I'm In Love with the Memory of You." That song is significant because it was Loesser's first published effort; also because its composer was a young hopeful named William Schuman, who today is one of America's major serious composers, besides being president of the Julliard School of Music.

Loesser's first successful lyric was "I Wish I Were Twins," to music by Joseph Meyer. It was responsible for bringing him to Hollywood, where, with Irving Actman, he wrote some songs for Grade B Universal pictures. When Universal failed to renew his contract, Loesser passed on to Paramount, and it was for this organization that he wrote his first important lyrics. To Burton Lane's music he wrote "Says My Heart" in the *Cocoanut Grove;* with Hoagy Carmichael he wrote "Small Fry," sung by Bing Crosby in *Sing You Sinners,* and "Two Sleepy People" made famous by Bob Hope in *Thanks for the Memory;* with Arthur Schwartz he wrote "They're Either Too Young or Too Old" in *Thank Your Lucky Stars;* with Joseph J. Lilley, he did "Jingle, Jangle, Jingle" in *The Forest Rangers.* The last of these was intended by Loesser as a jocular song in Western style, but it was treated seriously in the picture. Stylistically it is interesting because it was written in the two-voice canon form of several later hits.

Not until Loesser wrote a dummy tune for his war song, "Praise the Lord and Pass the Ammunition"—the circumstances surrounding this event are described in the first chapter—did he get the confidence to write his own music. Since then, like Irving Berlin and Cole Porter, he has been writing both the music and words for most of his songs. After the war, he became the author of many individual song hits meant for neither the Broadway stage nor the Hollywood screen, among them being the successful "On a Slow Boat to China." But others no less popular first appeared in motion pictures: "Tallahassee" in the *Varsity Girl;* "Now That I Need You" in *Red, Hot and Blue;* "I Wish I Didn't Love You So" in *Perils of Pauline;* and the Academy Award winning "Baby, it's Cold Outside," in the two-voice canon form. In 1952, his delightful score for the Danny Kaye screen play, *Hans Christian Andersen,* was singled out by some critics as one of the reasons for the charm and appeal of this unusual picture. One of these songs, "Thumbelina," was nominated for the 1953 Academy Award.

Like Loesser, Jule Styne—who in 1954 won the Academy Award for "Three Coins in a Fountain" (Sammy Cahn)—wrote his first songs during World War II. And once again like Loesser he first became famous in Hollywood. He was born in London, England, in 1905, and came to Chicago when he was only eight. A piano prodigy, he made concert appearances with the Detroit Symphony and Chicago Orchestra, and attended Chicago Musical College on a scholarship. But he soon listened and responded to the siren call of popular music. In 1931 he organized his own dance band which played in various Chicago hotels and night clubs. The arrangements he made for his band attracted attention. Hollywood called him to make arrangements and write background music for several films. He also filled a post as vocal coach for 20th Century-Fox, where he worked with such stars as Alice Faye, Linda Darnell, and Shirley Temple.

His musical activities in Hollywood would probably never have broken down the walls of anonymity surrounding him if he had not met Sammy Cahn, a young lyricist, and begun writing melodies for him. Their very first song together was a winner, "I've Heard that Song Before," which Frank Sinatra sang in a short movie subject about racial intolerance. The new song partnership continued to prosper in 1945 with "Poor Little Rhode Island" (since become the official song of that state), "It's Been a Long, Long Time," and "Let It Snow, Let It Snow"—none intended for motion pictures. But among those written for the screen was one of the most moving ballads of World War II, "I'll Walk Alone," introduced by Frank Sinatra in *Follow the Boys*. After that came "There Goes That Song Again" in *Carolina Blues;* "Love Me" in *Stork Club;* "Give Me Five Minutes More" in *The Sweetheart of Sigma Chi;* "I Love an Old-Fashioned Song" in *The Kid from Brooklyn;* and "I've Never Forgotten" in the *Earl Carroll Sketch Book*.

The Academy Award "Three Coins in a Fountain" was something of a sleeper. It was intended for and utilized as background music in the picture of the same name, particularly in the opening sequence, which was a camera profile of the Eternal City. Apparently, the song was regarded so lightly by the motion-picture producers that its performer, Frank Sinatra, was not even given screen credit. But it caught on and became one of Styne's biggest money-makers.

The songs of Jimmy Van Heusen, whose career in Hollywood began in 1940, are often associated with the voice of Bing Crosby who introduced and popularized so many of them. It was for Crosby's pictures that Van Heusen realized his greatest successes, always to Johnny Burke's lyrics, including the one that won him an Academy Award in 1944, "Swinging on a Star" in *Going My Way*, a picture which itself won the Academy Award as the best of that year. Van Heusen also provided songs for several of the "Road" pictures in which Crosby appeared with Bob Hope and Dorothy Lamour: "Moonlight Becomes You" in *The Road to Morocco*, "Personality" in *The Road to Utopia*, and "But Beautiful" in *The Road to Rio*, all to lyrics by Johnny Burke, are some of the best. In other Crosby pictures, the star introduced such other Van Heusen-Johnny Burke items as "Sunday, Monday or Always" in *Dixie;* "Aren't You Glad You're You?" in *The Bells of St. Mary's;* "As Long as I'm Dreaming" in *Welcome Stranger;* "You're in Love with Someone" in *Top o' the Morning;* and "Sunshine Cake in *Riding High.*

Van Heusen was born in Syracuse, New York, in 1913. At the age of sixteen he played the piano and sang over local radio stations. For a year and a half he attended Syracuse University, where he wrote college shows with Harold Arlen's younger brother. The elder Arlen urged Van Heusen to come to New York. He came in 1931 and soon wrote music for various Broadway productions and revues at the Cotton Club in Harlem. Nonetheless, he was unable to make a living through composition and had to take a job as staff pianist in Tin Pan Alley. There he met Jimmy Dorsey, with whom he wrote "It's the Dreamer in Me," which not only became one of the song hits of 1938 but also won an award form ASCAP. Van Heusen now wrote some more hits, this time without outside help, among which were "Heaven Can Wait" (Edgar De Lange) and "Oh, You Crazy Moon" and "Imagination" (Burke). The road now led to Hollywood and Bing Crosby.

One of Van Heusen's major songs was not for a Bing Crosby picture: "The Tender Trap" (Sammy Cahn), sung by Frank Sinatra in the picture of the same name in 1955. Another 1955 Van Heusen-Sammy Cahn hit was introduced over television. Engaged to write the songs for a musical adaptation of Thornton Wilder's *Our Town* scheduled for television, Van Heusen wrote one of the top tunes of the year in "Love and Marriage."

V

In 1936, a musical won the Motion Picture Academy Award as the best picture of the year for the second time. It was *The Great Ziegfeld*, an MGM production, which featured several songs by Walter Donaldson and with them Irving Berlin's "A Pretty Girl Is Like a Melody" from the *Ziegfeld Follies of 1919*.

Many other screen musicals now turned to the life stories of famous personalities of popular music and the theater. These life stories were often highly romanticized, sentimentalized, and only remotely related to biographical truth. In this trend, many popular-song composers of the past and present were given screen biographical treatment, their fictionalized lives serving as a convenient frame for the presentation of their best songs. In 1939 came *The Great Victor Herbert*, and a maudlin and frequently dull story about Stephen Foster called *Swanee*, starring Al Jolson. Three years later, *My Gal Sal* presented the life and best-known songs of Paul Dresser.

One of the best of these composer biographies was that of George Gershwin, *Rhapsody in Blue,* produced in 1945, eight years after the composer's premature death. The strength of this picture lay not in the story (much of which was a distortion of fact) but in Gershwin's music. Twenty-nine Gershwin numbers were heard, including parts of many of his major serious works; eighteen were given featured treatment.

Since success in Hollywood ever inspires imitation, *Rhapsody in Blue* encouraged many other screen biographies of the musical great of Tin Pan Alley and Broadway. Cole Porter's story was told in *Night and Day* and Jerome Kern's in *Till the Clouds Roll By,* in 1946. Two years later *Words and Music* highlighted the careers of Rodgers and Hart. After that came the screen biographies of Bert Kalmar and Harry Ruby in *Three Little Words,* Sigmund Romberg in *Deep in My Heart,* Gus Kahn in *I'll See You In My Dreams,* and John Philip Sousa in *Stars and Stripes Forever.*

The lives and careers of stage stars also provided a convenient hook on which to hang songs and dances. The dancing Castles, Vernon and Irene, were played by Fred Astaire and Ginger Rogers in *The Story of the Castles,* in 1939; Alice Faye was Lillian Russell in *Lillian Russell,* in 1940; George M. Cohan was portrayed by James Cagney in *Yankee Doodle Dandy,* in 1942; Ted Lewis, by Larry Parks in *Is Everybody Happy?,* in 1943. In 1944, Ann Sheridan played Nora Bayes in *Shine On, Harvest Moon,* and the Dolly Sisters returned in the shapes and voices of Betty Grable and June Haver in *The Dolly Sisters,* in 1945. Other and later film biographies of great stage personalities included those of Marilyn Miller (*Look for the Silver Lining*), the Dorseys (*The Fabulous Dorseys*), Jane Froman (*With a Song in My Heart*), Glenn Miller (*The Glenn Miller Story*), Eddie Cantor (*The Eddie Cantor Story*), Benny Goodman (*The Benny Goodman Story*), Ruth Etting (*Love Me Or Leave Me*), Eddie Foy (*The Seven Little Foys*), Eva Tanguay (*The I Don't Care Girl*), Lillian Roth (*I'll Cry*

Tomorrow), and De Sylva, Brown and Henderson (*The Best Things in Life are Free*).

What was probably the greatest box-office triumph among these biographical pictures was *The Jolson Story* in 1946. A stage star of first rank for over a decade—and after that a giant figure in the early years of the talking picture—Jolson had by 1945 been completely eclipsed both on Broadway and in Hollywood by younger stars. A succession of second-rate and third-rate motion pictures, and a radio program that never quite made the grade, led to the general belief that Jolson was through. He had even become something of an untouchable among those planning new musicals for stage or screen. At a benefit at the swank Hillcrest Country Club in Beverly Hills he was put on almost as an afterthought—as the closing number —an open confession that he was no longer an attraction deserving favorable placement. Despite the late hour (it was almost 1 A.M.), the fatigue of the audience, and the long and glittering procession of performers that had preceded him, Jolson was able to work his old magic and hold his audience rooted to their seats for over an hour. To Harry Cohn, head of Columbia Pictures, this was the proof he needed that Jolson was still a king of performers; and a suspicion was born with Cohn that night that to a new generation, who had never seen or heard Jolson, the performer might come as a revelation. It was then that Cohn decided to gamble on Jolson by starring him in a new picture built around the story of his fabulous career.

The studio finally decided to have Larry Parks, then young and unknown, play the part of Jolson, with Jolson himself singing on the sound-track many of the songs he had helped to make famous. To these old Jolson hits, a new one was added, "The Anniversary Song," which Jolson himself wrote with Saul Chaplin, the melody based upon an old European waltz, "The Waves of the Danube," by J. Ivanovici.

The Jolson Story grossed $8,000,000 and narrowly missed winning the Academy Award as the best picture of the year. A sequel was prepared in 1949, *Jolson Sings Again,* once more with Larry Parks as Jolson, and Jolson singing on the sound-track. This picture was a solid hit in its own right, with a gross of $5,000,000. The talking picture which originally had helped crown Jolson king of entertainers had now helped to re-store him to his rightful throne.

Impressive as are the grosses of both *The Jolson Story* and *Jolson Sings Again,* these are only two of almost twenty motion-picture musicals thus far to gross $5,000,000 or more at the box office. The greatest figure for a screen musical, and the third greatest for any motion picture, was reached by Irving Berlin's *White Christmas,* with almost $15,000,000. After that come *This Is the Army, The Bells of St. Mary's, The Jolson Story, The Glenn Miller Story, The Country Girl, Going My Way, Welcome Stranger, Hans Christian Andersen, A Star is Born, Blue Skies, Seven Brides for Seven Brothers, Meet Me in St. Louis, Show Boat, Jolson Sings Again, No Business Like Show Business,* and *Pete Kelly's Blues.*

===== ♯ ♯ =====

chapter fourteen

FROM MUSICAL COMEDY
TO MUSICAL PLAY

BETWEEN 1930 and the 1950s, the Broadway musical stage has followed two paths. One led to old familiar places, its destination being the more formal and the long accepted patterns and routines of musical comedy. The other broke new ground, evolving a new kind of musical theater in which play and music, comedy and dance were all integrated into an artistic entity.

Among the most important contributors to the more traditional kind of musical theater—besides men like Irving Berlin, George Gershwin, Sigmund Romberg, Cole Porter, whose major musical comedies and operattas have already been discussed—were Arthur Schwartz, Harold Arlen, Vernon Duke, Leonard Bernstein, and Richard Adler.

While Schwartz had acquired a pattern for success with smart revues, he was less fortunate in musical comedies. He suffered six successive failures with story books before winning his first hand. Only one of these failures had more than casual interest. *Revenge With Music*, in 1934, was an ambitious effort to give popular treatment to a delightful love intrigue previously used in a celebrated ballet (Manuel de Falla's *The Three-Cornered Hat*) and less effectively in an opera (Hugo Wolf's *Der Corregi-*

dor). But despite two really outstanding songs, words by Howard Dietz—"You and the Night and the Music" and "If There is Someone Lovelier Than You"—*Revenge With Music* missed its aim completely; and it once again missed when television suddenly and inexplicably revived it one evening in 1954.

Not until 1951 was Arthur Schwartz able to break the jinx dooming his musical comedies. *A Tree Grows in Brooklyn,* adapted from the best-selling novel of Betty Smith, and starring Shirley Booth as Cissie, was still no sweepstakes winner. The songs, with lyrics by Dorothy Fields, were, however, pleasing to the ear, just as the over-all production had an ingratiating warmth. The best songs were "I'll Buy a Star" and "Love Is the Reason."

By the Beautiful Sea, in 1954, counted even more heavily on nostalgia, sentiment, and Shirley Booth than did *A Tree Grows in Brooklyn.* Two songs—again to Dorothy Fields' lyrics —were above average: "Alone Too Long" and "Happy Habit."

When Harold Arlen came back to Broadway after seven fat years in Hollywood, it was with the only stage triumph of his career thus far, *Bloomer Girl,* a play that had a two-year run on Broadway. This was a sentimental portrait of America during the Civil War era, dominated by the arresting personality of the feminist, Dolly Bloomer. Arlen's score contained at least one number as good as those he had previously been writing for Hollywood: "I Got a Song" (Harburg), a melody in the dusky style that had made him one of our best living writers of Negro songs. Other pleasing numbers were "Evalina" and "I Never Was Born."

Arlen's next musical, *St. Louis Woman,* in 1946, started out as an authentic Negro play with music, but ended up as a formal musical comedy. It was at its best when the situations were emotionally intensified by songs like "Legalize My Name" and "A Woman's Prerogative," both to words by Johnny Mercer, and both magnetically sung by Pearl Bailey. But when *St. Louis Woman* digressed into an elaborate cakewalk routine, and adopted some of the slicker devices of the musical-comedy stage, it was neither fish nor fowl.

Despite its defects, *St. Louis Woman* represented for its composer a healthy step forward, away from standardized formats and toward newer ideas and orientations. This advance was also evident in *House of Flowers*, in 1954, a book and lyrics by Truman Capote. Here was a musical in which very little happened, but which was so rich in atmosphere, local color, and tender sentiments that it never really was static. The pervading charm had an almost Oriental delicacy. The spell was maintained in some of Arlen's songs, piquant with West-Indian spices and flavors: "Sleepin' Bee," "One Man," and "I Never Has Seen Snow," for example.

Harold Rome's divorce from political realities became complete with his entrance into musical comedy. *Wish You Were Here*, in 1952—a musical version of Arthur Kober's stage comedy, *Having Wonderful Time*, about adult camps in New York and the romances they inspire—did not win the complete approval of the critics. But apparently it did have audience appeal, for it stayed on for over a year. Rome's music and lyrics, much more in the accepted style of the musical-comedy theater than those he had once written for the smart revues, included one of the major song hits of his career, the title song.

The human equation had been lost in the scramble to make *Wish You Were Here* an elaborate musical; indeed, one of the attractions had been a huge, permanent swimming pool on the stage. Miraculously, the human equation survived a similarly ostentatious and fussy stage presentation in *Fanny*, in 1954. The heart-warming humanity and compassion found in the three plays by Marcel Pagnol on which *Fanny* was based were carried over skillfully into the new adaptation by S. N. Behrman, one of our ablest writers of stage comedy, here making his musical-comedy debut. And the humanity and compassion were underscored by the most spacious and the most versatile score of Rome's career. Some songs penetrated to the very core of the characters they interpreted: "To My Wife" (Panisse); "Restless Sea" (Marius); and "Welcome Home" (César). Sometimes his background music brought mellow overtones to a dramatic scene; and sometimes his ballet music had symphonic breadth. Yet in extending his horizon, Rome did not forget his way with a good tune, as in "Fanny" and "Love Is a Very Light Thing."

It was not until eight years after he wrote his music for his last revue that Vernon Duke appeared on Broadway with a musical comedy with a score entirely his own. That musical, *Cabin in the Sky,* is one of the ornaments of the musical theater of the 1940s, one of the most sensitive and understanding pictures of Negro life and psychology on the contemporary musical stage. Every element in the production maintained the quiet dignity and integrity of the Lynn Root play, particularly the earthy lyrics and balladry of John La Touche, and George Balanchine's choreography. Vernon Duke's music tapped a rich creative vein hitherto reserved only for his *alter ego,* the classical composer. Songs like "Cabin in the Sky," "Taking a Chance on Love," "Honey in the Honeycomb," and "Love Me Tomorrow" often have the vibrant overtones of Negro folk songs.

Like Vernon Duke, Leonard Bernstein is a composer of ambitious serious works performed by the great symphony orchestras of the world. On several occasions, however, he has gone popular, and written music for the Broadway musical stage. *On the Town, Wonderful Town,* and *Candide* have been received with resounding acclaim and scored box-office triumphs. Born in Lawrence, Massachusetts, in 1918, Bernstein revealed remarkable gifts for music from his childhood on, and consequently was given an all-embracing musical training together with his academic education. After studying conducting with Serge Koussevitzky at the Berkshire Music Centre in Lenox, Massachusetts, Bernstein made a sensational debut as conductor when, in the fall of 1943, he was a last-minute substitute for Bruno Walter at a concert of the New York Philhar-

monic Symphony. That was the beginning of a career with the
baton that brought him acclaim in every part of the musical
world. At the same time he wrote serious musical works which
have placed him in the vanguard of the younger American composers.

One of these serious works was a ballet, *Fancy Free*, introduced by the Ballet Theatre. Bernstein's first musical comedy
emerged from the embryo of this ballet. *Fancy Free* was about
three sailors on leave, on the hunt for girls. *On the Town*, in
1944, was an amplification of the same subject. Musically, too,
On the Town evolved naturally from *Fancy Free*. Bernstein's
experiments with a popular style in the ballet score proceeded
with increased zest in the musical comedy. In *On the Town* he
struck a happy mean between time-tried formulas and provocative innovations—particularly in the ballads "Lucky to Me"
and "Lonely Town," while his wit and satire had a rapier edge
in "Carried Away" and "I Can Cook, Too," all the lyrics by
Betty Comden and Adolph Green. He could be popular without abandoning either his personality or his background.
Within more spacious designs—the opening atmospheric scene,
"New York, New York"; the fantasy on the subway ride to
Coney Island; the ballet music—Bernstein was able to use his
advanced technique and symphonic thinking to good advantage
to produce some of the best sequences of the musical theater in
the 1940s.

Bernstein's second musical comedy, *Wonderful Town*, in
1953 literally swept Broadway off its feet. This was a musical-
comedy based on the delightful *My Sister Eileen*, which had
been adapted for the stage from stories of Ruth McKenney, appearing in the *New Yorker*. The breathless excitement of the
overture, followed by the equally frenetic rag-tag dance of
the Greenwich Villagers, was the starting point of a production which continued to accelerate in pace and grow in
highpitched nervousness until the final curtain. The dynamo
keeping these exciting proceedings continually charged with

electrical energy was Rosalind Russell, the same Rosalind Russell who had been the sedate and sophisticated lady of the screen. Together with her sister Eileen she expresses homesickness in a winsome little number called "Ohio" which Bernstein had intended as a tongue-in-the-cheek parody of all hometown songs but which was taken in all seriousness by audiences and subsequent radio, record, and television performers. There was, however, no mistaking the satirical intent of Bernstein's amusing Irish ballad, "My Darlin' Eileen," or the rowdy humor of "What a Waste" and "Pass the Football"—all lyrics by Betty Comden and Adolph Green. Other Bernstein numbers were in a more sentimental vein, and one of these, "A Quiet Girl," is one of the best love-songs he has written.

Frank Loesser came to Broadway with his first musical comedy comparatively late in his career, long after his position in American popular music was firmly established. That first musical was *Where's Charley?*, in 1948, adapted by George Abbott from an old chestnut by Brandon Thomas, *Charley's Aunt,* first served hot in 1893, and after that reheated in innumerable professional and amateur revivals. It hardly appeared likely that an appetizing meal could be prepared from this leftover dish, even with the introduction of the new spices of songs. And yet *Where's Charley?* managed to be highly diverting. Most of the credit for this achievement went to Ray Bolger as Charley. His genial and ingratiating manner with a song—as in "Once in Love With Amy," in which he had the audience participate—and his equally disarming way with a tap dance added dimensions to his hilarious performances. As for Loesser's score—while mildly appealing to the ear and at times insinuating to the memory, it was hardly of the stature expected of a man of his natural gifts. "Once in Love With Amy" and "My Darling" were songs that served the play well, but neither is a particularly distinguished love ballad. The score also contained a comedy song more appealing for lyric than for melody in "Make a Miracle," and a march tune with the unbelievable title of "The New Ashmolean Marching Society and Students' Conservatory Band."

One, then, accepts Loesser's music in *Where's Charley?* with major reservations. But *Guys and Dolls*, in 1950, Loesser's second contribution to the Broadway musical theater, is quite a different story. This is perhaps a model musical comedy, because it is a play in which every farcical episode, every routine, and every song is germane to the plot. Even where musical-comedy techniques are used, these are integral to the play. There is a big opening scene in the tradition of the musical theater; but it becomes a pantomime of Broadway life and characters, beautifully paced by George S. Kaufman's direction. There is ballet—choreography by Michael Kidd—but its theme, in line with the story and characters of the play, is a crap game. There are love songs and ballads, but "I'll Know" and "If I Were a Bell" and "I've Never Been in Love Before" are the kind of songs Damon Runyonesque characters would sing, and their lyrics are rich with the kind of Broadwayese jargon that spices all the dialogue in the play. Other Loesser songs develop organically out of the context of the play. They include several humorous items, each a gem of its kind: the opening "Fugue for Tinhorns," ("I've Got the Horse Right Here"), a three-voiced canon; Adelaide's lament about her psychosomatic sneezes; two night-club routines at the Hot Box, "A Bushel and a Peck" and "Take Back Your Mink."

No less vital is the picturesque, cynical, hard-boiled universe of Damon Runyon, whose stories provided the material and characters for this musical comedy. It is Runyon's Broadway characters—and the strange forces and impulses motivating their daily lives and philosophy—that, in the last analysis, dominate *Guys and Dolls* and helped make it as good as it was.

After a historic run of over 1,000 performances, which grossed more than $12,000,000, *Guys and Dolls* was bought for the screen by Samuel Goldwyn for the unprecedented sum of $1,000,000 against 10 per cent of the world-take. In the screen version—starring Frank Sinatra, Marlon Brando, and Jean Simmons—several new Loesser songs were introduced. One of these, "A Woman in Love," was a major hit of 1955 and early 1956.

A new songwriting team entered the big leagues with a big-league musical comedy in 1954, *Pajama Game.* Jerry Ross and Richard Adler were discovered by Frank Loesser when both men were still in their early twenties. Ross and Adler had been trying to write songs separately without making perceptible progress in getting them published and performed. Then, early in 1950, they were introduced to each other outside the Brill Building in New York. They decided to pool their talents and to work collaboratively on both the lyrics and the music. For a while they wrote some special material for various singers, while trying to peddle other songs to leading publishing houses. One of these publishers saw enough merit in them to introduce them to Frank Loesser who, in turn, placed the boys under contract.

One day, while discussing the talent of Eddie Fisher, Adler remarked to Ross: "Funny how this guy's gone from rags to riches." The phrase "rags to riches" struck a responsive chord with them and they proceeded to write a song with that title which ultimately reached the Hit Parade. This song led to an assignment to write music for John Murray Anderson's *Almanac,* which, in turn, resulted in an audition for George Abbott, who engaged them to write the music for *Pajama Game.*

Pajama Game is a musical comedy based on a novel of Richard Bissel, *7½¢,* about a small-town pajama factory. Excitingly paced and studded with striking dance numbers, *Pajama Game* became a leading musical hit. It had two songs which achieved enormous popularity, "Hey There," and a tango, "Hernando's Hideaway."

That this songwriting team was no flash in the pan was proved a year later with *Damn Yankees,* based on a novel by Douglass Wallop. Two more Hit Parade songs helped make the production a leader in 1955: "Heart" and "Whatever Lola Wants."

With two major shows running simultaneously on Broadway, and with five Hit Parade songs, Jerry Ross and Richard Adler certainly loomed as the most important new composers to appear on Broadway in several years. Tragically, this happy partnership was suddenly and prematurely broken up by death. Jerry Ross, long a victim of chronic bronchiectasis, died in 1955 before reaching his thirtieth birthday.

II

Since Victor Herbert's time the musical theater had given repeated hints that it could become good art as well as good theater. That hint became an outright statement on December 27, 1927 with Kern's *Show Boat*. This was much more than a vehicle for eye-filling and ear-filling entertainment. This was a musical play with dramatic truth, some sharp-lined characterizations, effective background and atmosphere, a logical story line, and music that was integral to the play. *Show Boat* revolutionized the musical theater.

Kern, inspired melodist though he had been in earlier productions, had never before arrived at such full maturity as a composer, nor was he ever before so abundantly lyrical in any of his scores. Joe's immortal hymn to the Mississippi, "Ol' Man River," was a modern Negro spiritual, with the fervor and tragic overtones of a folk song. The love music covered "Make Believe," "Why Do I Love You?" and "Can't Help Lovin' That Man," each with a distinct personality of its own.

Based on the best-selling novel of the same name by Edna Ferber, *Show Boat* was adapted by Oscar Hammerstein II, who also wrote the lyrics. Up to now, Hammerstein had been a skillful craftsman, but hardly more than that. In *Show Boat*, his writing acquired new grace, and was touched with a new poetic glow which was an omen of future achievement.

Show Boat was a monumental success in every possible way.

At the box office it grossed an average of $50,000 a week for almost two solid years in New York. After that it went on an extensive tour, always playing to sold-out houses. The critical acclaim was equally impressive. Robert Garland, for example, did not hesitate to call it an "American masterpiece."

A triumph in 1927, *Show Boat* has gone on to become a classic. It has often been revived in every part of the country, and on three different occasions it has been adapted for the screen. In 1952, a new concert version of the play, with special narrative, was given at the Lewisohn Stadium in New York, while some years earlier Jerome Kern had used its basic melodies for a large symphonic work called *Scenario*, and performed by most of the major American orchestras. On April 8, 1954, it was given for the first time in an opera house as part of its regular repertory: by the New York City Opera Company.

Two subsequent Kern musicals developed the musico-dramatic concept first realized by *Show Boat*. In 1931, in *The Cat and the Fiddle*, Kern temporarily parted with Hammerstein to resume an old collaboration with Otto Harbach. Once again, as in *Show Boat*, the chief concern of the author was the projection of a musical play without interference by chorus girls' routines, synthetic humor, and set numbers. The action moved fluidly. Kern's tuneful score—which included "The Night Was Made for Love" and "She Didn't Say Yes"—grew naturally out of the action.

Music in the Air, in 1932, for which Oscar Hammerstein II returned to write book and lyrics, was described by its authors as a "musical adventure." This adventure takes place in the little mountain town of Edendorff in Bavaria; and *Gemütlich* is the word to describe the setting. The picturesque background and atmosphere are enhanced by songs like "Egern on the Tegern Sea" which has the flavor of a German folk song, and the vivacious German beer-hall vocals of Dr. Lessing's choral group. The play derives an additional radiance from such background material as the "Scene Music" in the first act and such unforgettable melodies as "The Song Is You" and "I've Told Every Little Star."

So admirable is the fusion of music and play in *Music in the Air*—so naturally do the various parts fall into the over-all pattern—that the production represented to Brooks Atkinson "the emancipation of the musical drama." Atkinson had no cause to change his mind when the show was revived on Broadway in 1951. "Although ours is a graceless world," now wrote the critic of the New York *Times,* "the lovely Kern score is still full of friendship, patience, cheerfulness, and pleasure."

Kern did not altogether abandon the more traditional kind of musical comedy, the kind with which he had received the acclaim of critics and audiences in the 1910s and early 1920s. Between *Show Boat* and *The Cat and the Fiddle*, he wrote the music for *Sweet Adeline*, in 1929, a gay and sentimental romance of the Nineties, with Helen Morgan and Charles Butterworth. Here the authors of *Show Boat* (for Oscar Hammerstein II was once again responsible for book and lyrics) were turning back the clock by writing a show in the comparatively stilted and stylized manner of their earlier musical comedies. The audiences rejected it emphatically. Two Kern gems survived this box-office fiasco: "Why Was I Born?" and "Here Am I," both poignantly sung by Helen Morgan.

But *Roberta*, in 1933, once again a reversion to the styles of the past, had a happier history—and this largely due to a single song. The song was "Smoke Gets In Your Eyes," (Harbach) one of the most beautiful Kern ever wrote. It is generally conceded that it spelled the difference for *Roberta* between failure and success. From the opening night on, whenever Tamara as Stephanie sang the ballad in the second act she stopped the show. The song swept the country, and had one of the largest sales of sheet music and records of any Kern number. Two other excellent songs—"Yesterdays" and "The Touch Of Your

Hand"—lent an eminence to a production that otherwise would have been quite humdrum.

If a song masterpiece was able to make *Roberta* a box-office attraction, it was ineffectual for Kern's last Broadway musical, *Very Warm for May*, in 1939. "All the Things you Are" (Hammerstein) belongs not only with the best of Kern but also with the best of American popular music. Despite the subtlety of its structure and the comparative complexity of the enharmonic changes, "All the Things You Are" had immediate appeal. But the show itself was so stodgy that the popularity of a song could not lift the production out of the morass of a fifty-nine performance failure. And so Kern's long and historic association with Broadway ended after almost thirty years with a box-office fiasco.

After 1939, Kern worked exclusively for motion pictures. In 1945, after finishing the music for *Centennial Summer*, Kern planned to return to the Broadway stage, engaged by the producing team of Rodgers and Hammerstein to write the music for a show planned for the following season. However, on November 5, Kern collapsed in front of his Park Avenue apartment in New York, and six days later he died in Doctors Hospital. Irving Berlin, who came to visit Kern on November 11, had to be told that his friend had just died. It was Berlin who took over Kern's Broadway assignment and made it his greatest stage triumph—*Annie Get Your Gun*.

III

One of the composers who did most to advance the artistic importance of our musical theater was Kurt Weill. Before coming to America, Weill achieved success in Germany as a serious composer, particularly of operas. Immediately after settling in New York he directed his energy and industry not toward the opera house but to the Broadway musical stage. In a short time he became one of the most important composers in the American theater, because he was one of the best equipped, and because he never hesitated to use that equipment for the best interests of the musical theater.

He was born in Dessau, Germany, in 1900, and received his musical training at the Berlin Hochschule and privately from Busoni, one of the most esoteric musical thinkers of his day. Weill's first opera, *The Protagonist*, was written in 1924, on a surrealistic text by Georg Kaiser, and was produced by the Dresden Opera. Its success brought Weill a commission to write *The Royal Palace* for the Berlin State Opera, in which the composer introduced the sharp condiments of jazz techniques. The use of American popular materials grows ever bolder in Weill's next opera, *The Czar Has Himself Photographed*; and they become completely integrated into his style in *Mahagonny* and *The Three-Penny Opera*, the last being a modernization of *The Beggar's Opera*. The phenomenal success of the last-named work made Weill one of the most celebrated composers in Germany. It was seen several times in this country both on the stage and on the screen. A successful revival in New York in 1955 yielded a surprise entry into the Hit Prade sweepstakes, with "Moritat," which courses through the production as a theme song.

When Hitler came to power, Weill fled from Germany and, after a period in Paris, came to the United States in 1935 to write music for *The Eternal Road*, a pageant by Franz Werfel produced by Max Reinhardt. *The Eternal Road* hit one snag after another and was not produced until 1937. Consequently, when Weill made his entry into the American musical theater, it was with a play entirely different from a vast religious spectacle; and for that play he created a music completely different from the mystical, spiritual, and Semitic score he had prepared for the Werfel pageant. The play was *Johnny Johnson*, by Paul Green, a fable about World War I, produced by the Group Theatre in 1936. Songs and musical incidents were planned as an integral part of the story development. With remarkable resiliency that immediately gave hint of his versatility and flexibility, Weill, who had just completed a Hebrew score for *The Eternal Road,* veered sharply toward a Tin Pan Alley style in *Johnny Johnson.* Like the text, the music combined satire, caricature, and burlesque with bitterness and melodrama.

Weill's next important assignment was to write the music for *Knickerbocker Holiday,* book by Maxwell Anderson, who was here associated with the musical stage for the first time. *Knickerbocker Holiday* had, among other things, two happy elements. One was Walter Huston, who gave a hearty and infectious portrait of Peter Stuyvesant. The other was Weill's music, to Anderson's lyrics, the most tuneful he had thus far written, and which included one of his best-known numbers, "September Song."

The way he wrote "September Song" points up his *modus operandi,* with the needs of the theater always uppermost in mind. When Weill learned that Huston would star in the play, he wired the actor inquiring the range of his voice. Huston replied tersely: "No Voice. No Range." Subsequently, Huston suggested that Weill listen to an imminent broadcast emanating from Hollywood when, for Weill's benefit, he would try to sing a song. Weill listened, and heard the rasping, husky sounds Huston passed off as singing. Weill recognized that Huston's singing might be effective in a special kind of sad song with unusual progressions in the melody. He wrote "September Song" just for Huston, keeping in mind the individual quality of his voice. Because voice and song were so naturally suited to each other, both achieved relevance within the play.

In 1941, Weill was asked to write the music for Moss Hart's *Lady in the Dark,* a play about psychoanalysis. The originality of the subject, at least at that time, and the performances of Gertrude Lawrence and Danny Kaye were primary factors in the altogether remarkable success of this play. But Weill's music also contributed handsomely. His atmospheric music was so perfectly attuned to the dream situations that it seemed an inextricable part of them; and the theme song, "My Ship," was beautifully suited to these dream sequences through its individual, haunting melodic structure. But Weill's music also consisted of many outstanding individual numbers (all of them with excellent lyrics by Ira Gershwin), like the sultry "The Saga of Jenny," or "The Princess of Pure Delight," or "Oh, Fabulous One in Your Ivory Tower." Yet even these numbers were so much a part of the dramatic pattern that *Lady in the Dark* remains what Moss Hart originally called it, "A play with music."

Much more striking in its departure from earlier concepts of musical comedy was *Street Scene,* in 1947, a musical version of Elmer Rice's powerful Pulitzer Prize tragedy. This is, in essence, a folk play with music, the latter bringing new depth to the play. While Weill's music had a few numbers to haunt the memory—"Lonely House," "We'll Go Away Together," and "Somehow I Could Never Believe," all lyrics by Langston Hughes—it is no single number, or combination of numbers that gave the show its emotional urge and its artistic stature, but the integrated musical texture.

Lost in the Stars, in 1949, is once again stirring dramatic art. Maxwell Anderson made the adaptation of *Cry, The Beloved Country,* Alan Paton's best-selling novel of racial conflicts in South Africa. The musical text, like its source, was touching in its compassion, warm in humanity, stirring in its promise of a better life of tolerance and brotherly understanding. As in *Street Scene,* music endowed a human and at moments a profound play with richer and deeper overtones. Rarely before has our musical theater had such moving choral music as that provided by Weill for this play. Weill uses the chorus to provide commentary: in the overwhelming dirge, "Cry, the Beloved Country"; in a penetrating pyschological analysis of an emotional state, "Fear"; in a deeply affecting religious statement, "A Bird of Prey." The solo melodies—one is reluctant to call them songs, so fluidly do they arise from and ebb back into the dramatic situation—are no less expressive, bringing up the immeasurable sorrow of Kumalo when he realizes his son is a murderer ("O Tixo, Tixo" and "Lost in the Stars"), in sharply defining character (that of Linda in "Who'll Buy?", and that of Alex in "Big Mole"). So germane is Weill's music to the play, so integral to its message and meaning, that one readily comprehends the temptation of some critics to describe *Lost in the Stars* as an opera. (Lyrics to all musical numbers are by Anderson.)

When Kurt Weill died in New York City on April 3, 1950, he was in the front rank of composers writing for our stage. He was at the height of his creative powers, presumably with his best work yet to come.

IV

A significant chapter in the career of Richard Rodgers had ended in 1942 when his long and fruitful collaboration with Lorenz Hart terminated with *By Jupiter*. But an even more significant chapter began one year later when he found a new collaborator in Oscar Hammerstein II.

By 1943, Hammerstein had spent about a quarter of a century in the musical theater. He had written the books and/or lyrics for about twenty-five stage productions, and the words to several hundred songs. He had been a partner in the creation of several operettas and musical comedies that were major events in our theater: Vincent Youmans' *Wildflower*; Friml's *Rose Marie*; *Desert Song* and *New Moon* by Romberg; *Show Boat* and *Music in the Air* by Jerome Kern.

He had, then, his share of victories before 1943. But he also had had more than the normal quota of defeats. When he joined up with Rodgers he had suffered three disasters in succession, not to mention several minor calamities in London. When, at long last, he recovered a winning stride through that first collaboration with Rodgers, he ran an "ad" in *Variety* which had the following headline: "I've Done It Before and I

Can Do It Again." But under that heading Hammerstein listed not the succession of his triumphs but the procession of his recent failures: *Very Warm for May* (seven weeks); *Ball at Savoy* (five weeks); *Sunny River* (six weeks); *Three Sisters* (six weeks), and *Free for All* (three weeks).

One day, in 1943, he was invited by the Theatre Guild to work with Richard Rodgers in turning a folk play by Lynn Riggs, *Green Grow the Lilacs,* into a musical. Lorenz Hart had firmly bowed out as Rodgers' collaborator and the Guild suggested Hammerstein as a replacement. Hammerstein and Rodgers were, of course, no strangers to each other. As far back as 1920, Hammerstein had written verses for a Rodgers' melody, "There Is Always Room for One More," heard in a Columbia Varsity Show. After that they often met, often exchanged encouraging words for each other's activities. Richard Rodgers' father, as a matter of fact, was the obstetrician for Hammerstein's two children by a first marriage. But though they knew each other well, not until the Guild brought them together for the Riggs play did they collaborate professionally.

Tentatively entitled *Away We Go,* the new Theatre Guild musical inspired little enthusiasm among potential sponsors. Parties organized to raise the $85,000 needed for production costs were fruitless; only $2,500 trickled in. The remainder of the sum was procured through entreaties, cajolery, tears, insistence. Most of the money came from friends of the Guild who regarded their contribution as a gift rather than an investment.

A preview in New Haven, on March 11, 1943, was pretty much of a dud. Drastic revisions took place, and the show acquired the new name of *Oklahoma!* In Boston it now inspired raves from the critics. The raves did not subside when *Oklahoma!* came to New York on March 31. Lewis Nichols perhaps crystallized the critical reaction by calling it a "folk opera."

Apparently *Oklahoma!* had as strong an appeal to audiences as to critics, for while reaching for art Rodgers and Hammerstein had not lost the popular touch. The show shattered every record that had previously existed in the theater for a musical. It remained on Broadway five years and nine months, amassing the staggering—and for a musical play as yet unequaled—total of 2,248 performances. It is estimated that about twenty million people saw *Oklahoma!* during the 10,000 or so performances on Broadway; and many more millions saw it in performances by the national company (which stayed on the road eight years, visiting over 200 cities) and by the regular Broadway company which made a 70-city tour when the New York run was over. In London, it remained three and a half years, the second longest run in the history of the London musical stage. A South African company presented it in 1948-1949, and an Australian company between 1948 and 1951. It was acclaimed in Norway, Sweden, and Denmark, and a special company was organized to tour European army camps. The show grossed somewhere around $40,000,000; the recording of the complete score sold over a million albums; the published sheet music sold about a million copies. In 1955, *Oklahoma!* found still a new audience of many millions in its screen adaptation in the then new Todd-AO process.

The play had greater literacy than most musical-comedy books; and Hammerstein's homespun dialogue and lyrics had greater authenticity and relevancy. But it was the flavor of American folklore that gave the production its particularly piquant savor. This folk element was strongly emphasized in play and lyrics, setting and costuming, in the choreography of Agnes de Mille and the songs of Richard Rodgers.

For Rodgers, *Oklahoma!* represented a departure from older ways. Adapting himself resiliently to the folk play, and to the poetry of Hammerstein's lyric-writing, Rodgers came up with melodies so fresh in approach, so simple in style and content, so wholesome in manner, that they often have the character of folk songs. Yet Rodgers' own musical personality is never obscured. The best of the *Oklahoma!* songs include "People Will Say We're in Love," the title song, "Oh, What a Beautiful Morning," "Out of My Dreams," and "The Surrey With the Fringe on Top."

More than any other single musical that preceded it, *Oklahoma!* made the artistic musical play an established fact in our theater. Its success undoubtedly gave its own authors both the courage and the stimulation to continue working with unusual texts, and to treat them ever more ambitiously in scope and design.

Less than two months after *Oklahoma!* another experiment in the Broadway musical theater came, was seen, and conquered. This time Hammerstein temporarily parted company with Rodgers to collaborate with a music master of the past—Georges Bizet. The experiment was a modern all-Negro adaptation of *Carmen*, the French opera, renamed *Carmen Jones*. In the new version, the Mérimée story from which the opera was derived was shifted in setting to a Southern town in the United States, and in time to 1943. Carmen becomes Carmen Jones, an employee in a parachute factory; Don José, Joe, an American soldier; the matador Escamillo, Husky Miller, a pugilist. The Bizet music was used with respectful fidelity, adhering as closely to the original form as was possible and, with minor exceptions, sung in its original order. The celebrated Habanera became "Dat's Love"; the Seguidilla, "Dere's a Café on de Corner"; the Toreador Song, "Stan' Up and Fight"; the Flower Song, "Dis Flower"; Micaela's Air, "My Joe." It cannot be said that Hammerstein's racy and colloquial lyrics and the Bizet music always jelled, any more than did Bizet's pseudo-Spanish idioms with a Negro production. But *Carmen Jones* on the whole was an exciting and exhilarating stage adventure.

Hammerstein resumed operations with Rodgers in 1945 with *Carousel*, in many ways a finer, more deeply sensitive, and more poignantly beautiful play than *Oklahoma! Carousel* was Ferenc Molnar's *Liliom* under another name, with the setting transferred from Hungary to New England in 1873. There are tragic and deeply touching overtones to the musical play not

often encountered on the musical stage. With these overtones
we confront nostalgic moods, mystical scenes, tender sentiments, all combining to make theater magic. Ever deeper and
richer grows the poetry of Hammerstein's lines, both in lyrics
and in dialogue. Richard Rodgers' music also has new stature.
Together with songs of the hit variety—"June Is Bustin' Out
All Over" and "If I Loved You," the latter one of the most
exquisite love songs written by an American—there was a remarkable seven-minute recitative, "Soliloquy," made up of
eight different musical ideas; an effective waltz prelude of
symphonic breadth, with which the play opens; and a stirring
inspirational song which is one of the composer's own favorites,
"You'll Never Walk Alone."

There was even more daring innovation in *Allegro,* in 1947.
Formal scenery was dispensed with; unusual visual designs and
colors were thrown on a large screen to intensify moods; a
speaking chorus and a singing chorus appeared as interpreters
and commentators. These unorthodox procedures were used to
develop a comparatively simple tale—the biography of the
central character from birth, through adolescence, college,
medical school, and up through his success in Chicago. To many
critics, *Allegro* was a disappointment, for all its refreshing
novelty, and its many splendid moments. Rodgers' bountiful
score included "The Gentleman is a Dope," "A Fellow Needs a
Girl," and what became the hit of the show, "So Far."

A great deal of publicity, hullabaloo, and enthusiasm pre-
ceeded *Allegro* into New York. Unfortunately, the production
failed to live up completely to expectations. Even greater
publicity, hullabaloo, and enthusiasm—and a higher pitch of
excitement—set the stage for the première of *South Pacific* in
1949. Here was a new musical by Rodgers and Hammerstein
which was adapted from the Pulitzer Prize novel of James A.
Michener; in which Joshua Logan took charge of staging;
where the starring roles were assumed by Mary Martin and
Ezio Pinza, the latter stepping for the first time from the

Metropolitan Opera to the Broadway theater. Surely this was a veritable caravan of theatrical delights!

And there was nothing anticlimactic about that performance, on that enchanted evening of April 7. What the first-night audience witnessed was as nearly ideal a musical play as ingenuity, creative talent, imagination, artistic courage, and seemingly inexhaustible funds could produce. William Hawkins wrote that this was "the ultimate blending of music and the popular theatre to date, with the finest kind of balance between story and song, hilarity and heartbreak"; he was reflecting the prevailing critical and audience opinion.

South Pacific did not equal the fabulous run of *Oklahoma!*, but it came pretty close, with 1,925 performances. It did manage, however, to set a new mark at the box office by grossing over $2,500,000 in its first year. In that time tickets for each performance were in such demand that a full-size volume could be compiled of anecdotes about the various efforts to land a pair of tickets. During its entire Broadway run *South Pacific* was seen by over 3,500,000 theater-goers who passed more than $9,000,000 through the box office. It gathered more prizes than any previous stage production, about a dozen in all, including the Pulitzer Prize and the Drama Critics' Award.

In no other Rodgers and Hammerstein production did the music echo the background and characters so sensitively. Rodgers has explained that in writing many of his songs he was always conscious of the characters who sang them. He said: "I tried to weave his [De Becque's] personality into his songs—romantic, rather powerful, but not too involved." The result was "Some Enchanted Evening" and "This Nearly Was Mine." Rodgers said further: "Nellie Forbush is a Navy nurse out of Arkansas, a kid whose musical background probably had been limited to the movies, radio, and maybe a touring musical comedy. It gave me a chance for a change of pace, and the music I composed for her is light, contemporary, and rhythmic." And so Nellie sings "I'm Gonna Wash That Man Right

Outa My Hair" and "A Wonderful Guy." In the same way, "Bali Ha'i" and "Happy Talk" are as natural to Bloody Mary as the color of her skin; and there is an equal affinity between Lt. Cable and songs like "Younger than Springtime" and "Carefully Taught."

South Pacific, with a World War II setting on a Pacific island, represented a radical departure in plot, locale, characters and approach from *Allegro*, just as *Allegro* was so basically different from *Carousel* and *Oklahoma! The King and I*, in 1951, once again saw the authors in a drastic change of material. Now the setting is Siam, where two opposing cultures rub elbows; the principal characters include a semi-barbaric and swaggering monarch and a refined English schoolteacher. The point of origin was a novel by Margaret Landon, *Anna and the King of Siam*, previously made into a poignant motion picture starring Rex Harrison and Irene Dunne. Gertrude Lawrence and Yul Brynner were chosen for the leads in the stage musical. For Gertrude Lawrence the part of Anna was destined to be the last of her stage portrayals, the concluding chapter of her biography; while the play was still running, she died suddenly in New York in 1952.

Rodgers' score was another ambitious attempt to make music indispensable to the flow of the play. The device of using music and not speech in the beginning of the play, whenever Anna has to talk by means of an interpreter (the characters remain mute and the instruments speak for them) is one of several instances in which music and play are indivisible. The use of music as a provocative background to spoken dialogue, often to lead more naturally to a musical number, is another. Still a third is the remarkable ballet conceived by Jerome Robbins "The Small House of Uncle Thomas," in which the story of *Uncle Tom's Cabin* is retold in terms of the Siamese dance.

It is quite true that Rodgers' effort to inject Siamese or Oriental characteristics into his musical writing by using the pentatonic scale or percussive effects of the East does not always carry conviction. The march of the royal children and the background music for the main ballet is wonderful theater, to be sure. But much more admirable for their musical interest, and probably because they are more authentically Rodgers, are haunting songs like "I Whistle a Happy Tune," "Getting to Know You," "I Have Dreamed," "Hello, Young Lovers," "We Kiss in a Shadow," and the "Shall We Dance?" sequence, or the king's exciting recitative, "A Puzzlement."

In *Me and Juliet*, in 1953, and *Pipe Dream*, two years later, Rodgers and Hammerstein followed the ritual of the musical theater of the past more strictly than had previously been their custom. The first was a love letter by Rodgers and Hammerstein to the world they both knew and loved—the world of the theater. What is here portrayed is life both back-stage and on-stage during the period of the run of a musical comedy. *Pipe Dream*, based on John Steinbeck's *Sweet Thursday*, was built around the disreputable characters of Monterey County's Cannery Row in California.

The critics generally expressed disappointment with both productions; and the truth is that after *Oklahoma!*, *Carousel*, *South Pacific*, and *The King and I* they seemed anticlimactic. Nevertheless both shows were liked by audiences, and both had memorable songs. *Me and Juliet* had "No Other Love," one of the leading hits of Rodgers and Hammerstein; for this song, Rodgers used a melody he had previously woven with striking effect into the background music for the documentary film, *Victory at Sea*. Another delightful number in *Me and Juliet* was "Keep it Gay." *Pipe Dream* had two substantial hits: "All At Once You Love Her" and "Everybody's Got a Home But Me."

As for the tendency on the part of many critics to regard both *Me and Juliet* and *Pipe Dream* as failures—in spite of their many attractions—one columnist commented wisely: "They never used to cheer Babe Ruth when he hit a double."

V

Frank Loesser's return to Broadway after *Guys and Dolls* came with *The Most Happy Fella* in 1956, one of the most ambitious and expansive scores our popular musical theater has known. Loesser himself made the adaptation of Sidney Howard's 1925 Pulitzer Prize play, *They Knew What They Wanted;* this was Loesser's first effort at writing the text of a musical as well as its music and lyrics. The simple and poignant love story of an aging Italian winegrower and a young waitress he had wooed through correspondence was flooded with so much music that critics were at a loss whether to identify the final product as a musical play, a musical drama, or an opera. Certainly this is musical comedy no longer—not in the way *Guys and Dolls* was—but a play in which music is ever the driving force. As Brooks Atkinson reported the day after the première, "He has told everything of vital importance in terms of dramatic music." And the following Sunday Mr. Atkinson added: "His music drama . . . goes so much deeper into the souls of its leading characters than most Broadway shows and it has such an abundant and virtuoso score that it has to be taken on the level of theatre art."

There are so many musical numbers in *The Most Happy Fella* (over thirty) and they are so inextricable from the drama, that they are not listed separately at the end of the program, as is habitual with musical shows, any more than principal arias are listed at the end of an opera program. And the musical material is as varied as it is prolix. There are fat show tunes to remind us that *The Most Happy Fella* belongs to the popular theater. Indeed, disk jockeys throughout the country were happily spinning "Standing On the Corner" long before the show opened; and it was not long before other numbers like "Big D" and "Happy to Make Your Acquaintance" and "Young People" also caught on. Besides show tunes, the

score had recitatives, passionate arias and duets, choruses, parodies, dance music, musical interludes of all kinds—every character, situation, and mood found its musical equivalent—to
give the musical theater a new depth and dimension.

The abundance and variety of musical riches that made *The
Most Happy Fella* so good and so important were among the
reasons why *My Fair Lady,* also produced early in 1956, became
one of the outstanding musical plays of the past decade. *My
Fair Lady* is Alan Jay Lerner's musical-play version of Bernard
Shaw's *Pygmalion.* The Shaw play was essentially a romance, a
fact Lerner did not forget even while bringing to his adaptation
mockery, irony, and satire, together with a generous dose of
humanity and a suggestion of sentimentality. The many songs
which crop up through the play (they are by Frederick Loewe
to Lerner's lyrics, a combination that brought to Broadway in
1947 one of its great musical delights in the whimsical Scottish
fantasy, *Brigadoon*) are major contributors to the over-all en-
chantment. Like Loesser's play, *My Fair Lady* has its healthy
quota of song hits, two particularly: "I Could Have Danced All
Night" and "On the Street Where You Live." But while tunes
like these linger on the lips after the show, what remains in the
memory long afterward are moments like the "Rain in Spain"
sequence, or the ironical Ascot Gavotte, or Professor Higgins'
subtly dramatic number, "I'm an Ordinary Man" and Doo-
little's two hilarious ones, "With a Little Bit of Luck" and
"Get Me to the Church on Time." These and many other
musical pages made for sheer stage magic.

Like the best musical plays of Kurt Weill and Rodgers and
Hammerstein, *The Most Happy Fella* and *My Fair Lady* bring
the conviction that when great American opera is written it
will emerge not in the opera house but in our musical theater;
that in all probability it will be erected not on the cornerstones
of the classical operatic traditions, but on those of popular
music. And it is not beyond the realm of possibility that the
musical historian of the future will look upon plays like *Show*

Boat, Street Scene, Lost in the Stars, Oklahoma!, Carousel, The King and I, The Most Happy Fella and *My Fair Lady*— and, of course, to Gershwin's *Porgy and Bess*—as the beginnings of an American operatic tradition.

INDEX